A Good General

The Science of Leadership

DAG HEWARD-MILLS

Parchment House

A GOOD GENERAL: THE SCIENCE OF LEADERSHIP

Copyright © 2015 Dag Heward-Mills

First published 2015 by Parchment House
11th Printing 2018

[77]Find out more about Dag Heward Mills at:

Healing Jesus Campaign
Email: evangelist@daghewardmills.org
Website: www.daghewardmills.org
Facebook: Dag Heward-Mills
Twitter: @EvangelistDag

ISBN : 978–1–61395–559 – 8

Contents

The life of man upon earth is a warfare

Job 7:1

CHAPTER 1

A Good General Learns about Warfare

...in righteousness he doth judge and make war.

Revelation 19:11

War involves a lot of killing, sorrow, sadness and death. War is known as one of the most terrible things that can happen to men. War is therefore rarely associated with God. How could God ever be involved with a war? How could God want people to die? Does God want to kill people? Does God want to harm people? Certainly not!

God has no such evil plans. The rise of an enemy that needs to be crushed is what brings about war. God wages war in a righteous way and crushes His enemies. As Christians, we have an enemy that needs to be crushed and beaten. As ministers of the gospel, we have even more enemies and need to know how to overcome them, crush them and wipe them out. The Scripture says, "In righteousness he doth judge and make war". There is a godly way to make war. There is a wise way to wage war. God wants you to wage war in His way and in His wisdom.

This book is about how to wage war in a godly, spiritual and wise way. Anyone who thinks we are not at war lacks understanding. Satan would like you to have the mind that we are living in peace under the Prince of Peace. Satan would like you to think there is nothing to worry about. But God's Word is very clear that we are at war. God's Word is very clear that we are to war a good warfare and fight a good fight!

Ten Reasons to Learn about War

1. Jesus Christ leads the armies of Heaven and makes war in righteousness.

A lot of people do nothing in the ministry because they do not want to fight. If you want to follow Jesus, you have to join His army and you have to fight.

And I saw heaven opened, and behold a white horse; and he that sat upon him was called Faithful and True, and IN RIGHTEOUSNESS HE DOTH JUDGE AND MAKE WAR.

His eyes were as a flame of fire, and on his head were many crowns; and he had a name written, that no man knew, but he himself.

And he was clothed with a vesture dipped in blood: and his name is called The Word of God.

And THE ARMIES WHICH WERE IN HEAVEN followed him upon white horses, clothed in fine linen, white and clean. And out of his mouth goeth a sharp sword, that with it he should smite the nations: and he shall rule them with a rod of iron: and he treadeth the winepress of the fierceness and wrath of Almighty God.

Revelation 19:11-15

2.   Jesus Christ is a lamb who makes war.

The lamb made war on the ten kings who united themselves against Him and overcame them. Jesus Christ is a lamb who makes war. Don't you want to be like Jesus? If you want to be like Jesus you must learn to fight a war!

And the ten horns which thou sawest are ten kings, which have received no kingdom as yet; but receive power as kings one hour with the beast. These have one mind, and shall give their power and strength unto the beast.

These SHALL MAKE WAR WITH THE LAMB, and the Lamb shall overcome them: for he is Lord of lords, and King of kings: and they that are with him are called, and chosen, and faithful

Revelation 17:12-14

3.   God teaches our hands to war.

God wants to teach you how to fight a war. If you believe, you will be supernaturally enabled and guided on how to make war.

He TEACHETH MY HANDS TO WAR, so that a bow of steel is broken by mine arms.

Psalm 18:34

4.   We are instructed to fight a good fight.

There is a clear word in the Bible that says you must fight. God urges you to fight! A good fight is a good fight because you win. A good fight is a fight with a good purpose.

FIGHT THE GOOD FIGHT of faith, lay hold on eternal life, whereunto thou art also called, and hast professed a good profession before many witnesses.

1 Timothy 6:12

5.   We are instructed to war a good warfare.

We are actually told to be good at warfare. It is an instruction for every minister of the gospel. Timothy was one of the first pastors ever in the history of the church. And he was told to be good at warfare.

This charge I commit unto thee, son Timothy, according to the prophecies which went before on thee, that thou by them mightest WAR A GOOD WARFARE;

1 Timothy 1:18

6.   The ministry of the Lord Jesus is described as warfare.

Apostle Paul considered his ministry as warfare and asked an important question. Who goeth a warfare any time at his own charges?

WHO GOETH A WARFARE any time at his own charges? who planteth a vineyard, and eateth not of the fruit thereof? or who feedeth a flock, and eateth not of the milk of the flock?

1 Corinthians 9:7

7.   Paul described his life and ministry as a fight.

Paul was fighting constantly. If you are in the ministry, you are fighting! If you work for God, you are a fighter! Whether you like it or not, you are in a fight for your life. I have always felt that I was fighting for my life.

I therefore so run, not as uncertainly; SO FIGHT I, not as one that beateth the air:

1 Corinthians 9:26

I have fought A GOOD FIGHT, I have finished my course, I have kept the faith:

2 Timothy 4:7

8.   We are instructed to have weapons of warfare.

Paul, a minister of God, had weapons with which to fight his good fight. If Paul needed weapons, you will too.

For though we walk in the flesh, we do not war after the flesh: (For THE WEAPONS OF OUR WARFARE are not carnal, but mighty through God to the pulling down of strong holds;)

2 Corinthians 10:3-4

9.   We are instructed to be strong and to arm ourselves.

Why would we have to be armed if we were not going to fight? We are at war with principalities, powers, rulers of the darkness of the world. Gird up your loins and get ready for a good, long and difficult fight!

Finally, my brethren, BE STRONG in the Lord, and in the power of his might. Put on the WHOLE ARMOUR of God, that ye may be able to stand against the wiles of the devil.

For we WRESTLE not against flesh and blood, but against principalities, against powers, against the rulers of the darkness of this world, against spiritual wickedness in high places.

Ephesians 6:10-12

10. There is a war with the dragon and we are a part of it.

The dragon makes war against people who keep the commandments of God. Do you keep the commandments of God? If you do, then expect a dragon to take you on and fight with you.

And THE DRAGON was wroth with the woman, and went to MAKE WAR with the remnant of her seed, WHICH KEEP THE COMMANDMENTS OF GOD, and have the testimony of Jesus Christ.

Revelation 12:17

CHAPTER 2

A Good General Will
Avoid a Foolish Fight

Fight the good fight of faith . . .

1 Timothy 6:12

A good general is a trained fighter but he will not fight a foolish fight. The Bible teaches us to fight the good fight. It is a good thing to fight the good fight of faith. To fight means to strive vigorously for something. However, there are many foolish fights a person can get into. Are you into a foolish fight or are you into a good fight?

General Paulus and the Foolish Fight

In 1942, Adolf Hitler, the leader of Germany, invaded Soviet Union for the second time and tried to capture an important city called Stalingrad. Both Adolf Hitler and Stalin (the leader of Russia) were strong commanders and it seemed that they had met their match in Stalingrad. The German forces were under the command of General Paulus.

Stalin issued an order to his troops, which was: "Not one step back!" Everyone will fight to his death. This command directed that any commander who allowed retreat without permission from his superiors be subject to military tribunal. The order called for soldiers found guilty to be forced into "penal battalions". This means that they were sent to the most dangerous sections of the front lines. The order also directed the Russian soldiers to shoot fleeing panicked troops at the rear. In the first two months following the order, over 1,000 troops were shot by blocking units and over 130,000 troops were sent to penal battalions.

But Hitler had also forbidden his troops from retreating under any circumstances. Because of this, fighting moved street-by-street and block-by-block until the city was transformed into a ghost town. The Germans would launch repeated air raids involving 1,000 planes at a time. Troops from both sides took cover in bombed out buildings whilst Russian and German snipers hid in the ruins to pick out enemy soldiers.

On 24th January, General Paulus requested permission to surrender. He sent a message to Adolf Hitler, "Troops without ammunition or food. Effective command no longer possible. 18,000 wounded without any supplies or dressings or drugs.

Further defence senseless. Collapse inevitable. Army requests immediate permission to surrender in order to save lives of remaining troops."

Hitler refused to give permission for the German surrender saying they should stand fast to the last man. This refusal by Adolf Hitler to give General Paulus the permission to surrender was basically an instruction to fight a foolish fight.

But General Paulus would have none of that. In spite of Hitler promoting him to Field Marshal, he refused to continue in the nonsense. On the 31st January 1943, General Paulus surrendered in spite of Adolf Hitler's instruction to him to fight a foolish fight. As Russian infantrymen approached the German headquarters in the cellar of a wrecked department store, Field Marshal Paulus and his surviving staff officers simply came out and quietly surrendered. They completely ignored Hitler's order to fight a foolish fight to the last man.

Thus the Battle of Stalingrad ended with General Paulus refusing to fight on in a foolish fight that made no sense. After the defeat of Stalingrad, an embittered General Paulus turned against Hitler. He collaborated with the Russians, forming a National Committee for Free Germany and made radio broadcasts from Moscow urging German troops to give up fighting for Hitler.

My Foolish Fight

Years ago when I was in school I got into a fight with a bully in my school. Two things happened after the fight. First of all I thought I had won the fight or been equally matched with my opponent. But everyone around laughed at me and said I had been beaten.

Secondly, for all my efforts I received a black eye. The entire region around my eye became black and stayed that way for about a week. After this fight, I came to the conclusion that there was no point in fighting such useless fights with useless people and a useless audience who did not appreciate my boxing and fighting skills!

From then on, I decided to fight only good fights that were worth fighting. I would only fight for good causes and I would only fight for things that had a good outcome. This is why today I do not engage in the fight of politics or even in the fight for money. I learnt to avoid foolish fights many years ago in school. Today, I have discovered many good causes to fight for. The Word of God has shown me many good things that are worth fighting for. These things are worth the struggle and they are worth the effort. You can either fight for something good or fight for something foolish. Many people are engaged in foolish fights.

CHAPTER 3

A Good General Will Fight a Good Fight

Fight the good fight of faith . . .

1 Timothy 6:12

I t is important to identify good fights so that you do not retreat from them when the time comes for you to fight. Below is a list of fights that you should be ready to engage in. Prepare yourself to fight because you are a Christian. Prepare yourself to fight even more because you are a minister of the gospel.

Eighteen Good Fights

1.   Fight to be a strong Christian.

Most Christians are not strong in the Lord. It takes great effort to become a strong believer.

Finally, my brethren, be strong in the Lord, and in the power of his might.

Ephesians 6:10

2.   Fight to be led by the Holy Spirit and to be in the will of God.

It is a struggle to distinguish between the different voices that try to influence us. It is a fight to separate the voice of the flesh from the voice of the mind and the voice of the Spirit. The most important place to live is to live in the will of God. Many voices will vie for your attention. Many demons will fight to take you off-track. It is a real fight to be in the will of God. Sometimes, the voice or your spouse or the voice of your flesh can be so strong that you will have to rebuke it. Are you ready to fight with your closest friend so that you can be in the will of God?

There are, it may be, so many kinds of voices in the world, and none of them is without signification.

1 Corinthians 14:10

3.   Fight to be spiritual and not carnal. It is a fight to be a spiritual person.

It is more natural to follow the inclinations of your flesh. It is more natural to eat, to sleep, to rest and to have sex than it is to abstain from these things. All through your life you will fight to be a spiritual person. It is also a big fight to be prayerful. To rise up early and to wait on God is not natural. It takes the grace of God and the power of God to enter the realm of spirituality.

For to be carnally minded is death; but to be spiritually minded is life and peace.

Romans 8:6

4.   Fight for the fruit of the Spirit. Fight to walk in love.

It is a struggle to bear the fruit of love, joy and peace. It is more natural to be angry, bitter and disgruntled. You will have to fight against your very nature to bear the fruit of love, joy and peace.

But the fruit of the Spirit is love, joy, peace, longsuffering, gentleness, goodness, faith, meekness, temperance: against such there is no law.

Galatians 5:22-23

5.   Fight to enter the ministry.

One of the greatest fights is the fight to enter the ministry. This will be one of your greatest battles. It is very unnatural to leave a good secular profession for the priesthood. If you are ready to follow God and you want a good fight, then try the fight to enter the ministry of the Lord Jesus Christ.

And he said unto another, Follow me. But he said, Lord, suffer me first to go and bury my father.

Jesus said unto him, Let the dead bury their dead: but go thou and preach the kingdom of God.

Luke 9:59-60

6.   Fight to stay in your calling.

Once you get into the ministry, it is a struggle to stay on the right course in ministry. Some young missionaries had to take a job and become lay pastors so that they could support themselves in the mission field. Within a short time, their hearts had shifted from real ministry into secular business. When you are in the ministry, it is easy to slip and slide away from your real calling. When God blesses your ministry and you have a large church, it is easy to become a preacher of nonsense. When you have a large church, you may consider the basic truths of the Word of God as too basic to preach. You may have to fight a good fight to avoid becoming a motivational speaker.

For DEMAS HATH FORSAKEN ME, HAVING LOVED THIS PRESENT WORLD, and is departed unto Thessalonica; Crescens to Galatia, Titus unto Dalmatia.

2 Timothy 4:10

7.   Fight to associate with great men of God.

It is not easy to get close to men of God. I have tried to be close to several people but I have not always succeeded. It takes years of fighting, relating, flowing and humbling yourself to be close to anointed people. Most people are not prepared for this fight. Most people give up trying to associate with men of God when they realize that they have to fight to be close and also fight to maintain the close relationship. It is not easy to be associated. Elisha had to fight to be close to Elijah. It was a fight that he won. Are you ready to fight for the anointing?

And it came to pass, when the Lord would take up Elijah into heaven by a whirlwind, that Elijah went with Elisha from Gilgal.

2 Kings 2:1

And Elijah said unto Elisha, Tarry here, I pray thee; for the Lord hath sent me to Bethel. And Elisha said unto him, As the Lord liveth, and as thy soul liveth, I WILL NOT LEAVE thee. So they went down to Bethel.

2 Kings 2:2

And Elijah said unto him, Elisha, tarry here, I pray thee; for the Lord hath sent me to Jericho. And he said, as the Lord liveth, and as thy soul liveth, I WILL NOT LEAVE THEE. So they came to Jericho.

> 2 Kings 2:4

And Elijah said unto him, Tarry, I pray thee, here; for the Lord hath sent me to Jordan. And he said, as the Lord liveth, and as thy soul liveth, I WILL NOT LEAVE THEE. And they two went on.

> 2 Kings 2:6

8.   Fight to catch the anointing.

It is a fight to catch the anointing. That is why Elijah said to Elisha, "You have asked a hard thing." It is indeed a hard thing to catch the anointing and to become anointed. If you are not prepared for a fight, you cannot have the anointing. It is those who are ready to fight for the anointing who are worthy of the anointing!

And it came to pass, when they were gone over, that Elijah said unto Elisha, Ask what I shall do for thee, before I be taken away from thee. And Elisha said, I pray thee, let a double portion of thy spirit be upon me.

And he said, THOU HAST ASKED A HARD THING: nevertheless, if thou see me when I am taken from thee, it shall be so unto thee; but if not, it shall not be so.

> **2 Kings 2:9-10**

9.   Fight to find a good partner for your life.

It is a fight to find a spouse. Ruth fought hard to get Boaz's attention. It is also a fight to stay married. Most animals do not have one partner. Our animal instincts make us tend towards multiple partners. You must fight to prevent yourself from becoming a person with multiple partners.

And she went down unto the floor, and did according to all that her mother in law bade her. And when Boaz had eaten and drunk, and his heart was merry, he went to lie down at the end of the heap of corn: and she came softly, and uncovered his feet, and laid her down.

Ruth 3:6-7

10. Fight to prosper. Prosperity does not come easily.

You will have to fight to prosper. Riches are hidden in secret places. Treasures are hidden in dark places. Without a fight, you will never discover the riches that are all over this world. Phlegmatic, slow and lazy men do not easily become rich. This is because a strong fight is needed to cause the earth to yield its fruit. You have to fight to go to school. You have to fight to pass your exams. You have to fight to get a good job. Then you have to fight to be promoted. Again you have to fight to use your money wisely.

For he that hath, to him shall be given: and he that hath not, from him shall be taken even that which he hath.

Mark 4:25

11. Fight to build a house. You have to fight to build a house.

Most people do not own a house and will never own a house. It is a fight to become a house owner but it is worth fighting to become a house owner.

Through wisdom is an house builded; and by understanding it is established:

Proverbs 24:3

12. Fight to live long and to serve the Lord for a long time.

It is a fight to have good health, to stay alive and to serve the Lord for many years.

And they spake unto him, saying, If thou wilt be a servant unto this people this day, and wilt serve them, and answer them, and speak good words to them, then THEY WILL BE THY SERVANTS FOR EVER.

1 Kings 12:7

13. Fight against the negative aspects of your temperament.

Your phlegmatic temperament, your choleric temperament, your melancholic temperament and your sanguine temperament all have negative aspects.

The slowness and the dullness of a phlegmatic temperament will fight your ability to achieve anything in the ministry. The slowness and dullness of your temperament will make you not want to move or fight. It will tend to poverty.

The liberties of a sanguine will drive you into disorganization, confusion and fleshly sin.

The moodiness and depression of a melancholic will destroy relationships and dampen the atmosphere. The melancholy will cause you to be judgmental and to get rid of people when they make the slightest mistake.

The wickedness, sharpness and rudeness of a choleric will destroy your relationships. The hasty decisions of a choleric can lead him into rebellion. The busyness and the activity of a choleric will prevent him from waiting on God.

It is a fight to deny yourself of what you tend to do naturally! I find that this is the most difficult fight for many people: the fight to deny yourself. Fight the good fight to set aside your humanly inherited nature.

And when he had called the people unto him with his disciples also, he said unto them, Whosoever will come after me, let him deny himself, and take up his cross, and follow me.

Mark 8:34

17

14. Fight against your maleness or femaleness.

There is neither Jew nor Greek, there is neither bond nor free, there is NEITHER MALE NOR FEMALE: for ye are all one in Christ Jesus.

Galatians 3:28

If you are a man, you will find it difficult to stay with one partner. But you must fight this male tendency and figure out how to stay with one person. It is a fight for a man to be faithful. But this fight must be won! The maleness of a person is also expressed through the desire for sex. This heightened desire for sex can lead you into pornography, masturbation, fornication and adultery. If you do not fight to deny yourself, you will be in big trouble in the ministry.

Women will equally find themselves full of fears, jealousies and accusations. You must subdue your femaleness lest it cancels your ministry. It is important to control your maleness or femaleness until there is no difference, whether you are a male or a female.

15. Fight against tribal and national stereotypes.

One of themselves, even a prophet of their own, said, THE CRETIANS ARE ALWAY LIARS, evil beasts, slow bellies.
This witness is true. Wherefore rebuke them sharply, that they may be sound in the faith;

Titus 1:12-13

Every tribe, family or nation has its tendencies. In Ghana, Ashantis are well known for certain things and Ewes are equally well known for another set of things. When you go into the ministry, you must fight so that you are not "too Ewe" or "too Ashanti" in your presentation. If you come across as being either or the other, it will affect your ability to bear fruit on the other side. Some pastors are so nationalistic that they cannot reach outside their countries. Many Americans are so American that they are confined to America and are unable to minister in the rest of the world. Only five per cent of the world comes from North America and many American ministers of the gospel are now confined to ministering to five percent of the world. Amazingly, this five percent also has ninety percent of the ministers of the gospel.

Nigerians have given birth to many great churches. Nigerians also have a reputation for certain things. If you are a Nigerian minister, you must make efforts to distance yourself from any negative stereotypes. It is worth fighting to be more of a Christian than anything else.

Francophone countries are noted for certain practices. It is important to distance yourself from any negative stereotypes. You must be more of a Christian than a Francophone!

16. Fight against colour stereotypes.

And he said, Cursed be Canaan; a servant of servants shall he be unto his brethren.

And he said, Blessed be the LORD God of Shem; and Canaan shall be his servant.

God shall enlarge Japheth, and he shall dwell in the tents of Shem; and Canaan shall be his servant.

Genesis 9:25-27

Black people are noted for their lack of development, poverty, shabbiness, filth, confusion, disorganization and inability to prosper! White people are noted for their love of money, lack of relationships, homosexuality, divorce, gay marriages, atheism, smoking, alcoholism and high suicide rates!

Unfortunately, these stereotypes are real patterns that we need to fight. If you are a white man or a black man, fight to dissociate from these stereotypes. Distance yourself from any of these stereotypes. Take on the characteristics of a Christian rather than the characteristics of a black man or a white man. That is a good fight worth fighting for!

17. Fight against lust.

Flee also youthful lusts: but follow righteousness, faith, charity, peace, with them that call on the Lord out of a pure heart.

2 Timothy 2:22

Lust is a fire that burns away your holiness. It takes away from you spiritually. This is why Paul said it is better to marry than to burn. If you are burning, you are experiencing something that is not good. Your sexual desires are linked to your spirituality. Sexuality is supernatural because it is an almost a super-normal influence in a human being. Burning sexual desire is a negative thing and it takes away from you spiritually. You must fight lust with all your heart and with all your might.

The first way to fight lust is by preventing yourself from acquiring certain tastes. Once you have acquired the taste for certain sexual things, it is more difficult to control them.

Secondly, if you have already acquired the taste for certain sexual things like pornography, masturbation and homosexuality, you have to pray against it for the rest of your life.

The third thing to do to fight lust is to give your sexuality an outlet. This outlet can come through marriage, where you will be able to have regular sexual intercourse. Unfortunately, even in marriage, your sexuality may not be guaranteed an outlet if you have a bad wife. Whatever the case, you will have to fight against lust for the rest of your life.

18. Fight for fruitfulness.

For if these things be in you, and abound, they make you that ye shall neither be barren nor unfruitful in the knowledge of our Lord Jesus Christ.

2 Peter 1:8

The fight against spiritual barrenness is a long and difficult one. It involves galvanizing many hidden qualities and straightening your life out as you serve the Lord. You will notice that fruitfulness is connected to diligence, faith, godliness, temperance, knowledge, virtue and patience. These are all spiritual qualities that do not look like they are linked to fruitfulness. But they are! They are the real determinants of your fruitfulness. All through your life, you will fight for diligence, temperance, faith, knowledge, brotherly kindness and charity.

It is a good and worthwhile fight because it is a fight for fruitfulness.

CHAPTER 4

Get Used to the War Atmosphere

For every battle of the warrior is with confused noise, and garments rolled in blood; but this shall be with burning and fuel of fire.

Isaiah 9:5

We are in the last battle for the souls of men. If we do not get used to the battle atmosphere, we will never function properly. Listen to what the Bible says: "Every battle of the warrior has an atmosphere of confused noise, garments rolled in blood and the burning of fuel and fire."(Isaiah 9:5) This is not a tranquil atmosphere of peace, harmony and joy.

It is the war atmosphere of danger, risk, confusion, bewilderment, disorientation, stress, tension, unhappiness, fear, death, sorrow, pain, disappointment and shock. God is using us to spread His Word and to fight the deceptions and delusions that are leading the masses to Hell. We have an enemy who is not happy for the kingdom of God to advance. As soon as Jesus came on the scene, He was repeatedly attacked by the devil. Jesus Christ lived in the atmosphere of war. The devil was never far away. Jesus was attacked by a spirit of murder that wanted to wipe Him out before He could grow up. He was attacked in the wilderness whilst He fasted and prayed. He was attacked through the Pharisees and finally He was attacked through Judas Iscariot.

The Atmosphere of Ministry
Is the Atmosphere of War

Once you give heed to the high calling of God, you are entering into the very last battle for the kingdom of God. Jesus died on the cross and this began a serious campaign to save this world from a very wicked devil and his angels. The devil is that old serpent who has deceived this world for many years.

True ministry is war. The atmosphere of true ministry is the atmosphere of war. What is the atmosphere of war like? Is it an atmosphere of tranquility, calmness and peace? Certainly not! If peace and calm is what you are looking for, please do not come into the ministry. As soon as you start to obey God and live a godly life, you will begin to experience the different components of the war atmosphere. "Yea, and all that will live godly in Christ Jesus shall suffer persecution" (2 Timothy 3:12).

When war erupts, the atmosphere switches quickly into a characteristic mixture of *strife, confusion* and *disorientation*. When you are at war, you will always be under stress. There will be *fear*, there will be *tension* and there will be *uncertainty*. Can you operate under these conditions? Do surprises knock you out and silence you?

You will have to get used to the war atmosphere. A soldier cannot claim that he is *bewildered* because of the *turmoil* of war. The war atmosphere must not *overwhelm* a true soldier.

When I volunteered to be in the ministry, I was volunteering to live in the atmosphere of war. Every soldier who goes out to war is subjecting himself to great *risk* and *danger*. There will be *casualties,* there will be *turbulence*, there will be *hurts*, there will be *noise*, there will be *sorrow* and there will be *death*. This is the atmosphere of war! Get used to it! If you live for Jesus and try to do His will, this is going to be the atmosphere for your life.

One day, a pastor's wife asked her husband, *"You at all, when will you have peace?"* She wanted to know when her husband would have a normal and peaceful life. The answer is, "Never!" The ministry atmosphere is the war atmosphere.

CHAPTER 5

The Business of War is to Take New Territories, to Take Things by Force and to Defend Yourself

Rise ye up, take your journey, and pass over the river Arnon: behold, I have given into thine hand Sihon the Amorite, king of Heshbon, and his land: BEGIN TO POSSESS IT, AND CONTEND WITH HIM IN BATTLE.

Deuteronomy 2:24

1.   The business of war is to take new territories.

> Now after the death of Moses the servant of the LORD it
> came to pass, that the LORD spake unto Joshua the son of
> Nun, Moses' minister, saying, Moses my servant is dead;
> NOW THEREFORE ARISE, GO OVER THIS JORDAN,
> THOU, AND ALL THIS PEOPLE, UNTO THE LAND
> WHICH I DO GIVE TO THEM, even to the children of
> Israel. Every place that the sole of your foot shall tread
> upon, that have I given unto you, as I said unto Moses.
>
> From the wilderness and this Lebanon even unto the great
> river, the river Euphrates, all the land of the Hittites, and
> unto the great sea toward the going down of the sun, shall
> be your coast.
>
> Joshua 1:1-4

After the death of Moses, Joshua was commanded to take new territories for God. God is always telling His people to take new territories and advance into new areas. On many occasions, I have sensed the Lord leading me into new territories. It has always been a fight to take new territories. It is more difficult to take new territories than to simply enjoy the territories you already occupy.

If you want to have new territories, you have to fight a good fight! The lands on the earth are heavily guarded. No one gives up his land easily. The devil does not give up territory without a fight. Any form of expansion in your ministry will involve fighting a good fight. God has called us to take territories for Him.

We are to invade the enemy's kingdom and claim territories and cities for Him. This will not be done by calm, sleepy, sing-song Christians who just want to stay in one place and have nice worship times. It is nice to worship and sing songs of praise. But taking new territories is a completely different business. The business of war is the business of taking new territories.

Once the anointing for expansion is on your life, you will be taking new territories and you will always be in one battle or another. That is the meaning of war! It is the fight to take new territories!

2.   The business of war is to take things by force.

And from the days of John the Baptist until now the kingdom of heaven SUFFERETH VIOLENCE, and the violent take it by force.

Matthew 11:12

We must fight because some things are not given to us unless we take them by force. You must fight to overcome the resistance and the opposition to your goals. "Be sober, be vigilant; because your adversary the devil, as a roaring lion, walketh about, seeking whom he may devour: Whom resist stedfast in the faith, knowing that the same afflictions are accomplished in your brethren that are in the world" (1 Peter 5:8-9). The devil is called an adversary. This means he opposes your vision.

There are evil spirits as well as human beings who are intent on preventing you from accomplishing your aims. If your aims are fulfilled it may be harmful or detrimental to them. If you have an aim to win the lost, it will harm the devil. Satan will be negatively affected by your goal and he will decide to oppose you and make things difficult for you.

David wanted a headquarters for his ministry. He identified Jerusalem as a good place but the Jebusites who lived there decided to oppose David's new idea. King David launched a new war and crushed them, taking Jebus by force. That very spot which David took by force is called Jerusalem today. Jerusalem was not handed to David on a silver platter. David had to fight for every inch of Jerusalem. Your ministry will not be handed to you on a silver platter. You are going to have to fight for every inch of it. There are Jebusites who are going to say to you, "Thou shalt not come hither." You will not come here. We will fight you if you try to come!

And David and all Israel went to Jerusalem, which is Jebus; where the Jebusites were, the inhabitants of the land.

And the inhabitants of Jebus said to David, THOU SHALT NOT COME HITHER. Nevertheless David took the castle of Zion, which is the city of David.

And David said, Whosoever smiteth the Jebusites first shall be chief and captain. So Joab the son of Zeruiah went first up, and was chief. And David dwelt in the castle; therefore they called it the city of David. And he built the city round about, even from Millo round about: and Joab repaired the rest of the city.

1 Chronicles 11:4-8

3.   The business of war is to defend yourself.

The thief cometh not, but for TO STEAL, and TO KILL, and TO DESTROY...

John 10:10

There is a thief readying himself to steal, to kill and to destroy all that God has given you. We must fight to defend ourselves from aggressors who surprise us by launching attacks and wars against us. An enemy has come up against us to destroy all that we are and all that we have. We must fight because evil aggressors will come against us without any good cause. There are always aggressive people who attack good people for no good reason.

When Adolf Hitler decided to invade Europe, many countries simply succumbed to his wishes, but there were some who refused to allow Hitler to have his way. Winston Churchill was one of those people.

Winston Churchill Vows to Defend His Island

He said, "We shall prove ourselves once again able to defend our island home, to ride out the storm of war, and to outlive the menace of tyranny, if necessary for years, if necessary alone. That is the resolve of his majesty's government – every man of them. That is the will of parliament and the nation. The British Empire and the French Republic, linked together in their cause and in their need, will defend to the death their native soil, aiding each other like good comrades to the utmost of their strength. Even though large tracts of Europe and many old and famous states have fallen or may fall into the grip of the Gestapo and all the odious apparatus of Nazi rule, we shall not flag or fail.

We shall go on to the end, we shall fight in France, we shall fight on the seas and oceans, we shall fight with growing confidence and growing strength in the air, we shall defend our island whatever the cost may be, we shall fight on the beaches, we shall fight on the landing grounds, we shall fight in the fields and in the streets, we shall fight in the hills, we shall never surrender. And even if, which I do not for a moment believe, this island or a large part of it were subjugated and starving, then our empire beyond the seas, armed and guarded by the British fleet, would carry on the struggle until, in God's good time, the new world, with all its power and might, steps forth to the rescue and the liberation of the old."

Defend the Church

We, as ministers of the gospel, must defend the churches we are building. The enemy will rise up to destroy what God has used you to do. If you sit down calmly thinking that nothing bad can happen to the good work you have done, you are but a child. You will be attacked! The church will be attacked! Satan will fight to destroy all your fruits! He will come against the church using distinguished men in suits! Satan has no gentle plans for God's church. He is a wicked, merciless, heartless being!

You will have to put on your army uniform and fight hard to defend what God is doing. Once you build the church you must rise up and defend it against those who leave you, those who forget, those who pretend, those who are disloyal, those who are dangerous sons, those who are ignorant and those who accuse you.

When it is time for war, gentle, friendly, childlike attitudes will not help. It is time to mature and understand that Christians do have to fight to defend God's church. Today, homosexuality is invading the church. A strong stand is necessary to reject the perversion and destruction of the entire body of Christ. Today, a new attitude of prosperity, instead of salvation and soul winning is invading the church and weakening it. It is time to rise and defend the church against secularism and unspiritual teachings. It is time to defend the church from turning into an unspiritual "centre for motivational speeches".

The main mission of the Holy Spirit is to inspire us for soul winning. "But ye shall receive power after that the Holy Ghost is come upon you: and ye shall be witnesses unto me both in Jerusalem, and in all Judaea, and in Samaria, and unto the uttermost part of the earth" (Acts 1:8). That is why the Holy Spirit has been given! The main mission of the church is to win souls under the inspiration of the Holy Spirit. Today, the main mission of the church is to be happy, to be prosperous, to be excited and to stay in the safest, nicest cities of the world. Churches do not care much about the lost and dying people in this world. There is an invasion of an evil secular spirit. The church is under attack. It is time to defend the church against the spirit of the world. The spirit of the world is intent on destroying the mission of the Holy Spirit. It is time to rebuke the false, lukewarm spirit of the world that is destroying the church.

CHAPTER 6

Firmness Must Be Directed at Quieting, Humbling and Controlling Your Enemy

...for he is strong that executeth his word: for the day of the Lord is great and very terrible; and who can abide it?

Joel 2:11

I f you accept that you are at war, then you must practice the principles of war. When war erupts firmness, energy and physical effort must be directed at your enemy.

War is your effort to overcome something or someone. There is opposition to your vision and your dream. Your desire to serve the Lord will not be taken lightly by that old serpent and his angels.

The principles of war teach you to direct firmness at crushing something! A good soldier must direct firmness and energy at defeating the enemy.

The principles of war must be applied against those that agitate against you. To wage war is to *direct firmness at quieting something, humbling something, warning something* and *controlling something.*

War is a struggle. War is a conflict.

From the day I entered the ministry and tried to build a church, I have been struggling to control the church that I have built. I have been struggling to humble and discipline the enemies that naturally rise up against my calling.

You cannot be weak, uncertain or soft towards something that hates you! To be at war is to *direct firmness at quieting something, humbling something, warning something and controlling something.*

I tell you, there are men who can hurt your ministry so much that you may never be able to recover. They will take away your members, take away your income and destroy your life's work. If you joke with them, your heart will be broken and you may not be able to recover. They will repay your kindness with ingratitude and wickedness. Follow the principles of war. *Direct firmness at quieting humbling, warning* and *controlling disloyal people.*

It is time to direct firmness at controlling thieves in the church. There are people who are stealing the offering that you are receiving. You must direct firmness at humbling, warning and controlling these thieves in your ministry or business.

It is time to take the subject of war seriously. You are at war even if you do not realise it.

Sometimes it is your own spouse who is at war with you. Many men do not direct firmness at controlling their spouses. Their wives run amok and become like wild animals having a field day. It is time to direct firmness at quieting, humbling, warning and controlling your wife.

Neville Chamberlain without Firmness

Before the Second World War erupted, Britain's Prime Minister was Neville Chamberlain. He was determined to avert a war with Germany. His policy towards the mass murderer, Adolf Hitler, was one of appeasement. This meant that he was conciliatory towards the German government because he thought they had genuine grievances that needed to be addressed. He also thought that if he agreed to some of the demands of Adolf Hitler, he would avert another war.

The Prime Minister of England, Neville Chamberlain, was warned by the secret service that negotiations with Hitler would be fruitless and that the only way to deal with Germany was to stand firm. The Prime Minister of England was told that if he adopted a firm attitude and threatened war, Hitler could be stopped. But instead of *standing firm and directing firmness at quieting, humbling, warning* and *controlling Hitler*, the Prime Minister allowed Hitler to invade and annex both Austria and parts of Czechoslovakia.

A young historian living in Manchester by the name A.J.P. Taylor felt so strongly about the policy of appeasement towards Hitler that he made several speeches and addressed several meetings on the theme *"Stand up to Hitler."* He tried every possible argument but the crowd only responded in the same way: "What you are advocating means war. We want peace!" These people did not know that they were allowing a very evil person to grow in strength and power. Eventually, this policy of calm appeasement led the whole world into the worst conflagration ever known to man.

CHAPTER 7

Only an Equilibrium Leads to the Suspension of War So a Good General is Not Surprised at the Outbreak of War

Now the Philistines gathered together their armies to battle, and were gathered together at Shochoh, which belongeth to Judah, and pitched between Shochoh and Azekah, in Ephesdammim. And Saul and the men of Israel were gathered together, and pitched by the valley of Elah, and set the battle in array against the Philistines. And THE PHILISTINES STOOD ON A MOUNTAIN ON THE ONE SIDE, AND ISRAEL STOOD ON A MOUNTAIN ON THE OTHER SIDE: and there was a valley between them.

1 Samuel 17:1-3

Therefore David ran, and stood upon the Philistine, and took his sword, and drew it out of the sheath thereof, and slew him, and cut off his head therewith. And when the Philistines saw their champion was dead, they fled. AND THE MEN OF ISRAEL AND OF JUDAH AROSE, AND SHOUTED, AND PURSUED THE PHILISTINES, until thou come to the valley, and to the gates of Ekron. And the wounded of the Philistines fell down by the way to Shaaraim, even unto Gath, and unto Ekron.

1 Samuel 17:51-52

I t is not good for you to be surprised at the outbreak of war and trouble. A good general must expect war to erupt. A good general knows that there is peace only because there is equilibrium. A good general knows that a fight will soon erupt. A good general knows that a war will erupt when the balance of power changes. Do not be surprised when a war erupts or when there is a new battle.

A good general knows that peace exists only because there is equal strength on both sides of the divide. There is peace in Europe today, because Europe is an armed camp! Many nuclear powers lie silently by each other in Europe. All the key nations of Europe are armed to the teeth with the most sophisticated weapons ever known to man. Because of this, no one wants to attack the other.

The armies of Israel were in equilibrium with the armies of the Philistines. There was no breakthrough; there was a stalemate. Then suddenly, with the death of Goliath, Israel gained the upper hand and the equilibrium was broken. The suspended war was back in full force. The equilibrium was broken by the death of the Philistine giant.

Do not be surprised that you have to fight and fight and fight again. Do not think of resting or taking your ease whilst you are on this earth. As a teenager, you will fight to be a good Christian. When you are in your twenties, you will also fight to serve the Lord. In your thirties, you will have to fight the good fight of faith. There is a battle waiting for you at every stage of life. It is not a good thing that you should be surprised at the presence of conflict or difficulty. You should rather expect war, trouble, conflict and difficulty. To not expect war is to be simple minded. Many people say to themselves, "I am a good person with good motives. Why is this happening?" They say, "I have not hurt anyone. Why should anyone attack me? I am working for God."

What evil did Jesus do? Why did the Pharisees attack Him? Why did Pontius Pilate have Jesus crucified? Whom did He hurt?

Why was He persecuted so much? Was Jesus not a good person? Good people will have to fight too. Expect to fight on different levels. Expect to have to fight about different things. Expect war with almost anyone. Be prepared to fight and win. We are called to fight. Our Saviour is leading His armies into victory.

The Wars of Good People

1.   David was a good man but he had to fight with Saul.

Do not be surprised that you have to fight with a father. In the ministry, many fathers are insecure. Many fathers provoke their spiritual sons into conflict. Do not be surprised when you find yourself fighting a father.

> And SAUL SPAKE TO JONATHAN HIS SON, AND TO ALL HIS SERVANTS, THAT THEY SHOULD KILL DAVID.
>
> But Jonathan Saul's son delighted much in David: and Jonathan told David, saying, Saul my father seeketh to kill thee: now therefore, I pray thee, take heed to thyself until the morning, and abide in a secret place, and hide thyself:
>
> And I will go out and stand beside my father in the field where thou art, and I will commune with my father of thee; and what I see, that I will tell thee. And Jonathan spake good of David unto Saul his father, and said unto him, Let not the king sin against his servant, against David; because he hath not sinned against thee, and because his works have been to thee-ward very good:
>
> For he did put his life in his hand, and slew the Philistine, and the LORD wrought a great salvation for all Israel: thou sawest it, and didst rejoice: WHEREFORE THEN WILT THOU SIN AGAINST INNOCENT BLOOD, TO SLAY DAVID WITHOUT A CAUSE?
>
> 1 Samuel 19:1-5

2.   King David had to fight with his son Absalom.

Do not be surprised that you have to fight with a son. There are many sons who fight the fathers who raise them up. Do not be surprised if you have to fight with your own son in the ministry.

And David said to Abishai, and to all his servants, Behold, MY SON, WHICH CAME FORTH OF MY BOWELS, SEEKETH MY LIFE: how much more now may this Benjamite do it? let him alone, and let him curse; for the LORD hath bidden him.

2 Samuel 16:11

3.   David had to fight with people who reacted to his anointing.

People fought against David when they heard that he had been anointed. The anointing draws enemies and launches you into various new battles. Don't be surprised that you still have to fight when you are anointed. Many of the battles of your life are because of the anointing God has placed on you.

But WHEN THE PHILISTINES HEARD THAT THEY HAD ANOINTED DAVID king over Israel, all the Philistines came up to seek David; and David heard of it, and went down to the hold.

THE PHILISTINES ALSO CAME AND SPREAD THEMSELVES IN THE VALLEY OF REPHAIM.

And David enquired of the Lord, saying, Shall I go up to the Philistines? wilt thou deliver them into mine hand? And the Lord said unto David, Go up: for I will doubtless deliver the Philistines into thine hand.

2 Samuel 5:17-19

4.   Jehoshaphat had to fight with the ungrateful Ammonites.

Don't be surprised when you have to fight with people you have been kind to. There are many ungrateful people who will stir up battles in your life.

And now, BEHOLD, THE CHILDREN OF AMMON and Moab and mount Seir, whom thou wouldest not let Israel invade, when they came out of the land of Egypt, but they turned from them, and destroyed them not;

Behold, I say, HOW THEY REWARD US, TO COME TO CAST US OUT OF THY POSSESSION, which thou hast given us to inherit.

O our God, wilt thou not judge them? for we have no might against this great company that cometh against us; neither know we what to do: but our eyes are upon thee.

2 Chronicles 20:10-12

5.   Hezekiah had to fight with the king of Assyria.

Don't be surprised when you have to fight with a blasphemer and someone who does not respect God.

And it came to pass, when king Hezekiah heard it, that he rent his clothes, and covered himself with sackcloth, and went into the house of the LORD.

And he sent Eliakim, which was over the household, and Shebna the scribe, and the elders of the priests, covered with sackcloth, to Isaiah the prophet the son of Amoz.

And they said unto him, Thus saith Hezekiah, This day is a day of trouble, and of rebuke, and blasphemy: for the children are come to the birth, and there is not strength to bring forth.

It may be the LORD thy GOD WILL HEAR ALL THE WORDS OF RABSHAKEH, WHOM THE KING OF

ASSYRIA HIS MASTER HATH SENT TO REPROACH THE LIVING GOD; and will reprove the words which the LORD thy God hath heard: wherefore lift up thy prayer for the remnant that are left.

So the servants of king Hezekiah came to Isaiah.

And Isaiah said unto them, Thus shall ye say to your master, Thus saith the LORD, Be not afraid of the words which thou hast heard, with which the servants of the king of Assyria have blasphemed me.

2 Kings 19:1-6

6. Ahab the king of Israel had to fight with Benhadad of Syria.

Don't be surprised if you have to fight with troublemakers.

And Benhadad the king of Syria gathered all his host together: and there were thirty and two kings with him, and horses, and chariots: and he went up and besieged Samaria, and warred against it.

And he sent messengers to Ahab king of Israel into the city, and said unto him, Thus saith Benhadad,

Thy silver and thy gold is mine; thy wives also and thy children, even the goodliest, are mine.

And the king of Israel answered and said, My lord, O king, according to thy saying, I am thine, and all that I have.

And the messengers came again, and said, thus speaketh Benhadad, saying, Although I have sent unto thee, saying, Thou shalt deliver me thy silver, and thy gold, and thy wives, and thy children;

Yet I will send my servants unto thee to morrow about this time, and they shall search thine house, and the houses of thy servants; and it shall be, that whatsoever is pleasant in thine eyes, they shall put it in their hand, and take it away.

THEN THE KING OF ISRAEL CALLED ALL THE ELDERS OF THE LAND, AND SAID, MARK, I

PRAY YOU, AND SEE HOW THIS MAN SEEKETH MISCHIEF: FOR HE SENT UNTO ME FOR MY WIVES, AND FOR MY CHILDREN, AND FOR MY SILVER, AND FOR MY GOLD; and I denied him not.

1 Kings 20:1-7

CHAPTER 8

Selection and Maintenance of the Aim

Therefore, my beloved brethren, be ye stedfast, unmoveable, always abounding in the work of the Lord, forasmuch as ye know that your labour is not in vain in the Lord.

1 Corinthians 15:58

S election of the aim and maintenance of your aim is the number one principle of war! You must select your aim and keep at it. If your aim is to start and grow churches, stick to it! You must direct your efforts towards your objective.

A successful military operation is aimed at an objective that can be achieved. War is aimed at destroying the enemy's ability and will to fight!

The British military teaches that a single, unambiguous aim is the keystone of successful military operations. Selection and maintenance of the aim is regarded as the master principle of war. The Russian Armed Forces' doctrine calls this principle *Steadfastness*. Subordinate commanders are to carry out the mission in the spirit and the letter of the plan.

The American military calls this principle *Objective*. They are taught to direct every military operation toward a clearly defined, decisive and attainable objective.

Today, the church has largely set aside its one and only aim to win the lost souls of this world for Jesus Christ. Paul had this one aim: "For I determined not to know any thing among you, save Jesus Christ, and him crucified" (1 Corinthians 2:2). Today, very few ministers of the gospel have the aim of only talking about Jesus Christ and Him crucified. Most ministers have new aims and goals that are not the bringing of the lost to Christ. Many pastors have turned into motivational speakers and bankers.

The selected aim of the backslidden Christian church is to have a happy marriage, a successful career, lots of money and breakthroughs. The real aim of the church is to "Go ye into all the world and preach the gospel to every creature". Our aim has been selected by the Lord Jesus. When you shift away from your selected aim, you start to lose the war. Today, most of the church has set aside its original aim and Christianity is no more the fastest growing religion in the world.

It is important for an army to maintain its aim. What aims have you selected for your ministry? Is it church growth? Is it evangelism? Is it to catch the anointing? Is it to build a church building? The aim must be selected and it must be maintained! Throughout history, armies that violated this principle lost the wars. Remember that anyone who chases two rabbits will lose them both!

Large Christian areas of Africa have been taken over by other religions. Because the church has not maintained its aim of soul winning, preaching and evangelizing the world it is gradually losing the battle for the souls and lives of people. Large areas, which were formally Christian, have fallen almost completely to other religions. The aim "Go ye into all the world and preach the gospel" is a forgotten instruction in many churches today.

"Selection and Maintenance of the Aim" and the Invasion of Russia

Adolf Hitler, who caused the death of 50 million people, wrote a book, *Mein Kampf*. In this book he outlined his vision for the world. He stated his dreams, his anti-Semitic views and in particular, he stated his views on the need for Germany to acquire more land from where he could feed Germany.

He described this as "*lebensraum*" – living space. This vision of Hitler to acquire more "*lebensraum*" would be fulfilled if he invaded Soviet territory.

After capturing Ukraine, Adolf Hitler had really achieved his aim of acquiring more "*lebensraum*" or living space. With Ukraine under his control, he had the agricultural basket that he needed. If he had maintained his aim of just acquiring more living space as he wrote in his book, he would not have sent his armies to Moscow where they were destroyed. Hitler's demonic hatred for Russians inspired him to press on to his own destruction. It is wise to always remember and maintain your original aims.

In August 1941, the German forces were on the move to take Moscow. They captured the city of Smolensk, an important stronghold on the road to Moscow. The capture of Smolensk took the Germans two months to accomplish.

After the Germans had captured the city of Smolensk, Hitler ordered his forces to attack two key cities to the north and the south. These cities were Leningrad and Kiev. This change of plan greatly affected the Germans' ability to capture Moscow. This brought about a significant delay in the invasion of Moscow and caused a crisis in the German leadership. By the time the advance on Moscow was resumed in October 1941 German forces had been significantly weakened while the Russians had raised new forces for the defense of the city - changes that would greatly hinder the Russian offensive. Once again, not maintaining the original aim cost Germany the victory.

Most historians would agree that Hitler's decision to invade Russia was one of the main reasons that Germany lost the war. German forces were tied up in this conflict for years. It drained Germany's resources, destroyed their morale, and diverted its military presence from Western Europe, ultimately making it possible for British and American forces to invade and rescue Europe from Hitler's grip.

"Selection and Maintenance of the Aim" in the Gulf War

The first Gulf War was brought about by the invasion of Kuwait by Iraq. Iraq annexed Kuwait by invading a sovereign nation and simply taking it over. America responded by fighting Iraq and driving them out of Kuwait. This war was over in a few days as the Iraqi forces fled before the Americans invaded.

Even though the Americans could have pursued the Iraqis and destroyed the Iraqi army they did not do so. This would have been very possible for the Americans who were ready for a big fight. But they had to maintain the aim and the purpose of the war that they had embarked upon.

45

CHAPTER 9

A Good General and Maintenance of Morale

And Joshua the son of Nun, and Caleb the son of Jephunneh, which were of them that searched the land, rent their clothes:

And THEY SPAKE UNTO ALL THE COMPANY OF THE CHILDREN OF ISRAEL, SAYING, THE LAND, WHICH WE PASSED THROUGH TO SEARCH IT, IS AN EXCEEDING GOOD LAND.

IF THE LORD DELIGHT IN US, THEN HE WILL BRING US INTO THIS LAND, AND GIVE IT US; A LAND WHICH FLOWETH WITH MILK AND HONEY.

Only rebel not ye against the Lord, neither fear ye the people of the land; for they are bread for us: their defence is departed from them, and the Lord is with us: fear them not. But all the congregation bade stone them with stones. And the glory of the Lord appeared in the tabernacle of the congregation before all the children of Israel.

Numbers 14:6-10

46

Wars are won or lost by weakening the morale of the enemy. That is why maintaining the morale of the group is key to winning the battle. Joshua and Caleb are famous for their speech in which they sought to stabilize the congregation and encourage them to enter the Promised Land. Without enthusiasm and zeal you cannot do much for God. People must be happy to work for God. One day a brother remarked to me, "You make working for God exciting. Everyone is happy to be around and to be doing something." Without this positive feeling, negative thoughts quickly take over the hearts and minds of the team.

Maintenance of morale is the maintenance of cheerfulness, confidence and zeal especially in the face of battle. Morale is a positive state of mind derived from inspired leadership.

The morale of human beings reduces as time passes and events unfold. That is why the morale of younger people is usually higher than the morale of older people.

To maintain morale is to maintain zeal, enthusiasm, interest and confidence in something. It is easy to lose the morale as you take up the fight to follow the Lord in the ministry.

There are three main seasons of your life where you must maintain the zeal.

• You must maintain zeal and enthusiasm whilst in school.

• You must maintain your zeal as you go on in life. You need to be zealous during all the different boring phases of this life.

• You must be able to maintain zeal in times of crises. Crises have the greatest ability to reduce your zeal and confidence. Without good morale, you are likely to lose your war.

Indeed, many battles are directed at reducing the morale and enthusiasm of the troops. Many events are orchestrated by evil spirits with the intention of discouraging you from serving the Lord.

People leave the ministry because of discouragement more than any other single cause.

A good general knows how to raise the morale in the army. You must get the army to think less about themselves and more about what they are involved with. Motivate the troops and maintain their morale by making them think less about themselves and more about their hated enemy. You can raise the morale in the army of God's people by making them think less about themselves and more about the lost. You can raise the morale of the troops by talking to them.

Many leaders are famous for their speeches that raised the morale of their people. Leaders like Napoleon Bonaparte, Winston Churchill, Adolf Hitler, Martin Luther King, Ronald Reagan and Barrack Obama are famous for their motivational speeches. Leaders who do not speak to their troops fail to raise the morale of their troops. You must rise up and speak to your people. You must encourage them and tell them that it will be well. The morale of the people who are following you is very important. Your failure to raise their morale is your failure to lead.

Julius Caesar and the "Maintenance of Morale"

Julius Caesar was a famous general who won many battles on behalf of Rome. His most famous wars were fought in Gaul (France) and Britain. The Roman army was originally a part-time army. Many of the soldiers were farmers who would return to their original jobs after fighting in the Roman wars. Indeed, the armies of Rome had been run as a "lay army" before the time of Julius Caesar.

Julius Caesar changed all that by creating a professional organization with long terms of service far from home.

One of the things that Julius Caesar did was to boost the morale of his troops by promising the soldiers some land on which they could farm when they returned home. The soldiers were encouraged to fight in the Roman wars, knowing that when they returned home they would have land to farm on. This idea, to pay soldiers with land was a clever idea that greatly boosted the morale of Julius Caesar's soldiers. The high morale of Julius Caesar's troops contributed greatly to his success as a general.

Napoleon Bonaparte and the "Maintenance of Morale"

Napoleon Bonaparte, who lived in the eighteenth century, was another young but famous general. Napoleon is remembered for numerous campaigns and wars that he championed in Europe.

Napoleon was famous for boosting the morale of his troops through motivational speeches. In 1796, when he was only twenty-seven years old, he demonstrated his military genius in a war against Italy. Speeches were all that were needed to galvanize Napoleon's men into action. No wonder he was such a famous general because his loyal troops would go anywhere with him, ready to die for France. I want you to read Napoleon's speech as he motivated his armies to give their lives for the cause of France.

On the 27th of March 1796, Napoleon spoke to his men and said:

"Soldiers, you are naked, ill fed! The Government owes you much; it can give you nothing. Your patience, the courage you display in the midst of these rocks, are admirable; but they procure you no glory, no fame is reflected upon you. I seek to lead you into the most fertile plains in the world. Rich provinces, great cities will be in your power. There you will find honor, glory, and riches. Soldiers of Italy, would you be lacking in courage or constancy?"

A month later, on the 26th of April 1796, Napoleon charged his troops again calling on them:

"In a fortnight you have won six victories, taken twenty-one standards, fifty-five pieces, great of artillery, several strong positions, and conquered the richest part of Piedmont [a region in northern Italy]; you have captured 15,000 prisoners and killed or wounded more than 10,000 men. ...

You have won battles without cannon, crossed rivers without bridges, made forced marches without shoes, camped without brandy and often without bread. Soldiers of liberty, only republican phalanxes [infantry troops] could have endured what you have endured. Soldiers, you have our thanks! The grateful Patrie [nation] will owe its prosperity to you. . . .The two armies which but recently attacked you with audacity are fleeing before you in terror; the wicked men who laughed at your misery and rejoiced at the thought of the triumphs of your enemies are confounded and trembling. But, soldiers, as yet you have done nothing compared with what remains to be done. . . . undoubtedly the greatest obstacles have been overcome; but you still have battles to fight, cities to capture, rivers to cross. Is there one among you whose courage is abating? No. . . .

All of you are consumed with a desire to extend the glory of the French people; all of you long to humiliate those arrogant kings who dare to contemplate placing us in fetters; all of you desire to dictate a glorious peace, one which will indemnify the patrie for the immense sacrifices it has made; all of you wish to be able to say with pride as you return to your villages, 'I was with the victorious army of Italy!'"

"Maintenance of the Morale" in Rwanda

In Rwanda, there was a genocide in which 800,000 people were killed in a hundred days. The Hutus, a tribe in Rwanda, were able to carry out the mass killing of their neighbours and friends within three months. How did they do this? Were there any foreign troops there? Were there any interventionary forces stationed in the land that could have prevented this from happening? The answer is, "Yes." There were United Nations forces, Belgian forces and French forces present in the country. So why did they not do anything to prevent the genocide? The answer is simple: they refused to fight and simply abandoned Rwanda to its fate. So why did they leave? Their morale was severely weakened, leading to a mass evacuation of all foreign forces.

The story of this incredible genocide begins when the Germans colonized Rwanda in 1894. They felt the Tutsi had more European characteristics, such as lighter skin and a taller build so they put the Tutsis in roles of responsibility. Germany lost their colonies following the First World War and Belgium took over the control of Rwanda.

In 1933, the Belgians solidified the separation of the "Tutsi" and "Hutu" groups by instituting the use of an identity card for each person that labelled them Tutsi, Hutu, or Twa. (Twa is a very small group of hunter-gatherers who also live in Rwanda). Although the Tutsi constituted only about ten percent of Rwanda's population and the Hutu nearly 90 percent, the Belgians gave the Tutsi all the leadership positions. Land and power were in the hands of the minority Tutsi, whilst the Hutus were more of field workers. The Hutus were not happy with this.

From 1973 to 1993, President Habyarimana, a Hutu, run a government, which excluded all Tutsis from participating. However, in 1993 President Habyarimana signed the Arusha Accords that allowed Tutsis to participate in the government. This greatly upset Hutu extremists.

On April 6th, 1994, President Habyarimana of Rwanda was returning from a summit in Tanzania when a surface-to-air missile shot his plane out of the sky over Kigali. All on board were killed in the crash. Within 24 hours of the crash, some Hutu leaders took over the government and blamed the Tutsis for the air crash and begun the slaughter in Rwanda's capital city, Kigali.

These Hutu leaders killed both the Tutsis and moderate Hutus. They then proceeded to kill the lady Prime Minister Agathe Uwilingiyimana and her husband, as well as the ten Belgian soldiers assigned to protect them.

This dramatic episode in which ten Belgian soldiers were murdered drove Belgium into a state of depression and discouragement, causing Belgium to withdraw its troops from Rwanda. The Hutus, knowing that the Europeans would not want to have casualties among their ranks carried out this attack and thereby weakened the morale of all foreign nationals who were in the country.

The deaths of these Belgian troops caused the zeal and enthusiasm of all foreign nationals to plummet. They had no stomach to get involved in another African ethnic conflict. At that time, the memory of the Somalia war, with its American casualties was fresh in everyone's mind.

Indeed, all the foreign soldiers and embassies were evacuated from Rwanda, leaving the Hutus in absolute control. Without any checks or interventions, the Hutus carried out a systematic campaign to kill all the Tutsis they could find. They killed and killed until they could find no more Tutsis to kill. Their strategy had worked, breaking the morale of the foreigners by killing ten of their precious soldiers and making them leave the country. It worked like magic.

This is what the devil may be doing in your life. Events occur to break your interest and enthusiasm in the call of God and the ministry of Jesus Christ. Before long you are resigning and leaving your place in ministry. When there is an attack on your morale, you must rise up and fight. Do not allow yourself to be driven away from your place of ministry.

This is what happened to Elijah. Elijah was discouraged by the threat of Jezebel. He complained that he was the only one who believed in Jehovah. His discouragement and depression drove him to the end of his ministry. In this time of discouragement, he made mistakes, which led to the appointment of his successor.

"Maintenance of Morale" in the Vietnam War

Many of us do not understand why America was fighting a war in Vietnam. The Vietnam War came about because communists in the north of that country were determined to fight and take over the whole country for the cause of communism. This drew in the Americans who were determined to prevent Vietnam from becoming a communist country. The Americans pulled in more forces to fight with the communists in Vietnam. As the war progressed, the Vietnamese decided to launch a special attack on the Americans.

The North Vietnamese launched this massive surprise attack during the festival of the Vietnamese New Year, called "Tet". This attack was therefore called the "Tet Offensive." Thirty-six major cities and towns in South Vietnam were attacked at the same time. The morning after the first attack, around 80,000 Communist soldiers spread all over South Vietnam. More than 100 towns and cities were attacked. Most attacks were targeted at government buildings and military bases.

The city of Hue, for instance, was held for nearly a month by the North Vietnamese. During this time, several thousand civilians, who had cooperated with the U.S. and South Vietnam, were executed by the North Vietnamese. This was known as the "Hue Massacre". On February 26, when the U.S. and South Vietnam forces retook the city, 2,800 dead bodies were found and another 3,000 residents were missing.

On March 3, 1968, the North Vietnamese completely retreated out of Hue. They had lost about 2,400 to 8,000 troops while the South Vietnamese and U.S. had 668 dead and 3,707 wounded. As the conflicts occurred all over the country, many other towns and villages suffered badly. 627,000 Vietnamese were displaced.

The Tet offensive took the Americans by surprise but they were able to fight back and eventually regained control of

Vietnam. The news of the Tet Offensive and other battles began to be shown on American Television. Even though the Americans were firmly in control of the war and were superior to the communist forces, the morale of the American people was greatly affected by the pictures seen on television. Pictures of the dead Americans devastated the American populace so much that there was no more will to continue fighting what most Americans felt was a useless war. The American public began to call for the soldiers to be brought back home.

Even though the U.S.A did not lose any major battles, the American people could not stand the increasing loss of American lives. America was eventually forced by public pressure to start retreating out of Vietnam whilst South Vietnam surrendered to North Vietnam.

Public support for America's war in Vietnam plummeted from 50% in 1967 to as low as 26% right after the Tet Offensive in January 1968 whilst anti-war protests increased all over. A large percentage of Americans came to believe that America had made a mistake by sending troops to Vietnam. Although the Americans were not militarily defeated, their morale was completely weakened. In the end, the communist North Vietnamese prevailed over the American army simply by weakening their morale.

"Maintenance of Morale" in the First World War

The First World War was a complicated war fought between many different nations including Germany, Russia, France, Hungary, Britain and Austria. All these nations became involved because there were treaties and pacts between them. Because of these treaties, attacking one nation would mean getting into conflict with several other nations. One nation after another was pulled into this senseless conflict until virtually the whole world was involved.

But the First World War did not go as planned. New technology, especially the invention of new machine guns, were a surprise feature which caused the soldiers on both sides to dig trenches, take cover and hold their ground. Since the war was being fought across the length and breadth of Europe, the trenches eventually extended for over four hundred miles from the North Sea to Switzerland.

The young men of that day went out to battle with delusions of victory and glory. Instead of the glory they sought, the two sides were stuck in their trenches in an amazing stalemate. Can you believe that the soldiers lived in these protective trenches for four years? The two opposing sides faced each other across no man's land. During this prolonged period, the morale of the troops steadily declined. Many men died on their first day in the trench.

Rats, in their millions, infested the trenches. There were two main types of rats in the trenches: the black rat and the brown rat. Both were despised but the brown one was specially feared because they would disfigure dead bodies by eating their eyes and their liver. These rats could grow to the size of a cat. Lice were a never-ending problem, causing men to itch unceasingly. The lice caused Trench Fever that took some twelve weeks to recover from. Thousands of frogs were also found in the bases of the trenches. Trench Foot was a terrible fungal infection common to the soldiers.

Because most people had expected that this war would be over quickly, there had been an outburst of patriotic enthusiasm on the part of the soldiers headed to the war. Many young men had eagerly signed up to achieve the glory and honour associated with fighting for one's country.

However, when the trench warfare was in place, a sense of despair developed among the soldiers. Given the overwhelming conditions, hundreds of thousands of men fell victim to various emotional manifestations like panic, anxiety and insomnia, catatonia as well as physical symptoms like tremors, impaired vision, hearing and paralysis. Governments tried to prevent the news coming from the trenches. The messages from the soldiers contained messages of discouragement and depression. Indeed, the harsh realities in the trenches had a devastating effect on the morale of the soldiers on both sides.

An estimated 8.5million died in the First World War. Many of the survivors would never be the same again. The First World War was called the "War to End All Wars". Little did they know that in a few years time, the Second World War, which would cause the deaths of fifty million people, would be started by a man who himself fought in these very trenches.

CHAPTER 10

Never Forget about War in Times of Peace

And the prophet came to the king of Israel, and said unto him, GO, STRENGTHEN THYSELF, AND MARK, AND SEE WHAT THOU DOEST: FOR AT THE RETURN OF THE YEAR THE KING OF SYRIA WILL COME UP AGAINST THEE.

And the servants of the king of Syria said unto him, Their gods are gods of the hills; therefore they were stronger than we; but let us fight against them in the plain, and surely we shall be stronger than they.

And do this thing, Take the kings away, every man out of his place, and put captains in their rooms:

And number thee an army, like the army that thou hast lost, horse for horse, and chariot for chariot: and we will fight against them in the plain, and surely we shall be stronger than they. And he hearkened unto their voice, and did so.

AND IT CAME TO PASS AT THE RETURN OF THE YEAR, THAT BENHADAD NUMBERED THE SYRIANS, AND WENT UP TO APHEK, TO FIGHT AGAINST ISRAEL.

1 Kings 20:22-26

High Combat Readiness – Preparedness

Never forget about war in times of peace. High combat readiness is very important for every serious-minded Christian. The prophet warned the king of Israel to strengthen himself because he would be attacked the next year.

To be successful in your fight for the kingdom, you need to be prepared. Perhaps the key to preparedness is to believe that evil can happen to you. It is to believe that someone may be planning evil against you.

In the ministry, you must prepare for several different kinds of evil. You must believe that they can actually happen. When you do, you will begin to develop a high combat readiness in relation to those areas of evil. In the story below, the Second World War was about to begin. A mass murderer by the name of Adolf Hitler was gearing up to invade and senselessly kill fifty million people. Adolf Hitler was successful in causing the deaths of millions of people because Europe simply did not believe that such evil could be planned and implemented by any human being.

Poland shares a border with Germany. Whilst Germany was developing a vastly technologically superior arsenal of weapons, Poland did not prepare itself to combat such an onslaught.

Poland was completely unprepared for the war with Germany. Germany marched into Poland on September 1, 1939 with the most modern tanks, guns and planes.

Can you believe that the Polish army sent out soldiers on horseback to fight the Germans? But the horses and rifles were no match for the vastly superior armoured and mechanized German army. Poland was quickly overpowered.

The Polish armed forces did have some tanks and some aircrafts, but they were grossly inadequate. The Polish Army and Air Force were simply not ready for the kind of war Hitler unleashed on them. Millions of Polish people were murdered during the Second World War.

I think that the principle of combat readiness – 'think about war even in times of peace', cannot be over-emphasized. What evils have you prepared for? Have certain things even crossed your mind before? To be combat ready, you must allow your mind to run through certain possibilities. Then you must prepare yourself as though it could happen. You prepare yourself by asking questions and answering them realistically.

Questions for Combat-Readiness

Have you thought of yourself dying suddenly? What would be your response to that? How ready are you for that?

Have you thought of the possibility of becoming terminally ill and having to die slowly? What would be your response to that?

Have you thought of the possibility of never getting married?

Have you thought of the possibility of never having children even though you are married?

Have you thought of the possibility of a sudden financial crisis and poverty? What would be your response to that? How ready are you for that?

Have you thought of the possibility of being attacked by armed robbers? Is your dwelling place secure and combat ready?

Have you thought of the possibility of not being able to preach anymore? How would you survive? Do you have a successor? Do you have a replacement?

Have you thought of the possibility of your car tyre bursting when you are driving at top speed? What would be your response to that? Would you not prefer to slow down now?

Have you thought of the possibility of your house being burnt down? Is everything you value in one place?

Have you thought of the possibility of floods, storms, typhoons, hurricanes and cyclones? What would be your response to that? How ready are you for that?

Have you thought of the possibility of losing your child? What would be your response to that? How ready are you for that? Do you want to have more children in case you lose one?

Have you thought through the possibility of you falling into sin or becoming a homosexual? What measures have you taken to protect yourself from these? Do you think it is impossible? Better people than you have fallen for these things!

Have you thought of the possibility of the death of your spouse? What would be your response to that? Do you know how people's lives are destroyed when their spouses die? Have you seen the way it affects them?

Have you thought of the possibility of getting divorced? Do you know that higher and greater ministers have gotten divorced to their own surprise? Do you think they ever planned to be divorced? Do you think they had divorce on their minds when they first got married?

Have you thought of the possibility of the death of your good friends and workers? What would be your response to that? How ready are you for that?

Have you thought of the possibility of someone betraying you? What would be your response to that?

Prepare yourself for war. You are fighting an unimaginably wicked enemy who has ultimate wicked ideas for you. One day I sat down reflecting on a prominent city in Europe that had several thriving churches. I thought about each church and its pastor. To my shock, I realised that two of them had been to prison, two more had become homosexuals. Another of these prominent pastors has been displaced from his church and driven out of the city. Yet another pastor was being hounded by the government for various crimes. Satan had targeted the pastors of that city to destroy them. You must realise that the only plan that Satan has for you is wickedness to the highest degree. You must therefore prepare yourself to battle the highest kinds of ultimate evil. You must not rule things out of your mind and think that they cannot happen to you.

CHAPTER 11

Initiative - Offensive Action

So Gideon, and the hundred men that were with him, came unto the outside of the camp in the beginning of the middle watch; and they had but newly set the watch: and they blew the trumpets, and brake the pitchers that were in their hands. And the three companies blew the trumpets, and brake the pitchers, and held the lamps in their left hands, and the trumpets in their right hands to blow withal: and they cried, The sword of the Lord, and of Gideon. And they stood every man in his place round about the camp: and ALL THE HOST RAN, AND CRIED, AND FLED.

Judges 7:19-21

The story of Gideon attacking the Midianites and Amalekites is a good example of how offensive action confuses the enemy and gives you the upper hand. Offensive action speaks about taking the initiative. When a person takes the initiative he takes the first step and therefore controls what happens thereafter. All those who have succeeded in war have initiated action and moved forward aggressively.

Offensive action is the practical way in which a person seeks to gain advantage and sustain the momentum of the war. A good general must take the initiative by being decisive and aggressive. This surprises the enemy and enables you to continuously retain the upper hand in the conflict.

Defenders are often the losers! It is not easy, practical or possible to defend yourself for a long time. After a while, a mistake here and there will lead to your destruction. When you are a defender a single mistake can cost you everything, whereas the attacker can afford to make several mistakes.

In the ministry, it is important to take the initiative and not wait to defend yourself against obvious losses. You must know that the church will decline naturally if no offensive action is taken. Instead of waiting for the church to start reducing in size, it is better to take the initiative by aggressively and continuously inviting many people to the church.

Do you want to only have funerals in your church? Instead of waiting for your church to be occupied only by the elderly and dying, you must initiate your outreaches to younger people now.

When are you going to become an aggressive evangelist? Are you going to wait for your church to be empty? Remember that defenders are often the losers!

You must also initiate action against disloyalty. Do not wait for people to change into snakes before you initiate moves against their disloyalty. Take decisions about your leadership before people grow wings around you. Remember that Lucifer was perfect until sin was found in him. If Lucifer could fall, so can anyone!

Offensive operations are the best means by which a military force achieves great results. When you take the initiative, you force the enemy to panic and his reactions often help you to overcome him. Deny your enemies the ability to think and plan by taking the initiative.

Israeli Initiative in the Six-Day War

The Six-Day war was fought between Israel on one side, and Egypt, Jordan and Syria on the other.

Israel's 1967 Six-Day war is perhaps the best example of an army that took the initiative and won the war. Israel, surrounded by enemies, had no choice but to take the initiative and do the right things that make people win wars.

The United Nations had a special force that was stationed in the Suez Canal. On the 13th of May, President Nasser of Egypt dismissed the United Nations force from Sinai and deployed his own troops there instead. This meant that Egyptian forces were amassing on the border of Israel. This build-up of troops on the border sent a clear message to Israel that Egypt was getting ready to attack them.

Rather than waiting to be attacked, Israel took the initiative and launched an aggressive surprise attack on Egypt. Israel's armed forces, led by General Moshe Dayan, delivered themselves from impending destruction by Arab nations that surrounded them.

Egypt had by far the largest and the most modern of all the Arab air forces, consisting of about 420 combat aircraft all of them Soviet-built. Early in the morning, on the 5th of June, the Israeli Air Force flew to Egypt with a mission to wipe out all Egyptian aircrafts that would have been used to attack them. All but twelve of the Israeli warplanes headed out over the Mediterranean Sea, flying low to avoid radar detection, before turning toward Egypt. Others flew over the Red Sea. This attack wiped out virtually the entire Egyptian Air Force.

Three hundred and thirty-eight aircrafts were destroyed and a hundred pilots killed in this short but decisive attack. The numbers of Arab aircraft claimed destroyed by Israel were at first regarded as exaggerated. However, the fact that the Egyptian Air Force made practically no appearance for the remaining days of the war proved that the numbers were most likely authentic.

Because Israel took the initiative against its larger and stronger enemies, it ended up capturing several important regions in the Middle East. In six days, Israel captured the Sinai Peninsula, the Gaza Strip, the West Bank, the old city of Jerusalem and the Golan Heights. This war ended in a resounding military victory for Israel. What did Israel do right? They took the initiative by making the first and most critical move against the Egyptian Air Force!

Hannibal's Initiative

Hannibal was a famous military commander of the ancient nation of Carthage (present-day Tunisia). Hannibal was famous for a number of wars that he led. The world superpower in Hannibal's day was the Roman Empire. Hannibal, an African, is famous for having challenged the Romans in their own country for several years. Amazingly, Hannibal moved a force from Africa, through Spain, and across the Italian mountains and into Italy.

When Hannibal arrived in Italy, he fought several wars, advancing right up to the gates of Rome. Although he never invaded the city of Rome itself, he defeated the Romans soundly and memorably on a number of occasions. There are three notable victories of Hannibal you may want to remember: his victory at the *Trebia River*, his victory at *Trasimene,* and his victory at *Cannae.* Each of these battles gave Hannibal the reputation of being one of the greatest ever military commanders.

65

In the battle at the Trebia River, Hannibal's forces were on one side of the river and the entire Roman army was on the other side. Hannibal took the initiative by enticing the Roman army to come across the river and attack him. Hannibal did this by sending a small force to harass the Roman camp that was across the river.

The Roman commander fell into the trap and decided to send his forces across the river. This was a very bad decision because it was icy-cold and it was snowing. The Roman soldiers had not eaten and they were also tired. The river was freezing cold and these soldiers had to wade through breast-high icy cold water. By the time the Roman army came out of the water, they were frozen and unable to even hold their weapons. They were in no shape to fight with the well-prepared forces of Hannibal who had eaten, rested and had been warming themselves by the fire. Needles to say, the Roman army was soundly defeated at the Trebia River.

The Roman army was thoroughly vanquished at the river Trebia because Hannibal took the initiative to attack first and entice his enemy make a mistake.

This is the whole point about taking the initiative. You must move first! You must not wait until the crisis or problem is well developed. Take the initiative, make a move! Your enemies will always be confused whilst you are able to think and plan clearly!

CHAPTER 12

A Good General and Inexorability

For the Lord of hosts hath purposed, and WHO SHALL DISANNUL IT? And his hand is stretched out, and who shall turn it back?

Isaiah 14:27

Ged is inexorable! He has purposed a thing and who can disannul it? He has stretched forth His hand and who can turn it back? To be inexorable in your ministry is to approach the work of God with strength, courage and inflexible determination. To be inexorable, you must be conscious of the fact that ministry is a matter of life and death. There is no option for you to fail. You must succeed in obeying God and overcoming all obstacles that you meet.

When I entered the ministry, I was determined to stay on to the very end. I entered the ministry with no support from anyone. People I had looked up to as pastors and spiritual mentors did not believe in what I was doing. I could not even find a spiritual mentor or pastor to officiate my wedding. There was no one who could or would appoint me as a pastor. I had to appoint myself as a pastor and introduce myself as a bishop later on. I was simply an outcast, a renegade and an unwanted memory.

But I was inexorable in the mission. I could not be set aside or pushed away from my vision to become a pastor. People have always set me aside and pushed me away. But to be inexorable is to be unwavering, unfaltering, unflinching and relentless in pursuit of the will of God. You must have a relentless spirit when it comes to the things of God and the will of God. God must be sought with unwavering determination.

Just as you can see armies that will be defeated, you can also make out the pastors who are not going to succeed. Winning armies are unappeasable, hard, pitiless and relentless.

The posture of inexorability in the mission is important because it is a godly trait. Apostle Paul exhorted the church to "…be stedfast, unmoveable, always abounding in the work of the Lord, forasmuch as ye know that your labour is not in vain in the Lord" (1 Corinthians 15:58). This Scripture champions the principle of inexorability. Be unmovable!

As you can see from the Scripture above, God Almighty is inexorable in His purposes that He has purposed in the earth. He will not be moved, He will not be turned back and nothing will stop Him. This is an important principle in the art of war. You will need to be inexorable and unyielding when fighting the enemy. When dealing with disloyal elements and treacherous pastors, you need to be unyielding and resolute in your purpose. When it is time to dismiss such people and separate them from your life, you must not waver or show double-mindedness and weakness. Wars are won by people whose hands could not be turned back and who did not show weakness in the face of the enemy.

Inexorability in Moscow

Both Russians and Germans showed this great inexorability in their wars against each other. That is why they had so many casualties. No one was prepared to surrender.

The Russian army teaches "inexorability and decisiveness during the mission" as a principle of war. That is why they overcame the Germans during the Second World War. The Russians were unlike any of the armies that Germany faced during the Second World War. The German armed forces invaded and overcame Poland in just five weeks! The Germans invaded and overcame France in just six weeks! But the German invasion of Russia was to be a different story. *In Russia they were to meet an inexorable, unflinching, unwavering enemy.* The fight for Stalingrad alone would take six months, as the Russians were simply unwilling to surrender their city to the Germans.

At the beginning of the invasion of Russia, at 2.30 am on June 22, 1941 Adolf Hitler stated, *"Before three months have passed, we shall witness a collapse in Russia, the like of which has never been seen in history."*

But as the invasion of Russia progressed, Joseph Stalin, the leader of the Soviet Union pronounced on the 19th of October 1941, "Moscow will be defended to the last." Germany and Russia were to fight the bloodiest, most brutal and costly war for the next few years.

The invasion of Russia by Hitler involved a number of battles that were fought to capture prominent and important cities. Moscow and Stalingrad are two such cities of Russia that came under intense attack as Hitler sought to take over a nation that did not belong to him. In both Moscow and Stalingrad, the inexorable (relentless, pitiless, harsh, unyielding, unflinching, unwavering and unshakeable) attitude of both sides resulted in brutal wars in which millions of lives were lost.

When the Germans arrived at the gates of Moscow they met the inexorable defender of the city. Joseph Stalin had ordered thousands of Russians to dig row after row of trenches by hand, all the way around the city. Five thousand miles of trenches around the city of Moscow is what finally brought the German advance on Moscow to a halt. The Germans were stopped just twenty miles from the Kremlin. Stalin organised a row of soldiers to shoot down any Russians who would run away from the front lines. The Russians were therefore forced to stand and fight the Germans at the gates of Moscow.

In his attempt to defend Moscow, Stalin issued Order No. 270, demanding that any commanders who allowed retreat without permission be considered malicious deserters. The order required superiors to shoot these deserters on the spot. Stalin also conducted a purge of several military commanders that were shot for "cowardice" without a trial.

Inexorability in Stalingrad

After failing to take over Moscow, Hitler decided to invade the industrial city of Stalingrad. After an initial all-out assault on the city that killed 40,000 people, the Germans thought they would have the victory in Stalingrad within days.

They were mistaken! The inexorable nature of the defender of Stalingrad would turn this battle into one of the longest and bloodiest battles in history. This battle would last six months and the Germans would be soundly defeated in the end!

In July 1942, in attempts to defend Stalingrad, Stalin issued Order No. 227 that was: *"Not one step back!"*

This command directed that any commander who allowed retreat without permission from his superiors be subject to military tribunal. The order called for soldiers found guilty to be forced into "penal battalions", which were sent to the most dangerous sections of the front lines. The order also directed "blocking detachments" to shoot fleeing panicked troops at the rear. In the first two months following the order, over 1,000 troops were shot by blocking units and over 130,000 troops were forced to penal battalions.

In Stalingrad, both Stalin and Hitler had forbidden their troops from retreating under any circumstances. Because of this, fighting moved street-by-street and block-by-block until the city was transformed into a ghost town. The Germans would launch repeated air raids involving 1,000 planes at a time. Troops from both sides took cover in bombed out buildings whilst Russian and German snipers hid in the ruins to pick out enemy soldiers.

After some months of endless fighting in the cold winter, the German commander, Field Marshall Paulus, requested permission to break free and retreat. Adolf Hitler refused permission and ordered him to fight on even without food and supplies. Finally, Field Marshall Paulus decided to defy Hitler's orders and surrendered. It is estimated that two million people died in Stalingrad, about 800,000 Germans and 1.2million Russians. After the battle, there was little remaining of the city itself. The ghost town was the product of a battle between two inexorable and wicked commanders.

CHAPTER 13

When You Become a Defender, You Have Become a Loser

Now Jericho (a fenced town with high walls) was tightly closed because of the Israelites; no one went out or came in.

Joshua 6:1 (AMP)

No matter how well you defend yourself, you will eventually be the loser. The attacker is always at a great advantage and will defeat his enemy.

The great city of Jericho was heavily defended against the invading Israelites. The Israelites were on the attack but the people of Jericho were defending. What was the outcome of this epic battle? Disaster for the people of Jericho! You may feel safe within your walled and heavily defended cities, but it is just a matter of time.

When you become a defender, you have become a loser. No matter how well you defend yourself, you are likely to be the loser. If you prepare your defences and invest heavily in defending yourself, you will have to make sure that your enemy does not develop attacking mechanisms that are superior to what you are preparing for.

In the end, all your preparations and defences may fall apart because the enemy will have enough time to study you. When a church is grown, developed and established it usually sits back and becomes defensive.

An established church will try to defend itself against waning attendance. An established church will try to defend itself against breakaway factions. An established church will try to defend itself against mavericks who move independently within the establishment.

But no matter how the established church defends itself, it ends up reducing and losing the fight against mavericks and breakaway factions. A look at history will reveal how huge church establishments have had their membership and attendance eroded with time. Why is this? It is because the church stopped attacking and began defending itself. When a church is in the attacking mode, it reaches out, it evangelizes and it plants other churches. Many large ministries are dead as far as these attacking activities are concerned.

The church in America used to reach out to the world, sending the gospel through missionaries and travelling evangelists. Today, it is basically defending itself against the invasion of the spirit of abortion, homosexuality, gay marriage and other forms of sexual deviations.

Because of this, the church in America is on the decline whilst other religions are increasing their membership. Other religions in the world are advancing and even raising up prominent buildings everywhere.

The reality is that, the church is always under attack. It can choose to sit down and defend itself against invading demonic armies. On the other hand, the church can choose to reach out, evangelize more territories and build more churches. If we obey God, we will evangelize and build churches in Jerusalem, Judea, Samaria and in the uttermost parts of the world. It is time to stop defending ourselves. The outstanding generals in history did not become famous by defending towns and cities.

Alexander the Great, Hannibal, Napoleon and even Hitler conducted well-known wars and achieved legendary victories by attacking and not defending. Indeed, they became famous by invading and attacking. Which mode are you in? Are you in the attacking mode or the defending mode? I can predict the outcome of your war when I know which mode you are in.

Defenders of the Atlantic Wall

From 1939, Adolf Hitler spent his time invading one country after another. He had attacked Czechoslovakia, Austria, Poland, France, Holland, Belgium, England and Russia. He had been successful as the attacking force. Now, it was his turn to defend. His forces were thinly spread out and his attacks on Britain and Russia had not been successful.

As the Second World War progressed, Hitler's ability to attack other nations was diminished and he began to think about how to defend himself against an invasion. All the nations he had attacked were pulling themselves together to mount a decisive attack on him.

The Atlantic Wall was the name given to a massive coastal defensive wall that Adolf Hitler built to defend himself against his many enemies. This massive wall stretched all the way from Norway, along the Belgian and French coastline to the Spanish border. The Atlantic Wall covered a distance of 1,670 miles and was built between 1942 and 1944. This project was vast and mostly situated on the French coast, where the British and Americans were expected to land. This Atlantic wall was built purposely to repulse the British and American forces that were preparing to invade Europe.

But when the planned invasion of Europe eventually took place in June 1944, the wall was quickly overcome. The wall, which had taken over three years to build, was quickly overpowered within one week of fighting. The invasion started on the 6th of June and by the 11th of June all the major sections of the beach were under the control of the British and American forces. It took just five days to completely overcome this great defensive Atlantic wall. By the 11th of June, 326,000 troops and 100,000 tons of military equipment had crossed over.

This great defensive Atlantic Wall was overcome quickly. And that is how defending churches and ministries are overcome. Defensive ministries are overcome quickly and set aside. All the history behind a great ministry vanishes and provides no security against the onslaught of cruel enemies. It is time to rise and stop defending the ministry. You must attack and move forward into new territories.

CHAPTER 14

A Good General
and Surprises

For man also knoweth not his time: as the fishes that
are taken in an evil net, and as birds that are caught in
the snare: SO ARE THE SONS OF MEN SNARED IN
AN EVIL TIME, WHEN IT FALLETH SUDDENLY
upon them.

Ecclesiastes 9:12

S urprise is created when things happen suddenly! When negative things befall you suddenly, you have entered into an evil time. Surprise is the shock and confusion induced by the introduction of something unexpected. Most wars are won by the power of surprises! Many enemies are equally matched, so it is the element of surprise that changes the balance of power.

Surprise is a very important weapon of war. It is a weapon your enemy loves to use against you. When the enemy surprises you, you may be found wanting. Prepare for surprises! Use the weapon of surprise in your fight against the enemy.

Death can be a surprise! The death of a spouse can be a surprise! Not having a child is a surprise! Adultery can be a surprise! An unexpected illness may be a surprise! An unexpected divorce may be a surprise!

An army ought to prepare for surprises. Your enemy will strike at a time or place you are not prepared for.

Weak armies are defeated by military surprises. Weak governments are affected by economic surprises.

A fact about "surprise" in warfare is the fact that many surprises are not complete surprises. There are often warning signs that must be taken seriously. Sometimes God will reveal to you exactly what is going to happen but you cannot believe or imagine it happening. You must constantly be aware of a very evil devil with very wicked intentions. You can avert surprises by mounting counter surprises for every move of the devil against your life.

You can be surprised in the ministry through the death of a loved one. Many leaders' lives changed after the deaths of their spouses. The surprise and the shock overwhelmed them and made them change course forever.

Oral Roberts had the shock of his life when his daughter and son-in-law died in a plane crash. Aimee Semple MacPherson, the founder of Four-Square Gospel Church was surprised when her husband died on the mission field, leaving her as a pregnant widow.

It is important also to surprise your enemy. Surprise can decisively shift the balance of power. You must also seek to surprise your enemy. With surprise on your side your little strength can achieve great success against a powerful enemy.

You can surprise the enemy by saying sorry, repenting, changing your mind and making a U-turn. People never expect you to say "sorry". The devil does not expect you to apologize.

Another surprise move you can make is to forgive quickly. The devil expects you to remain bitter and unforgiving so that he can destroy you. Surprise the enemy by saying sorry. A sudden U-turn will always be a surprise to your enemy. No one is expecting you to make a U-turn.

You can also surprise the enemy by making sudden unannounced decisions in the ministry. Some major decisions such as transfers, dismissals and policy changes can have a better impact if they are surprises!

Surprise and Pearl Harbor

You must develop your defences so that nothing takes you by surprise. One of the greatest ever-military surprises was the Japanese attack on Pearl Harbor in Hawaii. In the build up to World War II, there was a strong anti-Western sentiment in Japan. Without the element of surprise, the Japanese would not have been able to destroy the American fleet.

Japan decided to bring a permanent end to Western interference in its affairs by wiping out the United States navy in the Pacific region.

In January 1941, a plan for attacking the U.S. fleet at Pearl Harbor was developed and training exercises were carried out. In October of the same year, the Japanese emperor, gave his general approval for the attack on the United States and it was eventually carried out on the 7th of December.

On the 25 of November, a large fleet of Japanese ships set sail from Japan, unseen by American spies in Japan. By December 7, 1941, unknown to the American government, a massive fleet of six aircraft carriers, twenty-five submarines, and over thirty additional support ships was just 200 miles north of the Hawaiian island of Oahu and ready to attack.

The first wave of attacking Japanese planes numbered more than 180. Although U.S. radar operators saw the massive formation nearly a full hour before the attack began, they raised no alarm, because they mistook the planes for a group of U.S. bombers expected to arrive from California around the same time.

The first wave arrived at the U.S. Navy base at Pearl Harbor at 7:55 a.m. and achieved complete surprise. The primary targets were major U.S. warships, most of which were docked close together in neat lines. These included eight of the nine battleships in the U.S. Pacific Fleet, along with several dozen other warships. The Japanese also targeted six nearby military airfields. A second attack wave of more than 160 planes followed just over an hour later.

In all, the attack on Pearl Harbor killed 2,402 Americans, destroyed five battleships completely, put three more out of commission, sank or seriously damaged at least eleven other warships, and destroyed nearly more than 180 aircrafts on the ground.

In addition to attacking Pearl Harbor that day, Japan also attacked the U.S. territories of Guam, the Philippines, Wake Island, and Midway Island, as well as British interests in Malaya and Hong Kong. As I said earlier, many surprises are not complete surprises. There are usually warnings. Unfortunately, it is sometimes incomprehensible to think of what the enemy plans to do to you. In the case of Pearl Harbor there were many warnings but most people simply could not believe the Japanese would carry out such an attack.

The first warning of a possible Japanese attack on Pearl Harbor came in a coded cablegram from the U.S. ambassador to Japan, Joseph C. Grew, to the U.S. State Department on January 27, 1941. Grew's cable told of a report that, "The Japanese military forces planned to attempt a surprise mass attack on Pearl Harbor." A State Department Japanese-language specialist believed the warning and urged his superiors to treat it as such. But both Grew and U.S. intelligence specialists dismissed the report as a wild rumour.

There were more warning signs in the months before the attack and notably, Admiral Turner, had been concerned that the Pearl Harbor base was particularly vulnerable to attack.

The United States was able to decode and read Japanese military communications until shortly before the attack, when Japan abruptly changed its military codes.

By the evening of December 6, 1941 U.S. military and government officials, including President Roosevelt, were certain that Japan was planning a major action against U.S. interests.

Indeed, the attack on Pearl Harbor was timed to take place after a 14-part message was delivered to the US Secretary of State by a Japanese envoy at 1.00pm on December 7, 1941. A meeting was even scheduled for 3:00 P.M. on December 7 to discuss the matter. Unfortunately, the target of the attack was unknown, and no one at Pearl Harbor was notified to be on alert.

CHAPTER 15

A Good General and the Concentration of Forces

...THIS ONE THING I DO, forgetting those things which are behind, and reaching forth unto those things which are before,

Philippians 3:13

Many Christians do not concentrate on what they are doing. When I was in school I joined one group and stuck to it. Many Christians belong to many things and therefore do not make an impact anywhere. Every war is won by concentrating on one thing at a time until it is conquered.

The British army teaches how "concentration of forces involves the decisive, synchronized application of superior fighting power to realize intended effects". The Russian Armed Forces simply describes this as the "decisive concentration of the essential force at the needed moment and in the most important direction to achieve the main mission."

The principle of concentration in war can be applied in many spheres of life. Concentrating your love on one person can give you a life-long relationship of happiness. Concentrating your forces on your marital problems and applying all efforts can make your marriage work out and help you avoid a divorce. Concentrating on church growth can make your church grow into a mega church. Most pastors do not concentrate on conquering the mystery of church growth. Concentrating on ministry as a job can lead to it becoming something great and important for you. Concentrating on the ministry as a career can bring you into full-time ministry.

At the end of 1991, the Holy Spirit spoke to me to give myself wholly to the ministry. This was simply an instruction to concentrate. It was God's command to me to wage war with the principle of concentration.

D-Day and the Concentration of Forces

To overcome a strong enemy, you will have to concentrate your forces on a single target until it is well and truly overcome. This is exactly what the British and Americans did to remove the German tyrant, Adolf Hitler. They concentrated all their forces on one purpose: to enter the mainland of Europe and get to Germany with enough military force to remove Hitler from his place of power. Hitler was no ordinary enemy. He had an iron grip on the European nations because he had spent many years building up the German army. The only way to remove the strong man from Europe was to concentrate all forces on that objective. This is what led to what is known as "D-day". D-day was the day that all the enemies of Germany concentrated their efforts at crossing the sea and placing a huge army in France that could march into Germany.

Remember that it is not easy to swim across the sea. Neither is it a small feat to have a boat that can take a hundred people across the sea. So imagine the number of boats and ships that are needed to carry thousands and thousands of soldiers across the sea. These soldiers needed to go across the sea with all their equipment, their food and their clothes. They also needed to go across the sea with cars, jeeps, buses, armoured tanks, heavy guns, fuel tankers and many other things.

D-day was the day all the forces were concentrated to make an actual landing in Normandy, France. First of all, 24,000 British, American, Canadian and French troops were parachuted into the area at midnight.

Early in the morning, 5,000 heavily loaded ships sailed in bringing troops and armoured divisions to France. Over 160,000 soldiers landed on 6th June, 1944, comprising 73,000 Americans, 61,715 British and 21,400 Canadians.

The principle of concentration was fully deployed as this invasion involved the use of air power and naval support for the transportation of soldiers and material from the United Kingdom.

This invasion of Europe marked the beginning of the end of Adolf Hitler's reign in Germany. As the British army was following the principle of concentration, Adolf Hitler was doing the opposite by dividing his forces into two major fronts. Half of his army was busy invading Russia whilst the other half had to face the concentrated forces of the British, Americans and Canadians.

When you face an intractable enemy, don't give up hope. When you face a wicked enemy, concentrate your forces and overcome him! There is a price to pay for victory and perhaps the price you have to pay is to concentrate on one thing.

CHAPTER 16

A Good General and the Economy of Effort

Either what woman having ten pieces of silver, if SHE LOSE ONE PIECE, DOTH not light a candle, and sweep the house, and SEEK DILIGENTLY TILL SHE FIND IT?

Luke 15:8

The American military calls this principle "Economy of Force". In other words, employ all combat power available in the most effective way possible. The British army calls this principle "Economy of Effort". Economy of effort is the judicious exploitation of manpower, material and time in relation to the achievement of objectives.

War is a very expensive thing. If you use your resources wisely, you will be able to fight on for many years. Your fight to serve the Lord is going to cost a lot of money. Ministry is a war. Ministry is expensive! If you do not learn how to use the principle of "Economy of Effort", you will not be able to sustain the war effort.

Many people do not know how difficult and expensive it is to build a church, to evangelize or to just be a full-time missionary. Building a church is like building an office on enemy territory. Satan is the god of this world and we are ambassadors of Christ in this dark and evil world. To wage a successful war, you must defeat your enemy and even build something in his capital city. Because wars are so expensive, a good general is always interested in minimizing the cost of his campaign so that he can continue.

When I began mass evangelistic crusades, I understood why there were few evangelists. Evangelism is an invasion into enemy territory to capture souls for our master. There are fewer and fewer evangelists but it is not because God has not called evangelists. It is because of the cost of evangelism.

The Expensive First World War

The First World War was a very expensive war in terms of the cost of lives of the soldiers. Many lives were wasted in trenches that were dug from the coast of Belgium to France. Many soldiers perished in these trenches over a period of four years as they maintained a virtual stalemate. Publicity for the British First World War film *For the Empire* included the slogan: "Damn the cost, we must win this war". But after this war, few people were ready to have another war. The cost of casualties and the lives of soldiers were taken into account in a way that was not done before the First World War.

In economic terms, the First World War was fought at an estimated cost of $208 billion. This war caused the greatest economic global depression of the 20th century. Debts were accrued by all of the major warring nations with the exception of America.

After the First World War, unemployment was rife. Inflation dramatically increased the cost of living - most famously in Weimar , Germany, where hyperinflation meant that by December 1923, a loaf of bread cost 428 billion marks. The First World War abruptly ended a period of relative economic prosperity, replacing it with two decades of economic misery.

In terms of loss of human life, the First World War was unprecedented. The number of people who died from the war was about 9.4 million. This means that an average of 6,000 people died every day of the war. From every nation that took part in the combat, most families had lost a relative in the war. It could be a brother, a son, a father, a nephew or an uncle. Some towns and villages lost all of their male members of fighting age. Also, because of the high death toll and wounded toll, many villages were robbed of skilled tradesman such as printers, smiths, and carpenters; skills that took a long time to learn and rebuilding required many of these people. This ruined the infrastructure and business practices of the local villages and crippled many rural areas.

Fifteen million men were also crippled by their service in the war. The First World War also created a series of refugee crises, as the conflict forced whole populations - Armenians, Belgians, and Jews in Russia's Polish provinces - to flee from their homes to safer areas.

A summary of the cost of the First World War is that, of the 65 million men who fought, 8 million men were killed in battle, 2 million died of illness and disease, 21.2 million were wounded,

7.8 million were taken prisoner or went missing in action. 6.6 million civilians were also killed.

The financial cost of war was ongoing for years after the ceasefire had been signed. Disabled soldiers had to be cared for whilst all the homes and industries had to be rebuilt. War memorials also had to built in every town, village and city of soldiers who had perished in battle. The bodies of thousands of soldiers who died in the war were removed from their shallow graves in the trenches and were taken to newly built cemeteries. Multitudes of graves and cemeteries had to be built for the soldiers who had perished in the War.

The Second World War caused the deaths of over fifty-five million people. That was the cost of the Second World War. A large number of cities like Cologne, Rotterdam, Calais, Dunkirk, Berlin, Dusseldorf, Hamburg, Hanover, Smolensk, Stalingrad, Kiev, Kharkov, Munich, Milan, Tokyo, Hiroshima, Nagasaki, were also totally razed to the ground. War is an expensive thing. Since ministry is war, ministry is also an expensive thing!

Jesus Taught on the Principle of "Economy of Everything"

Jesus taught His disciples to count the cost and do things as economically as possible. Without this principle of war, ("economy of everything") you will not be able to sustain this very expensive venture called "ministry".

Ministries come to a close because they are too expensive to run. Learn how to conduct your ministry as cheaply as possible. If your ministry becomes too expensive, you cannot do many things.

Remember that you can do everything that you are doing cheaper.

It is difficult and expensive to build a church. So plan to and devise methods to build the church in the most inexpensive way possible.

It is difficult and expensive to conduct crusades. So plan to and devise methods to conduct crusades in the most inexpensive way possible.

It is difficult and expensive to plant churches. So plan to and devise methods to plant churches in the most inexpensive way possible.

It is difficult and expensive to preach on television. So plan to and devise methods to be on television in the most inexpensive way possible.

It is difficult and expensive to preach on radio. So plan to and devise methods to be on radio in the most inexpensive way possible.

It is difficult and expensive to write books. So plan to and devise methods to write books in the most inexpensive way possible.

It is difficult and expensive to run a Bible school. So plan to and devise methods to run your Bible school in the most inexpensive way possible.

Do you know what will happen if you do not find the most economical way to do things? I can tell you free of charge! You will start your ministry well with great zeal and great support but the ministry will shut down before your vision is accomplished. You will be forced to shut down, not because the anointing is finished or your life is over but because you will not have money to sustain the ministry in a certain way.

Many great ministries started out planting churches but they had to stop because it is expensive to send people into foreign nations and sustain them with their families for years. This is why great nations which used to send missionaries no longer send missionaries. What they call missions are people going on a two-week holiday to help paint or do some repair works on a church building on the field. Perhaps they will donate a few oranges, bananas or Bibles whilst they are on the field.

These two to three-week forays have replaced lifetime missions where young men gave their whole life to establish the church of God in a foreign nation. It is not that the anointing and time for church planting is over. There is actually a greater need for church planting because there are more people in the world than ever before. The economical way to plant churches is to send lay men to find jobs in these towns. Another way is to send people who can do farming or teaching in these mission nations. This is how missions were done in the past.

One day, after a massive crusade in Nigeria, I met a senior Nigerian minister on a flight out of Lagos. He asked me about our ministry and I told him we had just had a massive crusade in a city in Nigeria. As we chatted, he asked me how much the crusade had cost us.

I told him and he laughed at me scornfully. I was taken aback.

"I can do several massive crusades with that money," he said. He mentioned a small fraction of the amount I had quoted and said he could have a larger, better attended crusade in more prominent cities in Nigeria. I knew he was telling the truth because I had seen his crusades on television. That discussion set me thinking.

How could I do my crusades more economically? I knew that this Nigerian minister was right. Americans have crusades in Africa that cost millions of dollars whilst the local ministers laugh at them in their heads knowing that everything could be done at a small fraction of the cost.

I once watched an American ministry have a crusade in an African country. They rented ninety-five rooms in a super-expensive five-star hotel. They came into the country with private jets and many employed members of staff. Obviously, this kind of crusade will cost a lot of money.

You may be able to do such things for a while, but many ministries usually fade out. Indeed, when the season changes, you may have to stop your ministry altogether.

Use the principle of economy of effort and you will be able to do a lot for God. If you use the principle of economy of effort, you will also be able to continue in the ministry for much longer.

Those who do not follow this principle will close down their Bible schools, stop writing books, stop having crusades and also stop planting churches. Do you want to stop your ministry before you die? Do you want to hang in there in the wilderness, doing nothing for God, and claiming that there are no resources? It is time you followed the principle of doing the ministry in the most economical way possible.

CHAPTER 17

A Good General and Flexibility

I know both how to be abased, and I know how to abound: every where and in all things I am instructed both to be full and to be hungry, both to abound and to suffer need. I CAN DO ALL THINGS through Christ which strengtheneth me.

Philippians 4:12-13

The United States Army calls this principle "manoeuvre". To manoeuvre is to place your enemy at a disadvantage through your flexible ways. When you are flexible, your enemy is thrown off balance. Flexibility is used to reduce your vulnerability. Your flexibility continually poses new problems for your enemy, eventually leading to his defeat.

Flexibility is your ability to change readily to meet new circumstances. To be flexible, you need agility, responsiveness, resilience and adaptability. If you are not flexible you will be replaced. When you are flexible you will keep your job. If you are flexible you will become the most important person to your superior. Things are always changing. What is valuable today may not be valuable tomorrow and what is done today may not be done tomorrow. If you cannot change and change quickly, you will become useless and irrelevant with time.

Vashti Lost Her Ministry through Inflexibility

On the seventh day, when the heart of the king was merry with wine, he commanded Mehuman, Biztha, Harbona, Bigtha, and Abagtha, Zethar, and Carcas, the seven chamberlains that served in the presence of Ahasuerus the king, To bring Vashti the queen before the king with the crown royal, to shew the people and the princes her beauty: for she was fair to look on.

But the QUEEN VASHTI REFUSED TO COME AT THE KING'S COMMANDMENT by his chamberlains: therefore was the king very wroth, and his anger burned in him.

Esther 1:10-12

A pastor had a vision of a huge ship going down a river. As the ship kept going down the river, it seemed to fill the entire river until the ship was squeezed in between the two banks on either side. Soon, the ship was virtually stuck in the river, unable to turn left, right or backwards. In the vision, God said to him, "Your ministry is this huge inflexible ship."

You have to work on your ministry to make it flexible, changeable and adaptable. If you do not, your ministry will perish. Sometimes as the ministry grows, you become stuck in your ways and you cannot accept a new way of doing old things.

Vashti, the queen, was inflexible, unbendable and unyielding. She lost her position as the queen and was replaced by a younger more flexible person. These are serious lessons that we learn from history. Could it be that you will lose your position as the leading pastor of your city because of inflexibility? Could it be that you will lose your position as the leading pastor of your city because of your refusal to adapt to new things that God is doing?

Could it be that you will lose your crusade ministry through your inflexible attitude towards miracles, healing and prophetic manifestations? Are you inflexible in your attitude towards technology and administration?

Napoleon was Successful Because of His Flexibility

Napoleon went to war against the Prussians who had a great history as descendants of Frederick the Great. They had not developed any new methods of war. Indeed, they were known to be very rigid. To them, success in war depended on organisation and discipline. Prussian soldiers drilled endlessly until they could perform elaborate manoeuvres as precisely as machines. Prussian generals studied the victories of Frederick the Great and to them, war was a mathematical affair.

Napoleon on the other hand, was a young and brilliant commander who was flexible and willing to do things that had never been done before.

In 1806, the Prussians, commanded by General Hohenlohe fought against Napoleon and were soundly defeated. The Prussian generals were old men who were rooted in the traditions and victories of Frederick the Great. Instead of responding to present circumstances, they were bent on repeating formulas that had worked in the past. But young Napoleon was full of innovative strategies and moved with speed and fluidity.

The Prussian army moved slowly and behaved like robots, even in parade. The Prussian army used slow-moving wagons that carried provisions for their troops. But young Napoleon's soldiers carried their supplies on their backs and moved with astonishing speed and fluidity.

In the actual battle, the numbers of both sides were the same. But the strategies were completely different.

The Prussian soldiers marched on an open plain with perfect parade order, drums beating and magnificent precision. Young Napoleon's men on the other hand, fought from behind gardens and from rooftops. They attacked as if from nowhere, and without a specific formation. Unlike the Prussians, they did not have a disciplined oblique formation. Like demons, they rushed forward from all sides, threatening to surround the Prussians. In a short while, the battle was over and the general ordered a retreat.

You see, flexibility is important. God is raising up His servants who are like young Napoleons. Men who do not have much respect or even knowledge of traditional ways of doing things! Every war is different and every battle is different. You cannot assume that what worked before will work today. Repetition must not replace the Holy Spirit's creativity. Rigidity must not replace flexibility. You must be led by the Spirit of God to do exactly what He wants you to do for today. Do not be rooted in the past, be rooted in the Holy Spirit! Do not be rooted in rigidity!

One day, a cat went out hunting on the farm and caught a bat. The bat pleaded for its life but the big farm cat would not listen. The cat explained to the bat that birds were natural enemies of the cat and that is why he the cat would eat the bird. The bat began wailing and explained to the cat that it was not a bird but actually a mouse. Upon believing that the bat was not a bird the cat released the bat to go free.

Unfortunately, the same bat was caught by another farm cat, later that night. The bat pleaded for its life but the second cat would have none of it because he said he detested mice and was happy to kill a mouse. The bat began wailing and explained to the cat that he was not a mouse but a bat. Eventually, the second farm cat became convinced that he was not a mouse but a bat and decided to set him free.

This bat was cleverer than many of us today. Many think that the strategy that worked yesterday must work today. On the first occasion, the bat escaped by claiming to be a mouse and on the second occasion, he escaped by claiming to be a bat! On two different occasions, two different strategies worked. Flexibility is preferred to rigidity! Be flexible, and you will win your wars.

CHAPTER 18

Avoid Pyrrhic Victories

Then Judas, which had betrayed him, when he saw that he was condemned, repented himself, and brought again the thirty pieces of silver to the chief priests and elders, Saying, I have sinned in that I have betrayed the innocent blood. And they said, what is that to us? See thou to that.

And he cast down the pieces of silver in the temple, and departed, and went and hanged himself.

Matthew 27:3-5

Judas Iscariot got his thirty pieces of silver all right. You could say that Judas was a successful businessman who had landed himself a very good deal. But at what price did he get this money? It cost him his position among the twelve apostles. It cost him his ministry and it cost him eternity.

A pyrrhic victory is a term for "a victory won at too high a cost". In the ministry, it is important to avoid pyrrhic victories. What really is a pyrrhic victory? A pyrrhic victory is a victory that comes with such devastating cost that ultimately nullifies the victory that has been achieved. Someone who wins a pyrrhic victory has been victorious, but the price of the victory can make you wish that you never won that fight.

The phrase "pyrrhic victory" came from a war between the Greeks and the Romans. King Pyrrhus of Epirus (north-western Greece) fought and defeated the Roman army. King Pyrrhus defeated the Romans at Heraclea in 280 BC and in Asculum in 279BC.

In both of Pyrrhus' victories, the Romans lost more men that Pyrrhus did. In other words, more Romans died than Greeks. But even though the Romans had more casualties, they had a larger reserve of men from which to draw soldiers. The losses to the Romans did not harm them as much as it did the Greeks. King Pyrrhus won the war but he lost so many soldiers in the fight that his army was virtually destroyed. His famous report was,

"If we are victorious in one more battle with the Romans we shall be utterly ruined."

King Pyrrhus

Even though he had won two famous battles against the Romans, he knew that these victories were actually ruining him.

Originally, Pyrrhus, king of Epirus in Greece, believed in the "win at any cost" battle strategy. However, by the end of his life, he had learnt that win at any cost is not the best strategy. A pyrrhic victory is often not worth having.

Pyrrhic Victories in the Ministry

Many ministers are drawn to fight in wars that lead to pyrrhic victories. Without realising it, they fight for their rights but lose everything else. The cost of such pyrrhic victories is too high.

Pyrrhic Luxury

What is the point in driving the most luxurious car of your childhood dreams if it costs you your credibility and support in the ministry? I have heard ministers arguing about why they deserve to have certain things. "I work very hard! I have worked for so many years! The labourer is worthy of his wages! Jesus came to give us abundant life! God takes pleasure in the prosperity of His servants! Neither Abraham, Isaac nor Jacob was poor! Jesus was not poor but wore seamless designer clothes that were too valuable to tear up! God wishes above all things that we will prosper! By now, everyone knows that I am worthy of this privilege!"

Surely, you have presented a brilliant array of reasons why you must drive a certain car, live in a certain house and have certain privileges. No one can argue with the fact that you have won the argument. But what is going to be the real cost of these things? Often such arguments only lead to a pyrrhic victory – a victory at too high a cost.

A Pyrrhic Beloved

Perhaps you are determined to marry this lady. Yes, she is nice, sweet, lively and fair-coloured. Your mother likes her and your father too. She has a guitar shape with nice swollen thighs. Her breasts appear in just the size that you prefer. But everyone is asking you whether this beautiful girl is born again or not. You may even have photographs of the day she walked forward to

99

the altar and gave her life to Jesus Christ. You may argue, "…
as many as received him to them he gave power to become sons
of God." Even though you have only known her for two weeks,
you explain that love is of God and that the love you have for her
was born of God.

Does this beautiful girl have the Holy Spirit? Yes, she does!
Even though she does not speak in tongues, you argue that she is
filled with the Holy Spirit. You are able to explain that speaking
in tongues is not the only sign of receiving the Holy Spirit. It is
a well-known fact that many denominations believe in the Holy
Spirit but do not speak in tongues. You argue that Billy Graham,
one of the world's great evangelists did not speak in tongues.
Indeed, your arguments are impeccable.

You may win the argument to marry this lady. But what
will be the cost of this victory? Years later, as you struggle in
your marriage with a virtual unbeliever witch who is in full
manifestation, you will wonder if it was worth arguing your way
into this marriage.

A Pyrrhic Divorce

Perhaps you have come up with a good reason to divorce your
wife and remarry another woman within seven days. You have
been married to her for some years and know that she is a witch.
You have received prophetic confirmation about the decision that
you are taking.

You have many biblical reasons for getting divorced.

You have seen in the Scriptures that God calls himself a
divorced person. If the Father will divorce Israel what is wrong
if you divorce your wife?

Adultery is given as a good enough reason to leave a wife.
Indeed, whoever looks upon a woman to lust after her has
committed adultery. You have therefore already committed
adultery because since you married you have looked at various

women and lusted after them. Also, both of you have committed adultery with different partners since you got married.

Indeed, you have a solid scriptural basis for your divorce. You also want to avoid falling into sin and therefore you are remarrying within seven days.

Dear friend, you may have good reasons and lots of Scripture to back your decision. But what is the point in being biblically and morally right about your divorce if the cost is too high for you to bear in the future. Perhaps walking in forgiveness and love may be a better way.

A Pyrrhic Project

Do not insist on doing things that have too high a cost. Perhaps you are buying land to build a house or a church. The cost of this land is so high that it will take away all the income of your ministry for the next ten years. You may succeed in getting a loan from the bank through a twenty-five year mortgage. Yes, you will have your million-dollar project. But at what cost? You may be tied down as a church, unable to breathe or do anything important. Your hand may be forced to steal because of this loan. You may be turned into a businessman because of this project.

You may become a money preacher because you always need to raise funds to pay up your debts. You may lose your health and your peace of mind over this million-dollar project. Indeed, you may be successful in accomplishing this million-dollar project but what will be the cost? Can't you see that you may be utterly ruined by this pyrrhic project?

Napoleon's Pyrrhic Victory

Napoleon's destruction began with a pyrrhic victory that he won in Russia. Technically speaking, Napoleon defeated the Russians and entered Moscow. But by the time he got back to France, his army was virtually destroyed, leaving him severely weakened and unable to maintain his power base.

When Napoleaon invaded Russia, the Russians recognized his strength and began to retreat into Russia so that they could avoid a confrontation. As Napoleon's army was forced deeper into Russia, he became entrenched in a long war that he had not really prepared for. Persistent hunger and long distances from the supply lines caused Napoleon's army to be severely weakened.

The Russians eventually decided to take on Napoleon on the 7th of September, 1812 in a town called Borodino near Moscow. The Battle of Borodino would decide whether Napoleon would be able to enter Moscow and claim it.

Over 250,000 men went to war in what was the largest and bloodiest single day for Napoleon's wars. It seemed as though all hell had been set loose. In the end, the Russian field marshal, Kutuzov, refused to weaken his army any further by continuing to fight. He retreated from the battle, leaving Napoleon free to take Moscow. Over 70,000 men were killed in the horrific Battle of Borodino.

Napoleon, with a severely weakened army marched into Moscow and found it empty. Everyone had fled. The Tsar of Russia and all the citizenry had fled Moscow leaving an empty city for Napoleon to rule over. Before they left, they released all prisoners of Moscow to burn down the city. Napoleon spent a month in Moscow waiting for the Tsar to return so that he would kneel down before Napoleon and declare him victorious but this never happened.

After a month, Napoleon was forced to retreat from Moscow and march through the harsh and dangerous winter to France. On the long march back, his army was attacked by the Russians who had been in hiding. The hungry, cold and severely weakened French men were thoroughly harassed, attacked and destroyed on their long march back to France. Napoleon himself came under attack during the journey back to France and had to escape for his very life.

Yes indeed Napoleon won the battle of Borodino. Yes Napoleon entered Moscow. But at what cost? Out of 650,000 soldiers who marched confidently into Russia, only 40,000 remained alive and crossed back into France. From then on, Napoleon's Grand Army was a weakened version of what it had been. That was the beginning of the demise of Napoleon.

Napoleon's victory was a pyrrhic one. During his exile many years later, Napoleon wrote that of the 50 battles of his life, Borodino was where "the greatest valour was displayed and the least success gained".

CHAPTER 19

Unity at All Levels

And Jesus knew their thoughts, and said unto them,
EVERY KINGDOM DIVIDED AGAINST ITSELF
IS BROUGHT TO DESOLATION; and every city or
house divided against itself shall not stand:

Matthew 12:25

The American principles of war include the "unity of command". This principle of war teaches that for every objective, seek unity of command and unity of effort. The principle urges that in all levels of war, the army should employ military force toward a common objective. Winning a war requires unity of command and unity of effort. To follow this principle of war, there must be a single commander with the authority to direct all forces in unity.

Indeed, every army that is not united in its purpose is doomed to eventual defeat.

Every church must have a leader who is united with his assistants and with the congregation. A leader must have scanning eyes that are looking for the signs of disunity and disloyalty. The unity of the team is crucial if we are going to win the wars that are before us.

One of the strongest armies ever was the German army (the Wehrmacht). They, however, suffered for a lot of disunity and internal disagreements with Hitler's policies.

Jesus Prayed for Unity at All Levels

Neither pray I for these alone, but for them also which shall believe on me through their word;

THAT THEY ALL MAY BE ONE; as thou, Father, art in me, and I in thee, that they also may be one in us: that the world may believe that thou hast sent me.

John 17:20-21

Do you see how Jesus prayed for unity at all levels? He knew that a lot depended on the unity of the body. The kind of unity that the Word of God describes is the type that forces us to join into a body of inseparable parts. You have not achieved unity until your separation from your co-worker is like separation of a part of your body. That is why we are called the body of Christ. Our joining together is the joining of body parts into one inseparable unit. Think about it.

How easy is it for you to be separated from your Christian brother? How easy is it for your kidney, your breast or your leg to be separated from your body? It is a very difficult, complicated process because the parts of the body are well and truly connected to each other. That is how we must be connected to each other. Stay connected! Develop connections between yourself and all the essential people that God has placed in your life and ministry! Connections that will be difficult to break and separate! That is the meaning of unity at all levels!

Adolf Hitler was the Germany's leader who the started the Second World War. To a large extent, Hitler's following was not united at all levels. On the outside everything in the German army seemed to be perfect but there was internal disunity. This kind of internal disunity is sure to bring down any regime. Can you believe that a total of forty-two attempts were made on the life of Adolf Hitler? Unfortunately, the details surrounding most of these attempts are sketchy and some stories are unsubstantiated. How many leaders have 42 recorded assassination attempts on their lives within six years? Adolf Hitler had entire battalions assigned to his security whilst Winston Churchill needed just a few bodyguards.

Opposition to Adolf Hitler within Germany clearly existed from 1933 to 1945. The opposition to Hitler took place at civilian, church and military levels. Although none of this opposition to the Nazi regime of Adolf Hitler was successful it reveals how there was disunity at all levels. There were however several well-documented attempts that came very close to succeeding.

The most famous example of men who were willing to overthrow Adolf Hitler was the famous July Bomb Plot of 1944. Claus von Stauffenburg was the man who actually set off the bomb at Hitler's East Prussian stronghold but there were many other men behind the plot. Many of these were in the military. Even Field Marshal Rommel was implicated in this plot but was allowed to commit suicide rather than face a very public and humiliating trial.

According to statistics the most common form of opposition came from those ideologically opposed to the Nazis such as communists and socialists. Of the 32,500 death sentences ordered for political reasons, 20,000 of the victims were communists.

With such levels of disunity and confusion, it is no wonder that the German campaign in the Second World War was defeated after six years. Do you want your vision and your ministry to be cut short? I don't think so! Fight for unity at all levels! To war a good warfare, you must have unity at all levels.

CHAPTER 20

A Good General and the Sustainability of the Mission

Or what king, going to make war against another king, sitteth not down first, and consulteth WHETHER HE BE ABLE with ten thousand to meet him that cometh against him with twenty thousand?

Luke 14:31

Sustainability of the mission" is one of the main principles taught by the British Armed Forces. Sustainability of the mission means that you have the power to maintain your fighting forces on the field.

The Russian Armed Forces calls this principle "logistics". Under this principle, the Russians teach about the "restoration of reserves". The principle teaches that the army must be capable of restoring its combat abilities in the modern and fast paced battlefield.

The Unsustainable Mission

During the Second World War, the German army invaded Russia on the 22nd of June in an operation code named "Operation Barbarossa". This was a mighty and massive undertaking involving 3 million men. The frontier of hostilities was an amazing one thousand six hundred kilometres long and the invasion into Russia was almost one thousand kilometres deep.

At the outset of this invasion, there was a shortage of vehicles for the campaign because the German industry was unable to keep up with the car production to supply the war effort. This resulted in the invasion depending on horses and wagons to transport supplies to the soldiers to the frontline. During this invasion 625,000 horses were relied upon to move artillery, wagons and everything else that was needed at the front.

Unfortunately, by August the ability to supply ammunition and fuel was compromised. Military operations had to be curtailed as they waited for re-supply from the rear.

The supply of food was also compromised. It is no easy task to feed 3 million men every day. Commanders in the field were forced to slaughter local livestock to feed the soldiers. They also began to slaughter and eat the very horses that were pulling their supplies.

The Germans also did not consider their ability to sustain the war in the extremely cold winter of Russia so no provisions were made to protect the men from the extremely cold temperatures. It is not easy to provide winter clothing for 3 million men. Fuel that was needed to keep trucks moving froze. There were no supplies of essential anti-freeze grease, oil and lubricants, which are needed to keep guns and other weapons in action.

No provision was made for winter clothing as it was assumed that these would not be needed. Troops resorted to stuffing newspapers into their summer uniforms to keep warm. About 14,000 amputations resulting from frostbite were conducted. By December 6th 1941, after 168 days of continuous fighting and within 30 kilometres of Moscow the mighty German army was exhausted. They were starved, frozen; out of fuel and ammunition. Their supply lines stretched a distance of 1600 kilometres. As a result of this, the Wehrmacht was unable to continue and sustain the invasion of Russia.

The German invasion of Russia collapsed over this one principle of "sustainability of the mission".

No matter how mighty you are, you must be able to sustain the mission you embark on. Jesus taught us to count the cost and see if the mission was sustainable. Sustainability of the mission is a mighty consideration in your calling. Will you be able to pay for it? If God has called you to evangelise the world and plant a church, will you be able to sustain it? Will you be able to carry on the ministry into your old age?

Many pastors are unable to sustain their churches into their old age because they do not have their own church buildings. They keep renting halls and moving from one place to the other when they should have built their own church buildings. Today, Bible schools have turned into secular universities because they were unable to sustain the ministry of teaching the Word of God at no cost. Today, many evangelists have turned into pastors because they were unable to sustain the ministry of evangelism.

It is time to consider the sustainability of your calling! Will you be able to persist into the future? What are you doing today that you will not be able to continue doing tomorrow?

CHAPTER 21

A Good General and Decisiveness

A double minded man is unstable in all his ways.

James 1:8

Be decisive! You will always have to take decisions. You will be blamed or rewarded for your decisions. You must know how to take decisions.

Double-minded people are unstable and indecisive. There is nothing worse than being under the leadership of someone who is indecisive. It is time to make up your mind and take the crucial decisions that God wants you to make. Why do some people not take decisions?

Some people do not take decisions because of their phlegmatic temperaments. Phlegmatic people are slow thinking men whose first option is to rest or do nothing. It takes great effort for them to rise out of their inertia and take a step.

People are indecisive because they have not thought through their plans carefully.

People are indecisive because they do not want to follow things through to their logical conclusions. A lot of your indecision would be overcome if you understand that you are already committed and there is no way out. Stopping in the middle is madness. You might as well finish what you started because you have one leg in the boat already.

In war, indecision can cost you everything.

The Indecision of Germany in the Second World War

Adolf Hitler, an evil man, lost the Second World War because he wavered at the most critical moment when victory was served to him on a silver platter.

The Second World War was started by Adolf Hitler when he invaded Poland on the 1st of September 1939. After the invasion of Poland, England sent its armies into France to help contain the German aggression. But after their quick victory in Poland, Germany decided to invade France, Holland and Belgium. The English armies had crossed into France to join the war and fight Germany. But they were no match for the modern and well-prepared German armies. The entire British army was pushed back to the sea and encircled at a place called Dunkirk. The British army was now a virtual prisoner of the German army and could have been easily wiped out at Dunkirk. But that is not what happened.

The British were effectively trapped at the seaside with nowhere to go. It was at this point that Hitler, acted strangely and became indecisive. The Panzer divisions asked for permission to attack but permission was not given.

Adolf Hitler was gripped by indecision and wavered between destroying the British armies and allowing them to escape across the sea. Whilst Adolf Hitler wavered, the entire British army escaped across the sea. They entered into ships and sailed across to safety, where they would re-group and return to defeat Germany a few years later. Adolf Hitler missed the opportunity to wipe out his greatest enemies in one swoop. This mistake cost Germany the Second World War.

When it was too late, Hitler had a change of mind and decided to attack England in what was called Operation Sea Lion. But he had missed his chance to defeat the British when they were at his mercy. His decision to attack England was too late and Operation Sea Lion ended up being a massive failure.

Indecision in Ministry

Many pastors do not take decisions when they should. They waver when they should strike firmly and decisively. When a person shows signs of disloyalty and should be dismissed, many leaders play around with the decision of dismissing them. But disloyalty is a leadership emergency and must be dealt with decisively. The best place to kill a cobra is in the egg. When you have a good chance to deal with certain things you must act decisively.

There are people who have opportunities to begin churches. But they are simply indecisive. I started my church when I was a student in Medical School. That was the good and opportune time for me to take a decision to be in the ministry. If I had failed to start the ministry at that time, I would have missed the opportunity of a lifetime. Years later, I would meet people who tried to start churches in their middle age. Some of them really struggled and became bitter at God. I remember a brother who claimed that God had asked him to start a church in London. He lived in London for years and got himself into great difficulty before he eventually started his ministry. By the time he got going, he was laden and burdened with problems that destroyed the church he started.

Do not make the mistake of indecision when you must act quickly.

CHAPTER 22

Fight Extremes with Extremes

How art thou fallen from heaven, O Lucifer, son of the morning! How art thou cut down to the ground, which didst weaken the nations! For thou hast said in thine heart, I will ascend into heaven, I will exalt my throne above the stars of God: I will sit also upon the mount of the congregation, in the sides of the north:

I will ascend above the heights of the clouds; I will be like the most High. Yet thou shalt be brought down to hell, to the sides of the pit. They that see thee shall narrowly look upon thee, and consider thee, saying, is this the man that made the earth to tremble, that did shake kingdoms;

THAT MADE THE WORLD AS A WILDERNESS, and destroyed the cities thereof; that opened not the house of his prisoners?

Isaiah 14:12-17

Satan's plans for you are extreme. Be extreme in your battles and strategies. The cross of Jesus Christ was an extreme response to the devil who has turned the world into a wilderness. Watch God's response to the devil's attempt to destroy His creation. He sent His Son, Jesus Christ, to die on a cross for us all. This is an extreme response from God and by God. To give up your only begotten son and to use His blood as a weapon to fight your enemy, is to fight extremes with extremes.

Perhaps most ministers do not recognize the extreme plans that Satan has for them. If we did, we would be more extreme in the measures taken against the devil, his agents and his plans. One day, the Holy Spirit impressed upon me the need to fight extremes with extremes. He showed me a group of ministers of the gospel living in one of the prominent cities of the world. As I thought of these ministers, I realised that extreme attacks had taken place on their lives. Two of the pastors of large churches were in prison. One of them was in prison for apparently having sex with an underaged lady. Another was in prison for having sex with young boys. One of the pastors of a mega church was dismissed and disconnected from his church, living in poverty and in need. Another pastor of a huge church died of a mysterious illness in the midst of his years, whilst yet another battled with the authorities over various accusations and investigations.

It was only in observing the pattern of afflictions and attacks of ministers of big churches that I realised how extreme Satan's attack and intentions are. Satan wants you to go to prison! Satan wants to kill you! Satan wants to silence you! Watch closely and keep your heart open and you will see that there is an extremely evil enemy planning great extremes against you and your future.

This is the essence of this book. We must fight the war of extremes. We have no choice because we have an extremely radical enemy with extremely radical plans for you and I. In the Second World War, Germany's neighbours could not imagine the evil that was developing next door. Poland could not envisage or imagine the kind of murder and onslaught that was about to be unleashed on them. Millions of Poles died like dogs at the hands of the murderous German army. Most of the world could not imagine the kind of murder Hitler was about to unleash on everyone. He needed to be stopped and no half-hearted measures would suffice. Extremes had to be fought with extremes.

Every country which dealt mildly with Germany before the Second World War lived to regret their weak, half-hearted approach towards Adolf Hitler. Nerville Chamberlain, the Prime Minister of Britain tried to appease Adolf Hitler, making concessions and agreeing to many of Hitler's demands. Stalin initially cooperated with Adolf Hitler, never imagining that he would be attacked and millions of Russians would die needlessly. When Winston Churchill became the Prime Minister of England, he vowed to fight Adolf Hitler to the very end. Churchill was the extreme that was needed to fight Hitler's extremes.

Stalin was far more resistant and resilient than Hitler expected. The Russians were not easy to fight and were never defeated by Germany. Adolf Hitler was fought on two fronts by two men who were equally extreme in their posture against him.

I have watched as pastors fight disloyal people with mild, half-hearted efforts, trying to counsel people who have turned in their hearts against them. If God did not counsel Lucifer but cast him out of Heaven, why would you try to counsel a disloyal person? When I share the need to sack some people, some think it is too extreme. You will think it is extreme because you are not experienced. Today, Europe is a nuclear storehouse with many countries armed to the teeth. Most of the countries in Europe are nuclear powers and capable of destroying each other within the first few hours of any war. They have learnt their lesson from Hitler and are ready to meet any extreme attack with extremes.

Israel is another example of a nation that has learnt to fight extremes with extremes. The people of Israel were attacked by Adolf Hitler and six million of them were murdered in cold blood. Today, they are an extreme force, ready to fight the extremes of other Arab nations. Indeed, the nation of Israel has learnt that the extreme hatred that people have against Jews must not be taken lightly. If you notice an extreme you must fight it with another extreme! Israel is known to have acquired nuclear weapons and all other extreme but necessary arms to fight the nations around them whose aim is to extinguish them. You, O man of God, must take extreme measures to defend yourself and fight the enemy who wants to kill you.

The devil wants to put you in a grave so that you truly shut up. You must take every extreme measure to be well.

The devil wants to put you in prison. You must take every extreme measure to ensure that no financial or moral issue puts you into prison.

The devil want to close down your church and take away all your members. You must fight these ideas with extreme messages on loyalty and an extreme stance against disloyalty.

Rise up now and fight extremes with extremes. It may be your only chance to deliver yourself from extreme plans of your enemy.

Imitate God who has countered the devil's extreme plan by sending His Son to die on the cross.

CHAPTER 23

A Good General Identifies Dangerous Enemies by their Lies

And when the inhabitants of Gibeon heard what Joshua had done unto Jericho and to Ai, They did work wilily, and went and made as if they had been ambassadors, and took old sacks upon their asses, and wine bottles, old, and rent, and bound up;

And old shoes and clouted upon their feet, and old garments upon them; and all the bread of their provision was dry and mouldy. And they went to Joshua unto the camp at Gilgal, and said unto him, and to the men of Israel, we be come from a far country: now therefore make ye a league with us.

And the men of Israel said unto the Hivites, Peradventure ye dwell among us; and how shall we make a league with you?

Joshua 9:3-7

Joshua's Greatest Mistake

The greatest mistake of Joshua, the General was made when he fell for the lies and deception of his enemy. He was dealing with his enemy, someone he should have destroyed. But they deceived him into thinking they were friends. Joshua was deceived because he did not investigate whether the people were liars or not. You must investigate whether people around you are liars or not. Many people around leaders do not tell the truth. Everyone wants to rise up and be favoured by the leader. Because of this, leaders are often surrounded by clever deceivers. This is why heads of state often do the wrong thing. There are liars around the leader. But you must not accept deceivers in your cabinet. Identify them and stop them. The deception will eventually feed back against you.

A dangerous enemy is identified by his lies and deception.

Your deadly enemy must be noticed by his lies and deception. The liar in your life is the person you must learn to mark as your deadly enemy.

Although most people tell lies effortlessly, lies remain the significant sign of the presence of Satan. Jesus said, "He was a murderer from the beginning, and abode not in the truth, because there is no truth in him. When he speaketh a lie, he speaketh of his own: for he is a liar, and the father of it" (John 8:44). This Scripture reveals that Satan is actually a killer and a murderer who tells lies. Satan wants to kill you and destroy you. The sign of the presence of the devil is always some kind of deception, lying or covering up of something. A pastor and a Christian must be very wary of telling lies because it is a step into demonic territory.

It is sad to see how lying and deception has become a part of the ministry. It is a sign of the presence of the devil in the ministry. If you are a man of God, do not tell lies or say things, which are not true. Do not make promises that you will not fulfil. Each time you do that, you reveal that there is some infiltration of demons in your life. Satan is a part of your life and ministry when lying and deception are a part of your life and ministry.

As a leader, you must watch out for signs of deception and traces of lies in those around you. Do not be deceived by innocent faces and nice presentations of people. Do not be deceived by the looks of a good liar. Be more conscious of whether someone has told the truth and whether he always tells the truth. A good general identifies enemies and marks them out by their lying and deceiving ways! The Bible has no kind remarks for deceivers of any sort. King David prayed that he would be rescued from liars!

Rescue me, O Lord, from liars and from all deceitful people. O deceptive tongue, what will God do to you? How will he increase your punishment? You will be pierced with sharp arrows and burned with glowing coals.

Psalm 120:2-4 (NLT)

Mind you, good liars are impressive! That is why it is difficult to believe that they are lying. Do not think that a liar cannot look you straight in the eye and tell a lie. Expert liars can lie to you without blinking. They can act the part and pretend to be anything they are not. Expert liars can undergo interrogation and even torture without ever changing their story. Years will pass by as they maintain their lying stories. Always remember; when you are dealing with a liar, you are dealing with a dangerous person. Apart from everything else, many politicians are liars. Adolf Hitler lied to the German people and led them to Hell. Through his lies he caused the deaths of fifty million people.

The Lies of a Head of State

The lies of Adolf Hitler were the greatest revelation of whom he really was. The lies he told in his speeches revealed the presence of a strong satanic force. Wherever there are lies and deception, you can be assured you are dealing with an evil presence. It is worth investigating, asking questions, searching and querying until you are sure you are not being told any kind of lies.

In this section, I want you to notice the many different lies that Adolf Hitler told. He said one thing in public and a completely different thing in private. He was lying all the time and the lies he told revealed that a great evil was preparing to manifest itself to the world. If you are sensitive to lying and deception you may save yourself from accepting the wrong people in your life.

Great liars are also great murderers. Adolf Hitler is a classic example of the fact that, "If you tell a big enough lie and tell it frequently enough, it will be believed." "Make the lie big, make it simple, keep saying it and eventually they will believe it."

How Hitler Lied about Invading Poland

Publicly Adolf Hitler lied and said:

"Poland is about to invade Germany. The Polish state has refused a peaceful settlement. Germans in Poland have been persecuted with bloodied terror and driven from their homes. A series of violations along the German-Polish border has proved that Poland is not longer willing to respect the frontiers of the Reich. Does anyone really believe that the German nation will stand for that act from such a ridiculous state: To put an end to this lunacy, I have no other choice than to meet force with force."

To the German military he said,

"Close your heart to pity. Act brutally. Eighteen million people must obtain what is their right. The strongest man is always right."

After destroying Poland in eighteen days of fighting, eighteen days of fire and killing 50,000 Poles, Hitler invited foreign journalists to view the destruction of Poland. Adolf Hitler then said:

"A great crime has been committed here. The Polish military went mad and look at the crime against their own people. They were drunk with power and talked of marching on Berlin. Then

*they barricaded themselves in the city, and look at Warsaw now!
Sheer sympathy for women and children caused me to make an
offer to those in command in Warsaw to, at least, let the civilian
inhabitants leave the city."*

In truth, Hitler ordered a special SS unit to follow the army
across the city. It was their job to murder any living Pole they
could find. Doctors, police, the clergy, Jews, landlords and the
nobility were all butchered. Less than three percent of the Polish
upper class remained alive after the attack.

How Adolf Hitler Lied about France

Publicly Adolf Hitler lied and said:

*"I have declared that the frontier between Germany and France
is a final one. I have repeatedly offered friendship and the closest
cooperation with Britain. Germany has no interest in the West
and we have no aims there for the future. With this assurance
we are in solemn earnest. As long as others do not violate the
neutrality of Holland and Belgium, we will take every care to
respect it."*

But in private Hitler said:

*"My decision is unchangeable. I shall attack France and England
at the earliest favourable moment. The neutrality of Holland
and Belgium is of no importance. If France and England strike,
let them do so. It is a matter of complete indifference to me.
Today is Tuesday. By Monday, we may be at war with someone."*

How Adolf Hitler Lied about Russia

Since the beginning of his political career, Hitler had
considered communism one of the world's greatest evils and
frequently insisted that any cooperation with Russia was out of
the question.

Publicly Adolf Hitler lied and said:

"The government of the Reich is ready to cultivate with the Soviet Union friendly relations profitable to both parties. Given the fact that Soviet Russia has no intention of exporting its doctrine to Germany, I no longer see any reason why we should still oppose one another."

But privately, Adolf Hitler said:

"We will crush Soviet Russia. The German Armed Forces must be prepared, even before the conclusion of the war against England, to crush Soviet Russia in a rapid campaign. We need only kick in the front door and the whole rotten edifice of communism will come crashing down. What matters is that Bolshevism be exterminated. Moscow, as the centre of the doctrine must disappear from the earth's surface. No organized Russian state must be allowed to exist."

How Adolf Hitler Lied about England

Publicly Adolf Hitler lied and said:

"I shall arrange an interview with foreign journalists of the British attempting to land on the coast of Europe. I will treat the subject in a manner that will come as a cold douche to the British. I will say that I do not believe in the possibility of an invasion."

But privately, he began preparing for the inevitable invasion.

"We must aim at securing a defensive line on Dutch soil because the war with England will be a life and death struggle. The idea that we can get off cheaply is dangerous. There is no such possibility. When the enemy invades in the West, it will be the moment of decision in this war and that moment we must turn to our advantage. I will emphasize the German military precision and thoroughness and ensure that we are prepared for every eventuality."

CHAPTER 24

Your Great Mistake is to Deal with the Enemy in the Spirit of Benevolence

NOW GO AND SMITE AMALEK, AND UTTERLY DESTROY ALL THAT THEY HAVE, AND SPARE THEM NOT; but slay both man and woman, infant and suckling, ox and sheep, camel and ass.

And Saul smote the Amalekites from Havilah until thou comest to Shur, that is over against Egypt.

And he took Agag the king of the Amalekites alive, and utterly destroyed all the people with the edge of the sword.

BUT SAUL AND THE PEOPLE SPARED AGAG, and the best of the sheep, and of the oxen, and of the fatlings, and the lambs, and all that was good, and would not utterly destroy them: but every thing that was vile and refuse, that they destroyed utterly.

1 Samuel 15:3, 7-9

The Amalekites attacked and harassed Israel as they made their way from Egypt to the Promised Land. The Amalekites are therefore a type of evil spirits who harass and attack the people of God on their journey to Heaven. The Amalekites, just like demons, attacked the Israelites from the rear where they were weak. This is characteristic of demons who use deceptive tactics to fight weak Christians.

God's response to the Amalekites was to utterly wipe them out. His instructions were clear, "Wipe out every single Amalekite." God was angry with Saul because he dealt with the Amalekites in the spirit of benevolence. That was his great mistake. Saul lost his ministry because he dealt with the Amalekites kindly, gently and mercifully. The spirit of benevolence is the spirit of kindness and mercy.

Many ministers lose their ministry because they deal with disloyalty in a kind, gentle and merciful way. Churches are destroyed, congregations are scattered because leaders are "kinder and more loving" than God.

God did not deal with the Amalekites in the spirit of benevolence and neither should you. It is a mistake to allow people who are clearly disloyal to flourish around you. To deal benevolently with a known enemy is a leadership mistake of great proportion. Your enemy has an extensive and extreme plan of action to kill you.

Know that your enemy will compel you to submit to his will if he gets the chance.

Your great mistake is therefore to deal with an enemy in the spirit of benevolence.

The Vision

I had a dream in which my associate pastors and I caught a massive viper in the fields. We were so delighted to have captured our enemy. We were even more delighted to have caught this terrible snake alive. We decided to tie the mouth of the snake so that it would not be able to bring out its huge fangs and poison anyone. We began to tie the mouth of the snake very firmly with rope and twine. As I looked at what was happening, it occurred to me that the rope could slip off the snake's triangularly shaped head.

I suddenly shouted to my assistants, "Why are we tying the mouth of this snake. If the ropes slips off it could bite us and we will be dead men."

"CUT OFF THE HEAD!" I shouted. "CUT OFF THE HEAD NOW! If you cut off the head you will be saved from all possible rebound attacks."

When I awoke out of that vision, the Lord showed me the need to wipe out the enemy without sparing or showing kindness. Don't leave behind an enemy who can rise up again and hurt you. Look at the way God dealt with Lucifer. He cast him out of Heaven and dealt with him permanently and conclusively. You are not kinder than God. You must be an imitator of God and deal with the devil and his agents conclusively and permanently.

And the great dragon was cast out, that old serpent, called the Devil, and Satan, which deceiveth the whole world: he was cast out into the earth, and his angels were cast out with him.

Revelation 12:9

Many of your unfinished projects are snakes whose mouths have been tied. A little bit of time and a little change in the circumstances can cause that enemy to resurface. Cut off the head! Finish the project! Obey God fully. Do all that is in your power to be obedient.

Certain relationships, especially with the opposite sex, are snakes that must have their heads cut off. Don't leave any traces of certain relationships in your life. Cut them off in totality. No texts! No Whatsapps! No calls! No Facebooking! No lunches! No visits! Be wise and win your war. Do not deal with your enemy in the spirit of benevolence. Do not deal gently with those who accuse you. Do not deal benevolently with those who are disloyal. Do not deal mildly with those who leave you and destroy your ministry as they leave. The spirit of benevolence will cause more of such people to arise and do more damage. Annihilation and extermination is the way to deal with deadly enemies.

CHAPTER 25

Extinguishment and Annihilation

And thou shalt consume all the people which the Lord thy God shall deliver thee; THINE EYE SHALL HAVE NO PITY UPON THEM: neither shalt thou serve their gods; for that will be a snare unto thee. If thou shalt say in thine heart, These nations are more than I; how can I dispossess them? Thou shalt not be afraid of them: but shalt well remember what the Lord thy God did unto Pharaoh, and unto all Egypt;

Deuteronomy 7:16-18

Joshua was under instruction to obliterate the Philistines. There was no other way to deal with the people in the Promised Land than with the principle of extinguishment and obliteration. Failure to obliterate Jericho would mean more deaths and more losses for the people of God in years to come.

History tells us that Joshua did fail to obliterate all the giants in Gaza, Gath and Ashdod. Indeed, because Joshua failed to obliterate the enemy, they lived to see the rise of certain characters from these very cities of Gath, Gaza and Ashdod. The people from these cities played significant roles in destroying the Israelites later.

The glory of God departed from Israel when the ark of God was captured by the people of Ashdod.

"And the Philistines took the ark of God, and brought it from Ebenezer unto Ashdod." (1 Samuel 5:1)

Years later, King David found himself fighting Goliath who came from Gath. "And there went out a champion out of the camp of the Philistines, named Goliath, of Gath, whose height was six cubits and a span" (1 Samuel 17:4).

At that time came Joshua, and cut off the Anakims from the mountains, from Hebron, from Debir, from Anab, and from all the mountains of Judah, and from all the mountains of Israel: Joshua destroyed them utterly with their cities
There was none of the Anakims left in the land of the children of Israel: only in GAZA, IN GATH, AND IN ASHDOD, there remained.

Joshua 11:21-22

The Russian Armed Forces have a principle of war called "annihilation". Annihilation speaks of the extinguishment, the obliteration, the demolition, the extermination, and the liquidation of your enemy.

Mind you, we are speaking about fighting a war and not just participating in some kind of Olympic games. When you fight a real war against a really deadly enemy, you will understand why the principle of annihilation is important.

Many enemies do not stop fighting you until they are actually annihilated and obliterated. War is often inevitable because there are people who will not back away from fighting. Many of these stubbornly fighting individuals are demonically inspired and want to kill, destroy and steal.

In the ministry, you equally have such belligerent fighters. They have no divine love, divine maturity or spiritual compassion. Like Judas Iscariot, they can do the unthinkable to destroy you and your ministry forever. If you have someone who will not go away on his own and who will not change his evil mind, you are left with no choice than to obliterate him from your life and ministry.

Just as God did not counsel Lucifer but wiped him out of Heaven, you must not waste your time counselling in certain situations. Be led by the Holy Spirit and you will know when you are dealing with an enemy who must be extinguished permanently and absolutely.

Cast out the scorner, and contention shall go out; yea, strife and reproach shall cease.

Proverbs 22:10

There are people who do not believe in you, and do not change their mind, no matter who you are and whom you become. You may be the greatest what not in the world but they will not be impressed. That is why the Bible teaches us to cast out (extinguish, obliterate, eliminate, annihilate) such people from your life and ministry.

I once tried to convert a scorner. This was a young pastor who was new to our ministry. I wanted him to see the extent of the ministry so that he would have respect for what God had done and decide to be a permanent part of the work. I sent him around many of the churches I had established in different parts of the world. But I was wasting my time because I had embarked on a project to impress a scorner.

Scorners cannot be converted. They must be cast out and contention will go. This scornful young man was not impressed by the programme I had laid out for him. In the end, he still became rebellious and left the church in a painful way. He destroyed the work of God and did not even understand what he had done wrong. I learnt a painful lesson there. You cannot counsel a scorner and you cannot advise a rebellious person. Cast them out as the Bible says. Eliminate and extinguish them forever from your life and you will be blessed.

Hiroshima

Japan continued to fight on in the Second World War even though the whole world wanted peace. Everyone was hoping that there would be no more bloodshed for American or British soldiers. An important and famous communication called the "Potsdam Declaration" was issued to the Japanese government advising, coaxing and pleading with them to stop fighting and surrender to the realities.

The Americans had developed the atomic bomb but did not wish to use it on fellow human beings.

The atomic bomb is a weapon of obliteration, extinguishment and annihilation. Many people had already died in the war. But talk as they did, the Japanese government refused to heed to the warnings. The American government went further to drop leaflets and make radio broadcasts to the Japanese people so that they would be aware of the request to stop fighting.

As I said earlier, some people will not stop fighting until they are completely obliterated. This ultimatum made good offers to the Japanese people. Below are a few of the points that were clearly communicated to the Japanese people before the atomic bomb was dropped on them.

- *"We do not intend that the Japanese shall be enslaved as a race or destroyed as a nation..." The Japanese government shall remove all obstacles to the revival and strengthening of democratic tendencies among the Japanese people. Freedom of speech, of religion and of thought, as well as respect for the fundamental human rights shall be established.*

- *Japan shall be permitted to maintain such industries as will sustain her economy and permit the exaction of just reparations in kind, but not those which would enable her to re-arm for war. To this end, access to, as distinguished from control of, raw materials shall be permitted. Eventual Japanese participation in world trade shall be permitted.*

- *The occupying forces of the allies shall be withdrawn from Japan as soon as these objectives have been accomplished and there has been established in accordance with the freely expressed will of the Japanese people, a peacefully inclined and responsible government.*

- *We call upon the government of Japan to proclaim now the unconditional surrender of all Japanese forces and to provide proper and adequate assurances of their good faith in such actions.*

- *The alternative for Japan is prompt and utter destruction.*

This communiqué is the pleading of a peaceful partner with the enemy; asking for humility and cessation of conflict. But there are people who do not cease conflict because of your pleadings, begging and good advice. This is a reality of life on earth. Many people continue fighting even when it does not make sense to fight. Many marriages experience mindless battles, upheavals and conflicts that destroy both parties.

Perhaps some of these people who fight mindlessly are not really human beings but evil spirits, para-humans and spiritual hybrids who are operating on earth to cause the mindless destruction of human beings. The government of Japan did not heed the advice, the pleading and the ultimatum given by America, Britain and China on the 26th of July 1945. A few days later, on the 6th of August 1945 America was forced to drop a weapon of extinguishment and obliteration on the Japanese city of Hiroshima. This bomb wiped out the entire city of Hiroshima. Can you believe that this did not lead to the surrender of Japan? It was only after another bomb was dropped on Nagasaki on the 9th of August 1945 that the Japanese surrendered.

Today, in our churches, we have people who rebel against the best of leaders and the noblest of fathers. Without reason and without any justifiable cause, they rise up against the ones who have loved them and counselled them. They fight, accuse, insult and destroy the character of their leader making him look ridiculous and stupid.

Often, such people cannot be counselled or advised to change. They must be obliterated, extinguished and wiped out of your life and ministry forever.

CHAPTER 26

Keep Your Plans as Dark as Night

... a wise man keepeth it in till afterwards.

Proverbs 29:11

I t is important to have secrets that are well kept from disloyal people who do not appreciate your love and care for them. You must have a system that protects the privacy and secrecy of vital issues. A good general seeks to know all about his enemy. You must assume that your enemy is trying to know a lot about you. You must keep as much information from him and let him know only what you want him to know. Without your systems of privacy and secrecy in place, your plans, purposes and pursuits can easily fail. As Christians, having secrets sounds a little unbiblical and even immoral. We teach a lot about confession, openness and honesty. Because of this, having secrets and keeping secrets seem to be a bad thing.

Yes, having secrets and keeping secrets in a civilian world is often evil. However, when you enter the realms of war, it is necessary to have secrets and guard them well. You must keep your enemy in the dark otherwise you will lose the war. Jesus Christ intentionally kept information and knowledge from the Pharisees and the Sadducees. Because they were hard-hearted evil men, it was necessary to keep them in the dark.

Jesus spoke in parables intentionally. It was no accident. He wanted to keep His enemies in darkness. The Pharisees were so hard-hearted and so wicked that they murdered Jesus Christ in cold blood when they had the chance.

When you have a hard-hearted enemy you must keep him in darkness about your life. It is important not to be open to a hard-hearted destroying devil. Keep your plans as dark as night when you are dealing with the enemy.

And the disciples came, and said unto him, Why speakest thou unto them in parables?

Therefore speak I to them in parables: because they seeing see not; and hearing they hear not, neither do they understand.

For this people's HEART IS WAXED GROSS, and their EARS ARE DULL of hearing, and their eyes they have closed; lest at any time they should see with their eyes, and hear with their ears, and should understand with their heart, and should be converted, and I should heal them.

Matthew 13:10, 13, 15

When there is a war going on, there are certainly occasions and reasons for keeping people in the dark. Enemies must be kept in the dark and must be given little information. Knowledge must be kept away from them and secrets must be kept from them. Don't let everyone know everything when you are at war.

Secrets are not always evil. On several occasions, the Scripture exhorts us to keep secrets.

Three Times We Learn to Keep Secrets

1. This Scripture teaches that it is foolishness to speak your whole mind.

    A fool uttereth all his mind: but a wise man keepeth it in till afterwards.

    Proverbs 29:11

2. The apostle Paul said that he had had revelations of things, which were unlawful to share.

    In other words, it was wrong to even speak about them. It is a sin (unlawful) to even reveal things that God has allowed you to know.

    I knew a man in Christ above fourteen years ago, (whether in the body, I cannot tell; or whether out of the body, I cannot tell: God knoweth;) such an one caught up to the third heaven. And I knew such a man, (whether in the body, or out of the body, I cannot tell: God knoweth;) How that he was caught up into paradise, and heard unspeakable words, WHICH IT IS NOT LAWFUL FOR A MAN TO UTTER.

    2 Corinthians 12:2-4

3.	Jesus sits at the right hand of the Father but does not know the day or the hour of His return.

The Father has kept that secret from the Son, even though He sits by Him.

But of that day and that hour knoweth no man, no, not the angels which are in heaven, neither the Son, but the Father.

Mark 13:32

Canaris

There was a man who was famous for serving his country at the highest level as the head of the secret service and yet he was a successful enemy of his own government. From his position as the head of the secret service, he fought against the German government and was not discovered until the last few days of the war. His name was Wilhelm Canaris. Canaris, a mystical figure, was full of plans as dark as night.

Canaris was a German naval officer and the head of the German military intelligence service from 1935 to 1944.

As at 1937, he was a staunch supporter of Hitler, considering him the only solution in the fight against communism in Germany. By 1938, however, he had realised that Hitler's policies would lead Germany to disaster and he secretly began to work against Hitler's regime.

After the outbreak of war between Germany and Poland in September 1939, Canaris visited the war front and witnessed examples of war crimes, including the burning of the synagogue in Bedzin, where the town's Jewish residents were burned to death. Other intelligence agents had also sent him reports about incidents of mass murder throughout Poland.

Canaris wanted to protest these atrocities and was shocked to learn that the atrocities were directed by Hitler himself. He was shocked by these incidents and started working actively to overthrow Hitler, whilst posing as a trusted man to Hitler.

Canaris only lost his job as the head of the German intelligence service in February 1944. There was no strong evidence that linked him to any of the coup and assassination attempts against Adolf Hitler. However, at the insistence of Heinrich Himmler, (Hitler's right-hand man) who had suspected Canaris for a long time, Hitler dismissed Canaris from the German intelligence service in February 1944.

On the 20th of July 1944, there was a major attempt to kill Adolf Hitler. Yet again, Canaris was not directly linked to this plot because he had been under house arrest and nothing linked him to the event.

Unfortunately, one of the officers involved in this plot, Werner Schrader, had kept a metal box in which the details of the plot, as well as fifteen other major plots to overthrow Hitler were discovered. For years, Canaris had also kept detailed records of Hitler's atrocities in his personal diary that he entrusted to Werner Schrader, a subordinate and fellow resistance member.

Following the uncovering of these documents, Canaris, and his deputies were arrested and tried. They were found guilty and were humiliated before witnesses. Canaris was executed a few days before the end of the war.

Canaris was led to the gallows barefoot and naked on the 9th April 1945, in the Flossenburg concentration camp. Meanwhile, his boss, Adolf Hitler himself was forced to commit suicide a few days later on the 30th of April 1945.

Amazingly, Adolf Hitler had employed a traitor as his chief spy for nine years. Canaris had kept his plans as dark as night. Even when his personal diary was discovered, the only link between him and the plotters was the fact that the names in the book were his friends.

In war, it is important to keep plans as dark as night if they are to succeed. The attack on Pearl Harbor was based on this principle of keeping plans as dark as night. The Tet Offensive which led to the defeat of the Americans in Vietnam was an absolute surprise because the plans were kept as dark as night. Secrecy is important in war! In times of peace, there is often no need for secrets. But when war erupts, secrecy becomes important.

Let Your Plans against Disloyal People Be As Dark As Night

The removal and transfer of disloyal and unreliable people must come as a surprise to them. Sometimes it is good for disloyal people to think that you do not know anything about their evil ways. It is good to shock them with unexpected moves that are well thought-through.

CHAPTER 27

To Subdue the Enemy without Fighting is the Height of Skill

Or what king, going to make war against another king, sitteth not down first, and consulteth whether he be able with ten thousand to meet him that cometh against him with twenty thousand? Or else, while the other is yet a great way off, he sendeth an ambassage, and desireth conditions of peace.

Luke 14:31-32

A good general must assess the battle that he has to fight. Are you going to win? Will you have the victory over your enemy? Can you handle what is coming your way? The Scripture teaches that you must offer conditions of peace when you see that you cannot win.

A good general accomplishes great victories by not fighting. To not actually fight a war may involve surrender, retreat or avoidance. You must know how to subdue an enemy without fighting. Retreat and surrender are often seen as signs of weakness. But sometimes retreat and surrender are not signs of weakness but signs of wisdom. It takes humility to accept the strategy of avoiding fighting, through retreat or surrender. You must accept that some enemies are too big, too strong or too erratic to fight. You must choose your fights carefully! If you choose your fights carefully you will win one hundred percent of your battles.

Refusing to employ uneducated and illiterate people is also a way to outthink the enemy. Many rebellious people are uneducated and illiterate. Many (not all) strikes, protests and campaigns of discontentment are led by such people. Once you have such people as employees, they can be the seed of complaints, rebellions and discontentment. Avoiding people who have little understanding is a good way of subduing an enemy without fighting him.

The Scripture teaches us to flee youthful lusts. "Flee also youthful lusts..." (2 Timothy 2:22). Fleeing youthful lusts is not a sign of weakness! It is a sign of great wisdom. There are always enemies who are stronger than we are.

Lust is a strong enemy that consumes and burns away at our lives. Deciding to marry so that you can discharge your burning lusts may be better than resisting your lusts every day. You may not win the battle against lust if you try fighting it. You may have to avoid lusts by leaking out a bit of that desire every day. It takes humility to accept a strategy, which does not involve violence and fighting.

How Napoleon Was Subdued without Fighting

Napoleon is well known for invading Russia and being soundly defeated for doing so. When Adolf Hitler tried to do the same, they were very conscious of the failure of Napoleon to conquer the Russians. The Russians destroyed Napoleon's army when he invaded Russia by constantly retreating and avoiding him. The Russians finally made a stand a few miles from Moscow and fought Napoleon, seriously weakening his army. When Napoleon eventually entered Moscow, the Russians had deserted the city and released all prisoners asking them to burn down Moscow, which they did. The Russian army and all the citizens of Moscow had disappeared into thin air!

Napoleon entered the absolutely empty city of Moscow and spent one month hoping to find an enemy he could defeat. But the enemy had fled. The Czar of Russia was nowhere to be found. He and his troops had made a fast retreat. Napoleon desperately needed to meet with the Czar of Russia and make him kneel down in defeat. But this never happened. Napoleon simply could not lay hands on anyone to defeat.

After one month of waiting, Napoleon had to leave Russia and head for France. He had not seen the Czar nor had he met anyone in Moscow whom he could claim to have conquered. On his long journey back to France, Napoleon's troops were attacked continuously by the Russians who had disappeared into thin air. Napoleon himself came under threat on the journey back. Eventually, only 40,000 out of 650,000 French soldiers survived and struggled back into France. The Russians had effectively defeated Napoleon by simply not fighting with him!

CHAPTER 28

It is More Important to Outthink Your Enemy than to Outfight Him

Wisdom strengtheneth the wise more than ten mighty men which are in the city.

Ecclesiastes 7:19

There was a little city, and few men within it; and there came a great king against it, and besieged it, and built great bulwarks against it: Now there was found in it a poor wise man, and HE BY HIS WISDOM DELIVERED THE CITY; yet no man remembered that same poor man. Then said I, Wisdom is better than strength: nevertheless the poor man's wisdom is despised, and his words are not heard.

Ecclesiastes 9:14-16

It is obvious that the poor wise man was able to outthink his enemy rather than outfight him. When you are surrounded and when you have little strength, you must start thinking. Brute force and old methods may not work anymore. It is better to outthink your enemy than to outfight him.

If you want to defeat your enemy, learn to outthink him. Think about the problem, seek advice, and seek counsel from others. "Every purpose is established by counsel: and with good advice make war" (Proverbs 20:18). You can listen to the advice and words of more experienced people. You can even seek counsel and good advice through books, CDs and videos. Your knowledge and understanding of history will be one of the greatest sources of counsel.

It is more important to *outthink* your enemy than to *outfight* him. Many of us do not pause to think much about anything. We are always on the move and have no time to think deeply about our problems and our battles.

We, as human beings have been able to overcome and defeat wild animals that are bigger and stronger than us. How is that possible? How do we overcome lions? How do we catch them? How do we subdue them? How do we imprison them? The answer is simple: we outthink them! Animals are very predictable. They do the same things all the times. That is why we can catch them. Human beings are superior in their thinking, understanding and planning. We can therefore catch elephants, lions, tigers, snakes and any animal we want to.

When people are in prison, there is not much human interaction so they get to think a lot. This is why many people turn to God when they are in prison! You must create a prison for yourself so you can think your way out of your problems. You can think your way into wisdom, knowledge and revelation of God. That is why Jesus went on retreats.

When you start to think, you will start to win the battles of life.

The Fabian Strategy

Hannibal was a great African commander hailing from Carthage. Carthage is modern-day Tunisia. Hannibal threatened and defeated the Roman Empire on several historic occasions.

Hannibal advanced all over Italy and threatened to attack Rome itself. This was the worst threat ever on the Roman Empire. The Roman generals struggled to contain this threat on their empire. Different Roman generals were appointed at different times to defeat Hannibal. After Hannibal had soundly defeated the Romans in famous battles at the Trebia River and the Lake Trasimene, a new Roman general called Quintus Fabius Maximus was appointed to fight Hannibal. It is at this point that Quintus Fabius Maximus instituted his famous "Fabian strategy" of avoiding major confrontations with Hannibal. He felt that it was better to outthink Hannibal than to outfight him, and he was right.

The Fabian Strategy was to avoid large battles in favour of minor harassing actions so as to break the enemy's will to keep fighting and to wear them out slowly. Fabius' troops shadowed and harassed the Cathaginian army while avoiding a major confrontation. Fabius also adopted a "scorched earth policy" that meant that he destroyed anything that was useful to the enemy such as food sources, farms and even people. The "scorched earth policy" was intended to starve Hannibal's troops and make life unbearable for them. Gradually, Fabius was able to achieve the desired result, keeping Hannibal in check.

The Battle of Cannae

Unfortunately for Fabius, the politicians in Rome did not accept his strategy as a right way to win a war. They desired an all-out confrontation that would defeat Hannibal. Fabius was removed from his position and an all-out confrontation between the Roman Empire and Hannibal took place. This famous confrontation was the Battle of Cannae. In this battle Hannibal decisively defeated the Roman Empire. The Roman army suffered over seventy thousand casualties whilst Hannibal's army lost only six thousand men. After this terrible defeat the Romans returned to the Fabian Strategy, realising that it was better to outthink their enemy than to outfight him. After all, they could not defeat Hannibal in battle.

In the Second World War, the French government wisely surrendered to Germany to avoid the city of Paris being destroyed. This surrender was a clever manoeuvre that enabled France to remain relatively intact during the war. Countries that fight a clearly superior enemy usually get destroyed. It is better to outthink your enemy when you cannot outfight him.

Independent Churches

Some denominations cleverly grant independence to branch churches. This decision completely averts any fights from independent-minded pastors who want to break away. The granting of independence to churches avoids conflict with rebellious men who want to break away. A branch pastor can say almost anything to a congregation and lead them along a path away from the rest of the denomination. Sometimes it is impossible to win a fight against such people because they have such control over the congregation.

You must consider the hidden cost of war. Every war will cost you time, money and human lives. In addition, every war creates bitter enemies who are bent on revenge in the future. Fight deadly enemies by strategic avoidance! That is the Fabian Strategy. It is better to outthink your enemy than to outfight him!

Avoid the conflict, avoid the war and avoid the issues and the arguments you cannot win.

CHAPTER 29

A Good General Does Not Advance Relying on Sheer Numbers

And the Lord said unto Gideon, The people that are with thee are too many for me to give the Midianites into their hands, lest Israel vaunt themselves against me, saying, Mine own hand hath saved me.

Now therefore go to, proclaim in the ears of the people, saying, Whosoever is fearful and afraid, let him return and depart early from mount Gilead. And there returned of the people TWENTY AND TWO THOUSAND; and THERE REMAINED TEN THOUSAND.

And the Lord said unto Gideon, The people are yet too many; bring them down unto the water, and I will try them for thee there: and it shall be, that of whom I say unto thee, This shall go with thee, the same shall go with thee; and of whomsoever I say unto thee, This shall not go with thee, the same shall not go.

So he brought down the people unto the water: and the Lord said unto Gideon, Every one that lappeth of the water with his tongue, as a dog lappeth, him shalt thou set by himself; likewise every one that boweth down upon his knees to drink.

And the number of them that lapped, putting their hand to their mouth, were THREE HUNDRED MEN:

but all the rest of the people bowed down upon their knees to drink water.

And the Lord said unto Gideon, BY THE THREE HUNDRED MEN THAT LAPPED WILL I SAVE YOU, and deliver the Midianites into thine hand: and let all the other people go every man unto his place.

Judges 7:2-7

Gideon is the best example of a commander who learnt not to rely on sheer numbers. Victory is never assured because you have a large force. Many times, a small committed group is better than a large, disloyal mixed multitude. In war, numbers alone confer no advantage. Do not advance relying on sheer military numbers.

Most pastors are comforted by the presence of large numbers of people. Indeed, the honour of the king is in the multitude of the people (Proverbs 14:28). However, there are also certain evils that creep in with the multitude of people. Most people are immature and carnally motivated. A large crowd of carnally inspired people is often a large crowd of people who have the wrong way of thinking. This is why democracy rarely chooses the best leader for the people. Look around you and you will see that the best leaders are rarely chosen by the democratic masses. The masses look at things like tribe, speeches, appearance and other irrelevant factors.

When it comes to real building and fighting, you do not need the masses. You need loyalty. You need a group of loyal people. It is not the size of the group that matters but the loyalty and commitment of the people you are with. Jesus dispensed with the masses and invested in a few disciples. He did not advance in His purpose of winning the world by depending on large numbers of people.

From that time many of his disciples went back, and walked no more with him. Then said Jesus unto the twelve, Will ye also go away?

John 6:66-67

If Jesus depended on large numbers of people He would have preached a different message that would attract them. But He had no time to waste on a large group of uncommitted men. In the early years of our church, I had to take a decision to dismiss certain people. I had discovered that many of the people in the church were criticising me and did not believe in my calling. I naturally wanted to be separated from the people who did not believe in me; but I had a problem.

My assistant, who was one of the people who were criticising was a very nice person whom everyone in the church liked. If I dismissed him, I would lose a large section of my small church. His leaving would trigger the departure of many others. But I took the decision and asked him to go.

Indeed, I lost many others and our small church became even smaller. I was saddened, depressed and confused by these events. I was now the leader of a very small group of loyalists. But over time, these few but committed people grew into a big, peaceful and harmonious church. I went further in ministry not with large numbers of people but with a few people.

Napoleon's Large Army

Napoleon, the famous French general, assembled the largest army known to mankind at the time. Napoleon invaded Russia with the largest army ever assembled in the history of mankind. Relying on the numbers that he had been able to gather, he thought the Russians would sue for peace and submit to his authority. But it was not to be so.

Unfortunately for Napoleon, the Russians did not sue for peace, neither did they surrender but rather enticed him, drawing him deeper and deeper into Russia until he was thousands of miles into hostile enemy territory. Napoleon, who had relied on the large size of his army then found himself having to manage and feed a huge force far away from home.

Napoleon's army of about six hundred and fifty thousand men was destroyed through this invasion. Only forty thousand soldiers remained when it was all over. Always remember, do not advance relying on sheer numbers! Numbers alone do not confer any advantage. With God on your side you are the majority! I have not regretted advancing with a small group of loyalists. It is one of the greatest wisdom steps of my life.

CHAPTER 30

Know Your Invisible Enemies

For we wrestle not against flesh and blood, but against principalities, against powers, against the rulers of the darkness of this world, against spiritual wickedness in high places.

Ephesians 6:12

Enemies come in two forms: visible and invisible. Christians must know the invisible enemy they are dealing with. To wage a war without knowing or understanding your invisible enemy is perhaps the greatest mistake you can ever make. Who are the enemies we are supposed to know. You must know all about the visible and invisible enemies of your life. Let us start with the invisible enemies.

Your invisible enemies occupy the dark and unseen world. The invisible enemies of your life are categorised in different ways to help you know and understand them. Knowing about them is very important to help you to fight them. Below is a list of invisible enemies that we have to deal with. These invisible enemies are spirits that exist in a realm that you cannot see. You must know about them and fight them if you are going to be successful in your war.

Spies, double agents, traitors, liars are all invisible enemies you must fight with. They will never come out openly and declare war on you. In fact, they will declare friendship with you but fight you secretly. Invisible enemies do not want you to expose their cover. They want to stay out of sight so they can be more effective. Evil spirits prefer you to believe that they do not exist. They are overjoyed when you say they are not there. Europeans claim there is no God and there is no devil and this has given Satan a free hand in Europe.

When it comes to dealing with invisible enemies, the more you talk about them and the more you expose their existence, the weaker they become. No spy would like you to even mention the subject of spies and spying. No spy would feel comfortable if an announcement is made that there is a spy amongst us. His mouth would become dry and he would immediately become nervous because people would start looking around and start wondering which one is the spy.

In the list below, you will find different types of evil spirits who do not want you to know they exist. Every single one of these spirits is real. They do not like the fact that I have listed them in this book. In another book, I shall be sharing even more details of their activities, manoeuvres, operations and how you can deal with them.

Invisible Enemies

1.   Fly and insect spirits:

But when the Pharisees heard it, they said, This fellow doth not cast out devils, but by BEELZEBUB THE PRINCE OF THE DEVILS.

And Jesus knew their thoughts, and said unto them, Every kingdom divided against itself is brought to desolation; and every city or house divided against itself shall not stand:

And if Satan cast out Satan, he is divided against himself; how shall then his kingdom stand?

And if I by Beelzebub cast out devils, by whom do your children cast them out? therefore they shall be your judges.

Matthew 12:24-27

2.   Unclean and hateful bird spirits:

And after these things I saw another angel come down from heaven, having great power; and the earth was lightened with his glory. And he cried mightily with a strong voice, saying, Babylon the great is fallen, is fallen, and is become the HABITATION OF DEVILS, and the hold of every foul spirit, and A CAGE OF EVERY UNCLEAN AND HATEFUL BIRD.

Revelation 18:1-2

3.   Unclean animal spirits:

And I saw THREE UNCLEAN SPIRITS LIKE FROGS come out of the mouth of the dragon, and out of the mouth of the beast, and out of the mouth of the false prophet. For they are the spirits of devils, working miracles, which go forth unto the kings of the earth and of the whole world, to gather them to the battle of that great day of God Almighty.

Revelation 16:13-14

And he became very hungry, and would have eaten: but while they made ready, he fell into a trance, And saw heaven opened, and a certain vessel descending unto him, as it had been a great sheet knit at the four corners, and let down to the earth: Wherein were all manner of FOURFOOTED BEASTS of the earth, and WILD BEASTS, AND CREEPING THINGS, AND FOWLS OF THE AIR. And there came a voice to him, Rise, Peter; kill, and eat. But Peter said, Not so, Lord; for I HAVE NEVER EATEN ANY THING THAT IS COMMON OR UNCLEAN.

Acts 10:10-14

4.   Sea and marine spirits:

And I stood upon the sand of the sea, and saw A BEAST RISE UP OUT OF THE SEA, having seven heads and ten horns, and upon his horns ten crowns, and upon his heads the name of blasphemy.

Revelation 13:1

Canst thou draw out leviathan with an hook? or his tongue with a cord which thou lettest down?

Job 41:1

There go the ships: there is that leviathan, whom thou hast made to play therein.

Psalms 104:26

5.　　Principalities

For we wrestle not against flesh and blood, but against PRINCIPALITIES, against powers, against the rulers of the darkness of this world, against spiritual wickedness in high places.

Ephesians 6:12

6.　　Powers

For we wrestle not against flesh and blood, but against principalities, against POWERS, against the rulers of the darkness of this world, against spiritual wickedness in high places.

Ephesians 6:12

7.　　Rulers of the dark world

For we wrestle not against flesh and blood, but against principalities, against powers, against the RULERS OF THE DARKNESS of this world, against spiritual wickedness in high places.

Ephesians 6:12

8.　　Wicked spirits in high places

For we wrestle not against flesh and blood, but against principalities, against powers, against the rulers of the darkness of this world, against SPIRITUAL WICKEDNESS in high places.

Ephesians 6:12

9.　　Thrones

For by him were all things created, that are in heaven, and that are in earth, visible and invisible, whether they be THRONES, or dominions, or principalities, or powers: all things were created by him, and for him:

Colossians 1:16

10. Dominions

For by him were all things created, that are in heaven, and that are in earth, visible and invisible, whether they be thrones, or DOMINIONS, or principalities, or powers: all things were created by him, and for him:

Colossians 1:16

11. Lucifer

How art thou fallen from heaven, O Lucifer, son of the morning! how art thou cut down to the ground, which didst weaken the nations!

For thou hast said in thine heart, I will ascend into heaven, I will exalt my throne above the stars of God: I will sit also upon the mount of the congregation, in the sides of the north:

I will ascend above the heights of the clouds; I will be like the most High. Yet thou shalt be brought down to hell, to the sides of the pit.

Isaiah 14:12-15

12. Fallen angels

And there was war in heaven: Michael and his angels fought against the dragon; and the dragon fought and his angels,

And prevailed not; neither was their place found any more in heaven. And the great dragon was cast out, that old serpent, called the Devil, and Satan, which deceiveth the whole world: HE WAS CAST OUT INTO THE EARTH, AND HIS ANGELS WERE CAST OUT WITH HIM.

Revelation 12:7-9

13. Fallen angel-human hybrids: The "Nephilim" - giants, bullies and tyrants

There were GIANTS (NEPHILIM) in the earth in those days; and also after that, when the sons of God came in unto the daughters of men, and they bare children to them, the same became mighty men which were of old, men of renown.

Genesis 6:4

14. Fallen angel-human hybrids: The "Gibborim" - strong, brave mighty men

There were giants in the earth in those days; and also after that, when the sons of God came in unto the daughters of men, and they bare children to them, the same became MIGHTY MEN (GIBBORIM) which were of old, men of renown.

Genesis 6:4

15. Fallen angel-human hybrids: The "Sem" - famous men

There were giants in the earth in those days; and also after that, when the sons of God came in unto the daughters of men, and they bare children to them, the same became mighty men which were of old, MEN OF RENOWN (SEM).

Genesis 6:4

16. Fallen angel-animal hybrids

But when he saw Jesus afar off, he ran and worshipped him, And cried with a loud voice, and said, What have I to do with thee, Jesus, thou Son of the most high God? I adjure thee by God, that thou torment me not.

For he said unto him, Come out of the man, thou unclean spirit. And he asked him, What is thy name? And he answered, saying, My name is Legion: for we are many.

And he besought him much that he would not send them away out of the country. Now there was there nigh unto the mountains a great herd of swine feeding.

And all the devils besought him, saying, Send us into the swine, that we may enter into them. And forthwith Jesus gave them leave. And the unclean spirits went out, and entered into the swine: and the herd ran violently down a steep place into the sea, (they were about two thousand;) and were choked in the sea.

Mark 5:6-13

CHAPTER 31

It is Essential to Seek out Enemy Agents Who Have Come to Spy against You

And Joshua the son of Nun sent out of Shittim two men to spy secretly, saying, Go view the land, even Jericho. And they went, and came into an harlot's house, named Rahab, and lodged there. And it was told the king of Jericho, saying, Behold, there came men in hither to night of the children of Israel to search out the country. And the king of Jericho sent unto Rahab, saying, BRING FORTH THE MEN THAT ARE COME TO THEE, WHICH ARE ENTERED INTO THINE HOUSE: FOR THEY BE COME TO SEARCH OUT ALL THE COUNTRY.

Joshua 2:1-3

The king of Jericho did the right thing to seek out the spies who had come to the house of Rahab. He knew that the presence of these enemies spelt his doom. And he was right! A good general is aware of conspiracies of all kinds and fights them continually. He develops a strong network of intelligence using his loyal people. Spies and conspirators are real. You may criticize someone who teaches against those who forget, those who pretend and those who are disloyal. You may criticise someone who teaches against those who leave you. Such teachings seek out and expose those who do not really belong to you.

It causes the disloyal to be exposed and vulnerable. Inappropriately positioned people can turn against you. You can dislodge conspirators by the re-positioning of troops and commanders. Transferring people within the church is the way to re-position troops and commanders. Conspiracies need time and planning with familiar faces. The changing of the jobs and the transferring of people destroys the plots and the plans of hidden enemies.

Fight conspiracies through the teaching of loyalty. Fight deception in the ranks by teaching against those who forget, those who pretend and those who conspire. Fight conspiracies by marking quiet people who don't speak their minds and those who are not open. Fight back by watching and taking note of people's bodily language. Watch out for those who do not speak much and claim that they are quiet by nature. Don't trust them! Watch out for those who chat happily with others but are quiet in your presence.

Watch out for those who look extra respectful in your presence. They are probably pretending and have a lot of negative thoughts and ideas in their heads. Don't be surprised if such people leave you. "They went out from us, but they were not of us; for if they had been of us, they would no doubt have continued with us: but they went out, that they might be made manifest that they were not all of us" (1 John 2:19).

Do not naively assume that everyone loves you. Many people stay in their position because they have nowhere else to go and not because they love you. Constantly searching, probing and questioning in such a way that exposes hidden disloyalty is important. Those who assume that all is well will only be surprised. To fight a good fight and to war a good warfare, you must constantly seek out disloyal people and strip them of their coverings.

Spies in Britain

During the Second World War, the German army launched a spying campaign against Britain in which they sent several spies to England to gather intelligence and perform other sabotaging military duties. Some of these spies entered England by swimming out of submarines, and some of them were secretly parachuted into England.

Part of this group of spies entered as refugees whilst others simply entered the country as individuals with false passports. But the British army knew about this campaign and actively sought out these spies who had infiltrated the country. Their search for these spies was so successful that none of the German spies escaped. Records after the war proved that the British captured all spies who were sent into England.

Upon capture, these agents were doomed as they were to be imprisoned and executed. But the British military offered them a chance to become double agents and turn against their own country. Most of the spies accepted the offer to work for the British, rather than to be executed. Through these captured spies, the British intelligence were able to determine what information the German military wanted. They were also able to actively mislead the Germans by feeding them with outdated, useless and false information.

Capturing these German spies and turning them against their masters proved to be crucial in the Second World War. Through these double agents, the British deceived the Germans about where exactly they would invade Europe. The Germans believed the deception and stationed most of their forces in the wrong places, allowing the British to invade Europe with much less resistance. Also, when the Germans launched special V-1 bombing attacks, the British made the captured spies report that the bombs had fallen at the wrong places. This made the Germans redirect their bombs away from the expected targets in London. Many lives were saved because the bombs were misdirected away from Central London.

Seeking out spies and enemies from your midst, indeed can save you and give you victory in any war.

CHAPTER 32

When a Falcon's Strike Breaks the Body of the Prey it is Because of Timing

Moreover Ahithophel said unto Absalom, Let me now choose out twelve thousand men, and I WILL ARISE AND PURSUE AFTER DAVID THIS NIGHT: And I will come upon him while he is weary and weak handed, and will make him afraid: and all the people that are with him shall flee; and I will smite the king only: And I will bring back all the people unto thee:the man whom thou seekest is as if all returned: so all the people shall be in peace.

2 Samuel 17:1-3

And shall lay thee even with the ground, and thy children within thee; and they shall not leave in thee one stone upon another; because thou knewest not THE TIME of thy visitation.

Luke 19:44

When a falcon strikes the prey, the falcon could go off balance, have an accident, and seriously injure itself. But when a falcon's strike breaks the body of the prey, it is because of excellent timing in all the different manoeuvres it makes during the strike. The success of the falcon's strike depends heavily on coordination and timing of different events. Your strike, your military strike, your spiritual strike, your move, the beginning of your ministry will be successful because of excellent timing.

All forms of ministry require the element of good timing. Without good timing many aspects of the ministry fail. You could have built a church and grown a large ministry if you had gotten the timing right. You could have gone on a mission when you were younger, fresher and more able to learn a language. Going on a mission as an older person is to do the same thing but with different timing. Wrong timing causes great visions to fall flat! When you get the timing wrong, it looks as though God never called you.

Ahithophel, the wise counsellor of David, knew the importance of timing. He knew that the same campaign with the same equipment would fall flat on its face if it was done at another time. Ahithophel advised Absalom to pursue after David that very night. "Don't wait for him to rest! If you attack David when he is rested you are attacking him at the wrong time and your campaign will fail!"

Absalom did not understand this great principle of timing and so he rejected the counsel that was based on the principle of proper timing. He chose to attack David at the wrong time when David had rested and recovered from the shock of being driven out of Jerusalem by his own son!

When your war is successful it is because of timing. When evangelism works it is because of timing. When marriage works it is because of timing. When you marry at the wrong time of your life, you may not meet the right partner. When you wait until you have prospered it may be difficult to find someone who really loves you for who you are. When you marry at the wrong time you may not be able to be pregnant because you have waited until the natural supply of sperms has dwindled. Your falcon's strike becomes unsuccessful in breaking the body of the prey, because of timing.

When full-time ministry works, it is because of timing! I came into full time ministry in my twenties and have been a pastor now for at least twenty-five years. When evangelism works it is because of timing. I began mass evangelism through Healing Jesus Crusades after planting hundreds of churches. I then had the support of many loyal churches. I did not begin mass evangelism at the beginning of my ministry. That would have been the wrong time. When the falcon's strike breaks the body of its prey it is because of timing.

Napoleon and Waterloo

Although Napoleon had won many wars and was a military genius, he was finally defeated at the famous battle of Waterloo, which is a small village near Brussels. The timing of the battle of Waterloo was such that Napoleon could be completely defeated. Napoleon graduated from the *Ecole Militaire* and became a confident and ambitious Second Lieutenant at the age of sixteen but at the Battle of Waterloo he was forty-six years old. This battle came at the end of a more-than-ten-year period filled with battles largely instigated by Napoleon. The timing of the falcon's strike was such that it would not be successful.

At this era of Napoleon's life, everything was different; Napoleon himself was older, pot bellied, married and was not feeling well on the morning of the battle. This was *the only time* Napoleon was prevented from directing his armies in the way that he preferred. Napoleon's usual practice was to keep a watchful eye on the progress of the battle by riding vigorously around the battlefield.

Unfortunately, on that morning he was acutely unwell and uncomfortable because he had an attack of piles (haemorrhoids).

Piles are a condition in which there can be bleeding from the anus. When a person has piles, a protruding, painful, itching and irritating lump can also stick out of the anus. Such a condition would make anyone extremely uncomfortable and a shadow of his usual self. It is no wonder that Napoleon was not riding vigorously around the battlefield as he usually did. Napoleon was obviously distracted on that morning! He had planned to attack at 6.00am, which was postponed to 9.00am and eventually to 11.20am.

Indeed, Napoleon, usually a driven personality, issued orders to his troops to start fighting *five hours later* than originally intended.

Napoleon's brilliant military career came to an end at Waterloo. It was the wrong time of his life to take on such a battle. He was old, tired, sick and depressed. The timing could not have been worse. When a falcon's strike breaks the body of the prey it is because of timing! When your ministry works, it is because of timing!

CHAPTER 33

A Good General Has a Surprise for Every Surprise

And yet again there was war at Gath, where was a man of great stature, whose fingers and toes were four and twenty, six on each hand, and six on each foot: and he also was the son of the giant. BUT WHEN HE DEFIED ISRAEL, JONATHAN THE SON OF SHIMEA DAVID'S BROTHER SLEW HIM.

1 Chronicles 20:6-7

Prepare a surprise for every possible surprise that the enemy can come up with. The enemy who thinks he is going to surprise you must receive a shock when he comes your way. The only way you can do that is by being prepared for it. Develop an equally nasty surprise for your enemy who thinks he is going to outwit you.

The enemy came up with giants who had twenty-four fingers and toes. They thought that no one would be able to defeat such giants. But there was a surprise for the surprise! Jonathan, the son of Shimea, was the surprise waiting for the giant who had twenty-four fingers and toes. What surprises do you have up your sleeve for every surprise of the enemy? Have you thought through what it would be like if the enemy attacked you in certain ways? What would your response be?

Surprise: The Prodigal Son

The father of the prodigal son was the first to receive a surprise when his son told him of his decision to leave the family. The whole family mourned the departure of this rebellious and ungrateful member. Everyone got used to him being away and no one expected him to come back, except the father. The Heavenly Father shocked everyone when He welcomed this worthless son back to His house, forgiving and accepting him. The Heavenly Father surprised the whole world when he actually promoted him, giving him a robe and a ring. All the evil spirits that had hoped for the total annihilation of this boy were dumbfounded at the response of the father.

You can shock the enemy by forgiving, accepting and loving those Satan never expects you to love again. Prepare a surprise for the enemy.

Forgiveness: Forgiveness of a wrongdoer is a surprise our enemy is never expecting. He never expects that you would forgive and forget about the past. You must surprise your enemy by forgiving and forgetting about old wounds.

Acceptance: Accepting certain people is a surprise that the enemy is not expecting. The devil knows our stereotypes. We have the people we like and we have the people we dislike. We have those we approve of and those we are prejudiced against. The acceptance of certain people into the fold is a shock and a surprise to the devil who has divided us. Satan has divided us into camps that do not relate with each other. Surprise the enemy by accepting all kinds of people into your fold.

Promotion: The promotion of an unworthy and forgiven offender is perhaps the greatest shock. Perhaps, you can forgive. Perhaps you can accept. But to promote such an individual is outrageous. In the promotion of certain individuals lies the defeat of the enemy. God has surprised the devil by promoting us and making us sons of God. In spite of our sins and our fallen nature, the blood of Jesus has lifted us to heights that surprise hardened, demonic entities.

Nuclear Weapons, a Surprise for Every Surprise

All over the world, nations have armed themselves with nuclear weapons. Everyone saw what happened at Hiroshima. No one wants to be another defenceless Hiroshima. Today, many nations actively seek to be nuclear powers.

The United States of America has 7,650 atomic warheads whilst Russia has 8,420 atomic bombs. Britain, not wanting to be left out has 225 atomic warheads and France has 300. In Asia, China has 240 warheads whilst India and Pakistan have a hundred each. North Korea, Israel and Iran are also up and coming nuclear nations.

Perhaps the principle behind the arming of nations with nuclear weapons is the principle of having "a surprise for every surprise". If you fire one of your nuclear weapons at me, I will fire two at you. Therefore, our whole world is an armed camp kept in a state of forced tranquillity and peace because everyone knows that a surprise will be met with another surprise.

Prepare yourself dear friend, for diverse attacks. If your friend nearby is attacked by the enemy do not think to yourself, "It cannot happen to me." Instead, prepare a deadly surprise response for the enemy in the event that you are attacked.

Surprise at Constantinople

During the siege of Constantinople, Mehmed II deployed all sorts of unconventional ideas to overcome the Christians within the city. After several inconclusive attacks, Mehmed's Ottoman forces sought to break through the walls by constructing underground tunnels. Many of the soldiers who dug up the mine were Germans. They were placed under the command of Zagan Pasha. As the Ottoman soldiers progressed through their German built tunnel, they did not know that the Christians had equally employed a German to build counter tunnels for them. A surprise for every surprise!

Indeed, the Christian men of Constantinople had a surprise for the Ottoman soldiers. They had also employed a German engineer named Johannes Grant to build counter mines. The Ottoman troops were intercepted in the tunnels and vigorously destroyed with fire and combat. When the Christian Byzantines eventually captured and tortured two Ottoman officers, they revealed the location of all their tunnels, which were then destroyed.

It is important to prepare a surprise for your enemy. All enemies are planning surprises. Your enemy thinks you are a fool. He thinks he will surprise you but you must give him the shock of his life. Have a surprise for every surprise!

CHAPTER 34

A Good General Expects an Attack of Depression

And David was greatly distressed; for the people spake of stoning him, because the soul of all the people was grieved, every man for his sons and for his daughters: but David encouraged himself in the Lord his God.

1 Samuel 30:6

Any kind of crisis can lead to discouragement and disillusionment. Repeated defeat leads to discouragement. Discouragement leads to depression. A good general must remain balanced and not allow discouragement and depression to overwhelm him.

Sometimes, the way out of difficulty is to choose the best of your bad options and to pursue it with the strength and zeal of someone who is pursuing a good thing even though it is a bad or unfortunate option.

If your wife is dead, find a new wife and make a new life! Many times you don't have an ideal situation. But how many things are ideal? Do not let depression destroy your life and ministry. Many great leaders are destroyed by depression.

I remember the story of a pastor of a church who lost his wife. The couple had 4 daughters. The husband, the widower, could not recover from his sorrow and depression. He died a year later and was buried in the same cemetery, near his wife. At the funeral, the caretaker of the cemetery remarked, "I am not surprised that this man is dead. Over the past year he has visited this cemetery every day to cry over his wife's grave."

Unfortunately, this man left behind four little daughters without father or mother.

Which is better, one parent or no parent? Do not let your sorrows overwhelm you. Rise up and press ahead. If you cannot have a child, pursue an adopted child with all your strength. Although adoption is not the ideal way of having your own child, pursue it as though it is the best.

If you don't get the highest educational qualification, pursue the next option as though it was the best. If you didn't marry your ideal partner, fight to have a second best marriage instead of pining away and complaining that you did not meet "Prince Charming".

If you cannot be a full-time minister, be a lay minister and serve the Lord with all your heart. Maybe one day it will be possible for you to be in full-time ministry. Do not let loneliness, depression, disappointment and disillusionment overwhelm you. There are many dark days and many sad things in this life. You must rise up and not be overcome by depression.

Shaka Zulu

Shaka Zulu was a great African warrior who united many tribes and fought many successful campaigns in South Africa. In spite of his success as a warrior he was affected by the loneliness and depression that afflicts many leaders.

Indeed, Shaka Zulu, the famous South African warrior struggled with depression and despondency after the death of his mother. Shaka the Zulu himself died relatively quickly after the death of his mother Nandi in October 1827 because of his strange and depressed behaviour.

According to the records, after Shaka Zulu's mother died, he ordered that no crops should be planted during the following year and that no milk was to be used by anyone. Meanwhile, milk was the basis of the Zulu diet at the time. In other words everyone was supposed to starve or fast because his mother had died.

He also ordered that any woman who became pregnant was to be killed along with her husband. Anyone who had had pleasure during his time of mourning was to be executed.

Also, Shaka Zulu noticed that some people were not as sad as he was and ordered some seven thousand whom he felt were not sufficiently grief-stricken to be executed!

Shaka Zulu did not restrict his depressive and erratic behaviour to human beings. He also ordered cows to be slaughtered so that their calves would know what losing a mother felt like. Obviously he was going mad in his loneliness and depression.

The depression of Shaka Zulu cost him his life. The leader of the Zulu tribe was clearly disliked and unpopular by the generalised murder he perpetrated when his mother died. Two of his half brothers conspired against him and assassinated him, dumping his body into a grain pit and covering his body with mud and stones.

You must see your wounds and problems as doors to ministry. Your pain and your wounds are the door to an effective ministry. If you have experienced any kind of darkness, remember that it may be the basis of your authority in that area. Remember that Jesus Christ is able to minister healing because of the wounds and stripes He received. Your wounds are the basis of your ministry. You minister out of what you have suffered and what you have been through. Paul explains why God comforts us! He shows us that your ministry is going to come out of your pain, your wounds and your experiences.

Blessed be the God and Father of our Lord Jesus Christ, the Father of mercies and God of all comfort, who comforts us in all our affliction SO THAT WE WILL BE ABLE TO COMFORT THOSE WHO ARE IN ANY AFFLICTION WITH THE COMFORT WITH WHICH WE OURSELVES ARE COMFORTED BY GOD.

For just as the sufferings of Christ are ours in abundance, so also our comfort is abundant through Christ.

But if we are afflicted, it is for your comfort and salvation; or if we are comforted, it is for your comfort, which is effective in the patient enduring of the same sufferings which we also suffer;

2 Corinthians 1:3-6 (NASB)

CHAPTER 35

Prepare Yourself to Meet a Cruel Enemy

Ye are of your father the devil, and the lusts of your father ye will do. HE WAS A MURDERER FROM THE BEGINNING, and abode not in the truth, because there is no truth in him. When he speaketh a lie, he speaketh of his own: for he is a liar, and the father of it.

John 8:44

S atan is described as a murderer. To murder someone is to brutally kill, destroy and put an end to his existence. This is what the devil wants to do to you and I. Satan wants to brutally kill you, destroy you and put an end to your existence.

You must prepare yourself for a cruel enemy. Satan is a cruel, evil, nasty, mean, pitiless, brutal, vindictive, merciless and heartless person. That is the kind of enemy you will face in your battles and in your wars. How do you know that your enemy is cruel? Watch what he does to others and you will have an idea of the kind of person you are dealing with.

It will give you an idea of what he can do to you if you fall into his hands. You must prepare adequately for your encounter with a cruel person. You must do all you can to prevent yourself from falling into the hands of a merciless enemy. Look around you and see what has happened to men of God who have fallen into the enemy's hands. Satan would love to turn every pastor into a fallen and withered branch.

I know a pastor who unknowingly married a beautiful lady who was HIV positive and died a couple of years later, leaving behind his large church.

I know a man of God who now lives under a bridge in East Africa, roaming the streets as a mad man. This is what Satan did to him.

I know of pastors who were turned into homosexuals and sent to prison. Satan would love to turn you into a homosexual and put you away in prison.

I know a pastor who lost his church to a rebellious pastor and even lost his ability to live a normal life and take care of his family.

I know a pastor who had five thousand members and lost them all until he now has only two hundred people.

I know at least two pastors who died divorced, alone and depressed in hotel rooms after taking some kinds of drugs or medicines.

I know pastors who have been disgraced and humiliated in public by the media and the church because of a mistake they made.

Satan is pitiless and cruel and you can have an idea of his plans for you by seeing what he did to other fellow ministers.

Julius Caesar

Julius Caesar was a cruel Roman dictator whose name lives on in notoriety. Although there were several Roman emperors, it is the name Julius Caesar that stands out among the names of the various emperors of Rome. Among his many qualities was cruelty!

The kind of cruelty he would mete out to his future enemies was portrayed in an incident that happened early in his career. His future enemies would have done well for themselves if they knew the kind of person he was. One day, as a young man, he was on a trip across the Aegean Sea when he was kidnapped by pirates and held prisoner. He fearlessly chatted with these pirates and told them that the ransom they had asked for was too low. They had asked for twenty talents of silver but he insisted that they ask for fifty. He pointed out to them that he was worth at least fifty talents. He also told them that if he was ever freed he would have them all executed. Eventually, the ransom was paid and he was freed by his new friends.

Instead of continuing thankfully on his journey, he raised a fleet and chased after the pirates. He eventually caught them and crucified them as he had promised them. Also, as a sign of clemency he allowed their throats to be cut before their crucifixion.

The calm way in which he kept his promise to kill the pirates who had virtually become his friends reveals his cruelty. This act spoke strongly about the kind of person he was growing up to be. In the years to come he would be responsible for killing thousands of people in many horrible ways. You can have an idea of the cruelty of your enemy by knowing what he has done to other people.

Dear Christian friend, you need no more evidence to convince you that Satan's plans are extremely cruel. Satan has no mild wishes for his enemies. He would like to destroy us all. We must do everything we can, not to fall into his hands.

CHAPTER 36

A Good General Uses Money as a Weapon

... money answereth all things

Ecclesiastes 10:19

How do you view money? Does money make you feel safe? Is money your source of pleasure, satisfaction and achievement? Well, you can also view money as a weapon that can be used against enemies. There are some problems that can be solved by money. Sometimes, a payment of money can reduce your stress and deliver you from a great evil. Fight, using money as a weapon whenever you have to.

You cannot save all the time!

What is the point in storing up riches for a day that you will never see? What do you need today? Do you have the money for what you need?

Will paying for something help you out of a crisis? Then pay for it! If buying something or spending money on something can help you out of your crisis then do it!

Spending money to buy the right car may save you much more money than you would gain by buying a cheaper car. When we started having crusades, we bought cheap used cars for our crusade directors. I was always excited at the low cost of these cars. But with time, I realised that my crusade directors were spending more time fixing their cars than preparing for a crusade. The Crusade directors were converted into "mechanics" and spent most of their time at the workshop waiting for their cars to be repaired. Also, their cars would break down at crucial moments in the build-up to the crusade. All these created crises situations that cost even more money to correct. At a point, I felt that evil spirits were attacking the crusades through these second-hand cars.

Indeed, it could have been evil spirits that were attacking the engines and the brain boxes of these cars. I could have fasted and bound these powers that were unleashed against the crusades. But I decided to fight back by buying brand new cars.

It seemed expensive initially, but it ended up being cheaper in the long run. Not only was it cheaper in the long term, but the attacks on the crusades came to an end. The enemy lost his power to prevent the crusades from coming on.

Every evil spirit, every entity, every demonic being and every principality lost its control over the crusades when I used money as a weapon. Remember that spending money can be a weapon to give you victory!

Atilla the Hun

Atilla the Hun was a fifth-century warrior who helped to unite the Hun kingdom. Atilla lived in an area that is now called Hungary. Atilla the Hun was a particularly brutal, plundering and devastating warrior. He was so brutal that he came to be known as the "scourge of God" because of the devastation he left in his wake. Atilla invaded a vast area that stretched through Germany, Russia, Poland and south-eastern Europe. He was so successful that he invaded the Roman Empire. At that time, the Roman Empire was divided into the eastern and the western part. The western part had its headquarters in Rome and the eastern part had its headquarters in Constantinople (Istanbul, Turkey). King Theodosius II ruled the eastern part of the Roman Empire.

Constantinople was a huge walled city that had been undefeated for several hundred years. It had withstood wave after wave of invaders and never fallen. But the Roman Empire, was in a weaker state and not ready for a war with somebody like Atilla the Hun. Instead of fighting with Atilla the Hun, the emperor of Constantinople constantly warded off Atilla the Hun by paying him higher and higher monthly payments.

Atilla the Hun entered into various treaties with the Romans. Each treaty involved higher sums of money to be paid by the emperor of Constantinople to Atilla the Hun. In one of the treaties, the Romans agreed to return the Hunnic fugitives, double their previous tribute to the Huns, open their markets to Hunnish traders and pay a ransom for each Roman taken prisoner by the Huns.

The Huns were so happy with the provisions of their treaties that they left the Roman Empire in peace and returned to their home in Hungary. Constantinople paid for peace with high amounts of money until Atilla the Hun eventually died. Through this tradition of paying for peace, they were able to avert a war with great losses.

King Theodosius II wisely used money to fight his wars with Atilla the Hun. Today, you must use money as a weapon when you have to.

CHAPTER 37

A Good General Can Achieve Greatness Beyond Ordinary Men through Foreknowledge

From that time Jesus began to show His disciples that He must go to Jerusalem, and suffer many things from the elders and chief priests and scribes, and be killed, and be raised up on the third day.

Matthew 16:21

Foreknowledge is to see and know about evils that lie ahead. A good general can attain greatness through foreknowledge. *Knowing what is going to happen takes away your enemy's ability to surprise you.* Jesus Christ knew that He would be arrested, tortured, manhandled and killed. Talking about this reality did not mean that he had no faith. It did not mean that He was not a man of God or a man of faith. He was a man of wisdom because He knew and accepted what was to happen.

Today, there are many Christians who do not accept the fact that they will die. They do not accept realities that God shows us. People die all around them but they think, "It can never be me." They will rebuke and curse you if you suggest things that God has determined. Many pastors do not set in order what should happen if they are to die. The ability to act on the foreknowledge of your certain death makes you greater than the ordinary.

What is the point in building a church that will fall into confusion after your departure? What is the point in doing a good work that will turn into a mountain of upheavals, quarrels and disunity when you leave? What is the point in striving hard to lay a foundation only for people to destroy it the day after you leave? Jesus told us to go out and bear fruits that would abide. Jesus is interested in long-lasting fruits.

The key to long lasting fruits is foreknowledge. A good general must be able to predict disunity, independence and confusion. You can prepare for these things by making everybody independent long before they fight you for it.

In the ministry, foreknowledge is given to us in two ways. The Holy Spirit ministers to us by impressing certain realities on our hearts. Holy Spirit also ministers to us through the word of knowledge! Impressions are not as sensational as prophetic revelation. However, common sense and wisdom are just as important. Most of us are given common sense, but some people are given special prophetic revelation that can make a difference in the battle. The prophet Elisha gave foreknowledge to his king through prophetic revelation. This foreknowledge made him win every battle. If you have the Holy Spirit, you can expect prophetic revelation in the form of dreams, revelations, words of knowledge and words of wisdom.

Then the king of Syria warred against Israel, and took counsel with his servants, saying, In such and such a place shall be my camp. And the man of God sent unto the king of Israel, saying, Beware that thou pass not such a place; for thither the Syrians are come down. And the king of Israel sent to the place which the man of God told him and warned him of, and saved himself there, not once nor twice.

Therefore the heart of the king of Syria was sore troubled for this thing; and he called his servants, and said unto them, Will ye not shew me which of us is for the king of Israel? And one of his servants said, None, my lord, O KING:BUT ELISHA, THE PROPHET THAT IS IN ISRAEL, TELLETH THE KING OF ISRAEL THE WORDS THAT THOU SPEAKEST IN THY BEDCHAMBER.

2 Kings 6:8-12

Elisha was of great assistance to the king of Israel in all his wars. He constantly revealed the whereabouts of the enemy troops, which led to repeated defeats of the Syrians. Through the prophetic ministry of seeing and knowing, you will be given foreknowledge about certain things. You are expected to move and take decisions according to the revelation God gives you.

Much military technology has been directed at acquiring foreknowledge. To know in advance, to prepare yourself, to be ready for enemy, will transform every military commander into a deadly fighting machine. "A prudent man foreseeth the evil, and hideth himself: but the simple pass on, and are punished" (Proverbs 22:3). The way a wise general can achieve greatness beyond ordinary men is to see the evil ahead!

Foreknowledge and the Six-Day War

The Six-Day War is the 1967 Arab-Israeli war that was fought between June 5 and June 10, 1967. It was the third significant Arab-Israeli war and involved Israel, Egypt, Jordan and Syria. The war began when Israel launched a surprise-bombing raid on Egyptian airfields. Within six days, Israel had won the war and gained control over several significant areas. Within these six days, Israel captured the places that we often hear about in the news: the Gaza strip, the Sinai Peninsula, East Jerusalem and the Golan heights.

How was the tiny nation of Israel able to win this war against all the Arab nations arrayed against it? What gave Israel the upper hand in these battles? Foreknowledge!

Israel had sent their secret agent Eli Cohen to infiltrate the Syrian government. Cohen the spy made many friends with high-ranking Syrian generals including the Prime Minister. The spy, Cohen, may even have been considered for the position of Syrian Deputy Minister of Defence. In this capacity, Cohen visited the Golan Heights and suggested that trees be planted where soldiers were stationed to shade them from the sun. He then secretly informed the Israeli army to use the trees as markers to locate and bomb the Syrian soldiers. Through Cohen the spy, Israel had foreknowledge about the creation of three successive lines of bunkers (instead of one). This kind of knowledge gave the Israeli army the upper hand when they attacked Syria.

Israel had also established a secret agent or an Egyptian informant in every Egyptian air force and military headquarters. Indeed three officers at the Egyptian high command were actually Israeli spies. Through the activities of these Israeli spies, the Israelis had foreknowledge of the impending war in the early part of 1967. By May of 1967, the Israelis knew the exact time they should launch their attack on the Egyptian air bases. The attack was launched at the exact time when there was a change in the shift and when the planes were parked on the tarmac waiting for their pilots to arrive at work. The Israeli attack was timed for when the pilots of the Egyptian Air Force were stuck in Cairo traffic unable to get to the airfield. Through foreknowledge, the Israelis simply bombed and blasted all the Egyptian planes as they were parked at the airport. Within a couple of hours, Egypt was neutralised through the power of foreknowledge.

Foreknowledge and the Submarines

During the Second World War, important supplies were brought to England from America. These supplies had to be transported across the Atlantic Ocean from America to Europe in large convoys of ships. These ships carrying important military equipment and other supplies sailed across the deep, wide Atlantic Ocean from New York to England. It was essential for Germany that they blocked the flow of supplies from America to England by attacking these convoys and sinking the ships that were carrying guns, tanks and planes to England.

Indeed, attacks by German submarines were devastating and many ships were sank and destroyed by German U-boats (submarines). Indeed, Winston Churchill confessed, "The only thing that ever really frightened me during the war was the U-boat peril."

The German submarines, otherwise known as U-boats were a most terrible menace to other ships. When the war broke out, the Germans had only 57 U-boats. But steadily increased this number until, by August 1942, it boasted of 300. The submarines operated in "wolf packs"— clusters of several vessels arrayed in a loose chain across the major shipping lines but within easy supporting distance, so that when one U-boat spotted a convoy, the others could quickly move in to join the attack. Convoys caught by wolf packs could suffer devastating losses in a matter of hours. The U-boats that were arranged in a chain across the shipping lines, would communicate with each other when they spotted a convoy. This way, a pack of submarines were quickly assembled to attack a convoy.

The British desperately needed a method to combat these hidden, deadly underwater attackers. The German submarines were destroying British and American convoys through foreknowledge.

The Germans had, unbeknownst to the British, cracked their royal navy codes and had been reading their communication for more than two years. Through this information the U-boats always knew where to find the British and American convoys.

The British also desperately needed to get the radio codes to the German submarines. If they had these codes they could understand what the Germans were communicating and would have foreknowledge about where the submarines were. Armed with this foreknowledge, the British would then be able to avoid the German submarines. With this foreknowledge, they would even be able to misdirect the U-boats away from the convoys by sending them messages with their own codes.

In October 1942, two British destroyers found and attacked a German submarine U-559 in the eastern Mediterranean Sea. After a barrage of more than 200 depth charges (under water bombs) the U-boat was forced to surface and the German crew abandoned the submarine. Three British men climbed into the U-boat control room, making their way to the captain's cabin. There, they used a machine gun to open its locked cabinets, then frantically grabbed some documents which contained the much needed radio codes. One of these three British sailors was able to escape from the German submarine with the codes in hand. The other two British soldiers drowned when the submarine abruptly sank. The codes were deciphered and the British began to have the much-needed foreknowledge about the location of German submarines. This foreknowledge brought about a dramatic change in the battle in the Atlantic Ocean.

The British and Americans now began to divert their convoys away from the packs of German submarines. The codes were used to locate and hunt down the German submarines and in a great reversal the hunters (U-boats) became the hunted.

By May 1943, U-boat losses were so heavy that the German high command withdrew their submarines from the North Atlantic. The foreknowledge acquired by the British and the Americans was said to be the most significant intelligence victory of the war and had a decisive impact on the outcome of the war.

What would have happened if the Allies had never had this foreknowledge? British planners estimated that Britain needed to import between 9.8 and 11.5 million tons of supplies per year. Unable to divert convoys around known German wolf packs, the Allies would have lost much of their supplies and never be able to find and destroy these menacing submarines.

CHAPTER 38

It is Essential for Victory that Generals are Unconstrained by People Around

And Saul said unto Samuel, I have sinned: for I have transgressed the commandment of the Lord, and thy words: because I FEARED THE PEOPLE, and obeyed their voice.

1 Samuel 15:24

Ageneral is a man of great authority. A man of great authority is a man of great importance. If you are God's general, you must not be constrained by the voices of the people around you. You must be controlled by God and God alone! Saul was a great general but he feared the people and was destroyed because of this fear. He no longer listened to God but followed the opinions of the masses. Generals who lead through the fear of people are often the worst kind of leaders.

A man of authority must follow God's voice and do what is right. Today, many leaders of nations come into power through democracy. Democracy is the choosing of the most popular person. The fact that you have to be liked by many people before you can be a leader is a very dangerous and unfortunate reality. It makes the leader please the masses and it also makes him please many little groups who are perceived to be important. Good leaders are often too busy with "good leadership" to make themselves popular or liked.

If you watch the decisions of people who are governed by the fear of man, you will sit back in amazement. You may even think that foolish, unlearned and inexperienced men were elected to rule. But that is not the case at all. Leaders who fear men take all the wrong decisions in order to be politically right and politically acceptable. Because everything is decided by the fear of man, such a leader is the worst possible thing that could happen to a nation.

Leaders who walk by the fear of man can act as though they do not know what is good and proper. But they do! They are actually very intelligent and very knowledgeable people. But when you fear men, you are unable to use most of the knowledge and intelligence you have. You simply cannot use the wisdom and knowledge you have because you fear the groups of men who surround you.

Do you want your leadership and your decisions to be comparable to that of an imbecile, a monkey or an idiot? I am sure you don't! Then do not allow the fear of man to dominate you. Do what is right! Do what God says and do what will help the people!

It is often better to watch a James Bond movie than to listen to the news in many countries. At least, in the James Bond movie you know that everyone is pretending. In the news, you are forced to watch pretenders, liars and men pleasers who claim to be telling the truth, when in fact they are all lying, pretending and playing politics with the lives of the multitudes.

If you look in certain countries today, you see the lack of the most basic things and you wonder whether brainless people are running the country. If you inquire further, you will find out that it is actually the brainiest men who are running the show. Governments are full of knowledgeable, brainy and clever people with many degrees. *Unfortunately, these people are not allowed to use their brains.* The fear of man has forced them to do everything that is opposite to what they know.

Such is the curse of being led by generals who are constrained by people around. It is a clear and age-old principle of war that a general cannot and must not be constrained by the people around. Democracy was intended to be a good thing to break the curse of domination by a few rich tyrants. Unfortunately, democracy has turned out to be something that produces puppets who cannot lead, because their hands are tied by many strings.

When God put Adam in charge of the Garden of Eden, He expected Adam to listen to Him. Unfortunately, Adam listened to his wife and did what his wife told him. This was a serious mistake because Adam was a man of great authority. When you are put in charge, you must be careful of whom you listen to. Listening to Eve was even more dangerous because she had been listening to the devil. By listening to his wife and obeying her, Adam was listening to the devil and obeying the devil. Without realising it, Adam put himself and the future of the whole world under the influence of the devil.

It is important that a man of great authority listens only to the one who sent him. Adam inadvertently put the entire human race under the influence of the devil. Adam lived to be almost a thousand years because sin and evil were not deeply rooted in man. As the years have gone by, the influence of the devil in human society has grown. This is why the evil and depravity of man has increased as the years have gone by.

Jesus Christ, on the other hand, did not listen to any other voice except the voice of His Father. Satan approached Jesus Christ, using exactly the same trick he had used on Adam. He came to Jesus through the voice of His closest and most trusted associate, Peter. The voice of Peter was strong, pleading and persuading. Peter did not want Jesus to go on the cross. But Jesus saw through it all. He knew that it was the devil. "But he turned, and said unto Peter, Get thee behind me, Satan: thou art an offence unto me: for thou savourest not the things that be of God, but those that be of men" (Matthew 16:23).

Adam had made a mistake of listening to the devil by listening to his wife. But Jesus would not make the mistake of listening to the devil by listening to Peter. You must be careful whom you listen to. The voice of the masses can be the voice of the devil. Jesus said to Peter, "You savour the things of the world." Satan's voice was the voice of the world.

Moses was a type of Christ. Moses was not popular. The masses voted against him in the wilderness. They voted to change him. They voted a new person into power when they did not see him for forty days. They murmured against Moses. Only two out of the twelve spies gave a positive report to Moses. Moses never enjoyed popular democratic support but he was always right and the masses were always wrong. If you have a desire to enjoy popular support, you open yourself up to demonic influence.

Whether it is the influence of the masses, the influence of a woman, the influence of your wife or the influence of your favourite associate, you must be careful to follow the voice of God. The fear of man will ruin every good leader.

Mark Antony Constrained by Cleopatra

Mark Antony was a famous Roman general who assisted Julius Caesar until his death. After Julius Caesar was assassinated, Mark Antony fought zealously to bring the killers of Julius Caesar to justice. Unfortunately for Mark Antony, Julius Caesar did not intend for him to become his successor. Julius Caesar had written a will and given his wealth, his name and position to his nephew, Octavian.

This surprise in Julius Caesar's Will, put Mark Antony in great difficulty. He was the natural successor, having been the right hand man of Julius Caesar. But Julius Caesar's Will did not give Mark Anthony the right to become his successor.

Mark Antony would now have to step aside for this young nephew called Octavian to rule the Roman Empire. This was difficult for Mark Antony and eventually there was conflict between Mark Antony and Octavian. After several years and much conflict, the showdown between Mark Antony and Octavian took place at the battle of Actium. Mark Antony was defeated in this battle and Octavian became the supreme leader of Rome and his name was changed to Augustus Caesar. This is the Caesar who was alive when Jesus was born.

Mark Antony's defeat and demise is often linked to his association with Cleopatra. Cleopatra was one of the girlfriends of Julius Caesar with whom he even had a child. Mark Antony, wishing to follow in his leader's footsteps, had also become involved with Cleopatra and was actually living under her influence in Egypt when the war erupted. Many historians blame Mark Antony for placing himself under the influence of Cleopatra.

Even though Mark Antony was an experienced general commanding troops on land, he strangely agreed to fight against Octavian's forces on the sea. This naval battle put Mark Antony at a disadvantage from the start. It seems the decision to use the navy rather than the land forces was taken in Cleopatra's tent. It seems Mark Antony was carried away by Cleopatra like a boy, in play and diversion, squandering and fooling away in enjoyment. But a good general must not be constrained by anyone. The people around are not the ones to give you the right decision.

CHAPTER 39

When Troops Flee or Are Routed in Battle, it is the Fault of the General

Now the Philistines fought against Israel: and THE MEN OF ISRAEL FLED FROM BEFORE THE PHILISTINES, AND FELL DOWN SLAIN in mount Gilboa. And the Philistines followed hard upon Saul and upon his sons; and the Philistines SLEW JONATHAN, AND ABINADAB, AND MALCHISHUA, SAUL'S SONS.

And the battle went sore against Saul, and the archers hit him; and HE WAS SORE WOUNDED of the archers. Then said Saul unto his armourbearer, Draw thy sword, and thrust me through therewith; lest these uncircumcised come and thrust me through, and abuse me.

But his armourbearer would not; for he was sore afraid. Therefore SAUL TOOK A SWORD, AND FELL UPON IT. And when his armourbearer saw that Saul was dead, he fell likewise upon his sword, and died with him.

1 Samuel 31:1-5

I n this account, the children of Israel fled from their enemies, the Philistines. The armies of Israel were routed in battle. Saul was wounded and died in the battle. Saul's sons were killed. These events always happen together: a captured general and a fleeing army.

A fleeing army is a pathetic sight. Often, the fleeing army perceives that it is about to experience total destruction. In fear and terror, they turn around and run for their very lives. Strong mighty men who could have fought, are convinced that there is nothing better to do than to escape the onslaught. But always remember: when troops flee or are routed in battle, it is the fault of the general.

Four Reasons Why Troops Flee

1. Troops flee or are routed because the general has not motivated them enough.

When the generals in the church do not even mention the importance of sacrifice, missions or evangelism, why would any of the troops be motivated to go out? It is the fault of the pastors and bishops that the troops are running away from true missions.

2. Troops flee or are routed because the general does not set a good example by fighting in the full view of all the other soldiers.

The absence of the general makes the soldiers wonder what they are fighting for. When the general himself is full of fear to do the works of God, how and why should the troops do anything? If the general needs to have a five-star hotel with an Olympic swimming pool and a special gym before he can go out to fight, why should the troops go out and do anything dangerous? If the generals are afraid to have a vaccination against a tropical disease or even receive one mosquito bite in a tropical country, why would the troops venture into the tropical world to preach the gospel?

3.   Troops flee or are routed because the general has surrendered or been captured by the enemy.

If the generals are in the captivity of the devil, living in sin, bondage, immorality, homosexuality, how can they speak out from behind their prison walls? This is the reason why many of the generals are silent. Many ministers of the gospel are in prison and in the captivity of the devil. They are unable to preach and speak out from the point of captivity.

4.   Troops flee or are routed because the general has been killed.

All troops know that the destruction of the general heralds their own destruction. When the general is spiritually dead to God and has no living communication with his Father, how will he hear the voice of the Spirit saying, "Go into all the world and preach the gospel"?

In the church today, the troops are routed and flee the mission field. The mission fields of the world lie empty and waiting for Christian soldiers to march there. Few people are really doing evangelism. If you suggest certain places or countries for missions, people will reject them.

Where are the brave Christians of yesteryear who used to leave the shores of England, Switzerland and America to the ends of the world to preach the gospel till they died?

Where are the brave American Christians who came to live in Ghana, Nigeria, Malaysia and Brazil when there were no mobile phones or internet for communication?

Where are all those types of Christians today? I have been to many countries and seen the fruits of the missionaries. I have personally seen the works of American missionaries in Colombia, Panama, Paraguay, Malaysia, Malawi, Ghana and Nigeria. These brave American missionary soldiers travelled out of their American comfort zone just to bring the gospel of Jesus Christ to others.

But today, such troops have fled. They cannot be found on any mission field any more. Yes, there are American television transmissions everywhere but there are no soldiers on the ground. Why is this?

When troops flee the battle or are routed it is the fault of the general. The missionaries have fled the battlefield because many of the generals are captured by the enemy and are living in sin and captivity. Because they live in sin they cannot preach the true hard gospel of repentance and sacrifice.

The troops are fled because they are not sufficiently motivated by the generals of today's church.

When Christians are no longer ready to go on missions to die for the Lord and to give up their lives, it is because of the pastor. As pastors, our teachings are seeds. We cannot expect a harvest of something that we did not sow. The Scripture teaches, "You are God's garden." If the church is full of immature, selfish, self-centred Christians who are willing to do absolutely nothing for God, it is the fault of the pastor.

The generals of today's church are preaching messages of the good life and giving promises of a better life today. The generals of today are not preaching about sacrificing our lives for missions. Neither are they sending any troops anywhere to do anything.

Because eternity is not spoken about there is no reason to give ourselves to eternal works. Today's Christians are earthly-minded and oriented towards worldly achievement. This is the fault of the general who has not sufficiently motivated the troops to go out and give their lives for a good cause.

The generals of today's church are often softies who cannot preach about sacrifice or sin.

Many of the generals themselves are in hiding, afraid to do many of the works of God themselves. Many of today's generals and pastors live in fear and lack the courage to go out and do anything that is dangerous.

Today's generals will ask, *"Is there a five-star hotel there?"*

"Is it safe? What is the weather like? Do I need any vaccinations?"

"What is security like? Is there a swimming pool? How large is the pool?"

"Is there a gym? Is there a sauna? Is there a French restaurant?"

"Do they have Thai food? Is there air conditioning?"

Dear friend, most of the world does not have these things. Because the church is being led by such captured, dead or fearful generals, it cannot and does not send troops to the battlefield.

CHAPTER 40

Wars Are Won by Lightning Strikes

And of the Gadites there separated themselves unto David into the hold to the wilderness men of might, and men of war fit for the battle, that could handle shield and buckler, whose faces were like the faces of lions, and were AS SWIFT AS THE ROES UPON THE MOUNTAINS;

1 Chronicles 12:8

W hen you enter into war mode you must move with the speed of lightning. Your decisions, your strikes, your actions must take place at high speed. On many occasions, speed alone will ensure victory.

When you are in the ministry you are in a war. Slowness and dullness give your enemy the upper hand. In my experience, pastors who are slow to act, slow in their thinking and slow in their reasoning, do not have successful ministries. The devil is waiting for no one. Life is not waiting for you to understand anything. Your age is not waiting for anything. Your very moments and days are ticking away. Nothing is waiting for you! Your slowness and dullness are very destructive for your life. Because slowness and dullness are not identified sins, they attach themselves to many ministers of the gospel.

When fighting a war, speed, coordination and movement help you to hit hard and move on instantly. Speed creates panic in the enemy's heart. Doubt, confusion and rumour spread within your enemy's camp because of your speed. As someone said, "Speed and still more speed and always speed was the secret..."

God is a God of movement. He is always moving. The Spirit is always moving. In Him we live and move and have our being. The Spirit moved over the surface of the earth and the Spirit is always moving. People who achieve something for God are movers and decision-takers. The commonest characteristic of failing ministers is their slowness to act and move on God's Word.

All God's commandments come with a time element. To serve the Lord properly, you must obey Him on time. If He has called you to the ministry what is the point if you give yourself to Him in your retirement? How much of the call of God can you fulfil when you have three more years to live? God called you and intended to use your entire life to minister to people. Your slowness in responding to God has destroyed your whole ministry. You will now fulfil only three percent of the things

God called you to do. Someone said, "You can always preach the Word of God. There is always time for that."

He continued, "Just focus on what is important now to build your life. As for the church it is always there. It is better to serve God when you are old and have fewer temptations. Throughout your life you will be falling into sin so wait until you are less likely to commit blunders."

This kind of advice takes away the speed and urgency that is necessary for true ministry. In war there is a race for victory. That is why it is called the arms race. Whoever gets the weapons first wins the war. You cannot afford to be slow when it comes to war. Remember that we are warring a good warfare and fighting a good fight of faith. War must be waged with lightning speed. Warring a good warfare means making war at high speed.

The Key to Speed

You must catch the anointing quickly!

You must learn how to preach quickly!

You must master the art of shepherding quickly!

You must learn how to pray for the sick quickly!

You must understand the ministry quickly!

None of these things should be done slowly. There is a lot to be done and there is a devil who is trying to outpace and outrun you. What is the master key to increasing your speed and achieving lightning strikes? The answer to speed is copying!

Copying, emulating, learning to be like someone is the key to rapid movement. All the poor nations, which have caught up with the rich nations did so by copying. All the nations which were two hundred years behind moved faster when they began to copy the richer nations. Look carefully and you will see how nations like Korea, Hong Kong, Taiwan, Malaysia, and Singapore have caught up with western nations like Germany, England, Holland and Italy. How did they do it? By copying and emulating those ahead!

Instead of spending your life discovering things that have already been discovered, you can humbly use the existing discovery and surge forward into something new. The key to achieving fast church growth is to copy those who have been able to build big churches. It may sound absurd to you, but I can assure you that great things are really very simple. The key to speed is copying. I have tried copying men of God I look up to and it made me move fast. I have practiced copying the fathers God gave to me and it has given me great speed. You can spend your life as a discoverer if you want to. Perhaps in Heaven you can sit by David Livingstone and share your discoveries with each other!

During the Second World War, the German army was well known for moving at lightning speed. Its lightning strikes were called blitzkrieg. Blitzkrieg is a German word that means lighting strikes. Several famous generals have moved with lightning speed, surprising their enemies and winning wars. Every minister who longs to please the Lord and fulfil his ministry must have the lightning speed mentality. You must have speed!

Alexander and Lightning Speed

Several famous generals were known for their speed. Alexander the Great, Napoleon and Adolf Hitler are some of the well-known generals who were associated with high-speed warfare. The speed of thought and movement were clearly keys that brought them victory.

In the Bible, Alexander the Great is depicted as a swift goat that came out of Greece. "The shaggy male goat represents the king of Greece, and the large horn between his eyes represents the first king of the Greek Empire" (Daniel 8:21, NLT). In the Bible, Alexander the Great is depicted as a goat that appeared from the western world (Greece) attacking the Persians (the ram) who were led by Darius the Great. Alexander displayed quickness of mind by turning his army around and arriving at the battleground before the enemy had fully prepared his defences.

The text below shows how the goat moved; crossing the land so swiftly that it did not even touch the ground. Such was the speed of Alexander the Great. He became the ruler of the known world. At the height of his power, when he was just thirty-three years old, he died suddenly and his kingdom was divided among his four generals. The Scripture shows how the large horn was broken and it was replaced with four prominent horns.

The ram butted everything out of his way to the west, to the north, and to the south, and no one could stand against him or help his victims. He did as he pleased and became very great.

While I was watching, suddenly A MALE GOAT APPEARED from the west, CROSSING THE LAND SO SWIFTLY THAT HE DIDN'T EVEN TOUCH THE GROUND. This goat, which had one very large horn between its eyes, headed toward the two-horned ram that I had seen standing beside the river, rushing at him in a rage. The goat charged furiously at the ram and struck him, breaking off both his horns. Now the ram was helpless, and the goat knocked him down and trampled him. No one could rescue the ram from the goat's power. The goat became very powerful. But at the height of his power, his large horn was broken off. In the large horn's place grew four prominent horns pointing in the four directions of the earth.

Daniel 8:4-8 (NLT)

Napoleon and Lightning Speed

The most outstanding feature of the Napoleonic system of warfare was undoubtedly its flexibility and limitless variation. The insistence on speed and mobility was the basic feature of Napoleon's campaigns from beginning to end.

It was Napoleon's emphasis on speed and mobility that confused and unsettled his enemies. Someone said, "The Emperor (Napoleon) has discovered a new way of waging war; he makes use of our legs instead of our bayonets." On one occasion, Napoleon moved the whole of the Grand Army of 210,000 men from its camps at Boulogne to the Rhine. From the Rhine he marched to the Danube and then to the outskirts of Ulm in just 17 days. When war begins, a good general will move with lightning speed.

Hitler and Lightning Speed

Adolf Hitler used a tactic called blitzkrieg, which means lightning war. This tactic depended on speed and surprise and needed the military force to be based along light tank units supported by planes and foot soldiers. This strategy was developed in Germany by an army officer called Heinz Guderian. He had developed a military pamphlet called Achtung Panzer which got into the hands of Adolf Hitler. Fighting with the speed of lightning was so successful that it resulted in the British and French armies being defeated in the first few weeks of the Second World War. Lightning strikes were used in the invasion of Russia and were very effective in capturing large expanses of land from the Russians within the first few weeks of the war.

Once again, moving with the speed of lightning gave the decisive advantage to the general. You must decide to become a commander who moves with lightning speed. Go into high speed as you decide to obey God and do His will completely.

It is time to stop giving excuses and calling for more meetings. It is time to stop planning for things to be done next week and the week after. If it must be done, it must be done now! It must be done with speed!

CHAPTER 41

Expect an Attack on Your Home Base

And it came to pass, when David and his men were come to Ziklag on the third day, that the Amalekites had invaded the south, and Ziklag, and smitten Ziklag, and burned it with fire; And had taken the women captives, that were therein: they slew not any, either great or small, but carried them away, and went on their way.

SO DAVID AND HIS MEN CAME TO THE CITY, AND, BEHOLD, IT WAS BURNED WITH FIRE; AND THEIR WIVES, AND THEIR SONS, AND THEIR DAUGHTERS, WERE TAKEN CAPTIVES. Then David and the people that were with him lifted up their voice and wept, until they had no more power to weep. And David's two wives were taken captives, Ahinoam the Jezreelitess, and Abigail the wife of Nabal the Carmelite.

1 Samuel 30:1-5

Whilst King David was out fighting, the enemy Amalekites had cleverly attacked his home base and burnt it down. All their wives, sons and daughters were taken captive. David was devastated, and that is to be expected. No matter how hardened a warrior is, he looks forward to going home, to a place of rest.

If you are fighting a war, you can expect your home base to come under fire. You must expect an attack on your home base. You must expect an attack on the family, friendships and alliances that are a source of your strength. Every attack on your home base, aides, alliances, friendships will have a significant impact on the war.

If you are a travelling minister, you can expect an attack on your home. The devil would like to leave you homeless. He would like to leave you without a place to come back to. Satan would like to attack your physical home and leave you without any solace or comfort. He would like to bomb your shelter so that you have nowhere to go to when you finish fighting. This is why many ministers have serious marital problems. It is an attack to bomb their shelters so that they have nowhere to go to. It is called a "de-housing" attack! Instead of pastors coming home to softness, comforts and delights, they come home to hardness, more hard work and arguments. Loving words are replaced with accusations, opposition and resistance. Soon, a minister of the gospel does not consider his house as a place of solace, comfort, softness and delights. He has been de-housed!

The Royal Airforce of England, under the command of "Bomber Harris" de-housed the citizens of Hamburg, Dresden, Berlin, Cologne and many other German cities. They did this by bombing and smashing the cities of Germany. Similarly, Satan has de-housed many pastors and preachers of the gospel.

This is also the reason why there are few evangelists. If you dare step out of your church and evangelise the world, your church can be taken over and you will have nowhere to come back to. You will also have no one to support you any more. Many evangelists are de-housed ministers, having no support, no more aid and no more aides.

Your family and your aides are very important for your mission. Their importance is spelt out by the fact that the enemy will target them and try to eliminate them. Do not be surprised if your home base of close aides and alliances come under attack. Often, your ministry cannot be completed without the input of these close aides and alliances. Do not be surprised if Satan tries to turn your aides into rebels. It is an attack on your home base. Stand up and defend your home base. Fight to maintain your house. Build bomb shelters so that you will not suffer a de-housing attack of the enemy.

How Hannibal was Defeated

Hannibal was the famous African general who invaded the Roman Empire with his elephants. He crossed the Italian Alps with his armies and elephants and entered deep into Italy. Hannibal defeated the Roman armies several times. Some of his famous victories were the victory at the Trebia River, the victory at Lake Trasimene and the victory at the Battle of Cannae. At the battle of Cannae he killed approximately eighty thousand Romans and won the proper respect of the Roman armed forces.

After the defeat of the Romans at Cannae, Hannibal was within striking distance of Rome. Everyone expected him to invade Rome but he did not. Instead, he stayed within the Roman territory for eight years. The Roman armies were not strong enough to defeat him so he had his way roaming around in Italy for this period.

The Roman armies had grown to have a proper respect for Hannibal and his elephants. These two mighty powers therefore stayed in equilibrium for eight years with Hannibal living in the Roman Empire and within striking distance of Rome, but not attacking it. Imagine having such a terrible enemy living with his armies in the neighbourhood. The Romans were terrified of his presence and expected an all-out invasion of Rome to start at any time.

Believe it or not, the Romans were never able to defeat Hannibal for eight whole years whilst he was in Italy. One day, they devised a strategy to get rid of him. The strategy was to invade Carthage (Tunisia), the home base of Hannibal. When Carthage came under serious attack, Hannibal was called back home to defend his own country. It was only when Hannibal was forced to return to Carthage to help defend his home country that the Romans were able to get him out of Roman territory.

When the Romans eventually fought with Hannibal in Carthage, they defeated him. Indeed, the mighty Carthaginian general who had brought the Roman Empire to its feet and lived for eight years within striking distance of Rome, was defeated by an attack on his home base.

CHAPTER 42

Expect an Attack on Your Aides, Friends and Relatives

And he that was over the household, and he that was over the city, the elders also, and they that brought up the children, sent to Jehu, saying, We are thy servants, and will do all that thou shalt bid us; we will not make any man king: do thou that which is good in thine eyes. Then he wrote a letter the second time to them, saying, If ye be on my side, and if ye will hearken unto my voice, take ye the heads of the men your master's sons, and come to me to Jezreel by to morrow this time. Now the king's sons, being seventy persons, were with the great men of the city, who brought them up.

And it came to pass, when the letter came to them, that THEY TOOK THE KING'S SONS, AND SLEW SEVENTY PERSONS, and put their heads in baskets, and sent him them to Jezreel. And there came a messenger, and told him, saying, they have brought the heads of the king's sons. And he said, Lay ye them in two heaps at the entering in of the gate until the morning.

And it came to pass in the morning, that he went out, and stood, and said to all the people, Ye be righteous: behold, I conspired against my master, and slew him: but who slew all these?

213

Know now that there shall fall unto the earth nothing of the word of the LORD, which the LORD spake

concerning the house of Ahab: for the LORD hath done that which he spake by his servant Elijah.

SO JEHU SLEW ALL THAT REMAINED OF THE HOUSE OF AHAB IN JEZREEL, AND ALL HIS GREAT MEN, AND HIS KINSFOLKS, AND HIS PRIESTS, UNTIL HE LEFT HIM NONE REMAINING.

2 Kings 10:5-11

J ehu, the commander, attacked the house of Ahab: all his sons, all his relatives, all his great men, all his priests until there was no alliance or friendship left. Jehu was fighting a war against Ahab. In war, people do not only target soldiers, tanks and military equipment. Aides, alliances, friends and relatives are all targeted. Attacks on your friends and friendships demoralise, embarrass and discourage you.

Many ministers of the gospel have experienced attacks on their families. The enemy can use your family to harass you. Your life can be made miserable because of your family. Your family is often an easy target for the enemy. It could be your wife, your husband or your children.

Many ministers are harassed by their children who turn away from God. A zealous missionary-minded pastor told me how his heart was broken by his son who became an atheist. Another pastor's heart was broken by his son who became a criminal and went to prison several times. He was dragged into the newspapers on several occasions because of his unruly and uncontrollable son. These attacks are spiritually orchestrated to embarrass, intimidate and silence the man of God.

Oral Roberts suffered terrible attacks through his children. His daughter, Rebecca, was happily married to a real estate developer called Marshall Nash. By the time they had been married for ten years, the couple were millionaires and strong supporters of Oral Robert's ministry. One morning, an administrative assistant arrived at the home of Oral Roberts in tears.

"I have some bad news. Marshall Nash and Rebecca died last night in a plane crash over the Kansas wheat fields on their way to Tulsa." They had spent a few days in Colorado and had been flying home in a private plane with friends. It was the duty of Oral Roberts and his wife, Evelyn Roberts to go over to Marshall and Rebecca's home to give their children the heart-breaking news. All three children were between the ages of five and thirteen. This was an attack of stupendous proportions.

Thousands of people reached out to help Oral Roberts and his family in grief. But this was not the end.

Ronnie, a son of Oral Roberts was extremely gifted by the Lord and Oral Roberts saw him as his successor to the ministry. They enrolled him in Stanford University where he developed independence and a desire to be removed from his father's presence and ministry. When their son eventually returned to Tulsa, it was clear he had fallen into drug addiction. His son had divorced and continued in his drug addiction. One day, Richard Roberts, Oral Roberts' son brought the news to his father: "The police have just informed us that they found Ronnie slumped over the steering wheel in his car, dead from a bullet wound. The police believed it had been suicide. Once again, the body of Christ around the world offered condolences to the grief-stricken family.

These attacks on God's honoured servants reflect the way in which Satan loves to attack men of God by attacking their families.

A man of God told me how he fasted for forty days and received the shock of his life after the fast. He said to me, "I was so lean that my shorts were falling off my body. Then somebody walked into my house and said to me, "Your wife is dead. She died last night in an accident."

This pastor said to me, "I did not know what to do or say. I walked out into the garden and lifted up my eyes and asked a simple question,

"What kind of God are you?"

He was devastated. The death of his wife marked the beginning of several crises in his life.

A way to overcome these attacks of the enemy is to see it for what it is: an attack of the enemy! God's power will give you the upper hand in every crisis. Protect your family and pray for your family because they are prime targets for the enemy. Any attack of the enemy on your family will turn your attention away from the war and side-track you from your real purpose.

Bomber Harris

In London today there is a controversial statue of Sir Arthur Travers Harris (Bomber Harris) who led a campaign to bomb German cities. He was the Air Chief Marshall during the latter part of World War II. At that time, it was discovered that bombing raids of the British air force were largely missing their targets. Only one out of three aircraft bombs were getting within five miles of their target. With the poor results of these bombing raids, it was decided to bomb large areas of ordinary civilian homes. This was indeed a controversial decision. But it amounted to attacking the friends, aides and relatives of the German military.

The bombing of these German cities was aimed at destroying as many homes and houses as possible. The aim was to de-house everybody in Germany. This de-housing exercise would displace the German workforce and reduce their ability to work. Bomber Harris believed that massive and sustained area bombing of the friends, relatives and families in Germany would force Germany to surrender. In this de-housing campaign, Bomber Harris bombed and flattened several cities of Germany such as Cologne, Hamburg, Dresden and Berlin.

After the war, information from Albert Speer, the armament minister under Hitler showed that the bombing raids at night had been very effective. Indeed, the attack on families, friends and alliances of the German army was truly effective. People had nowhere to go after the bombs destroyed their homes. People were unable to go to work in the factories to produce weapons because they had no homes. Nothing was normal because the Germans had been de-housed!

CHAPTER 43

Expect Your Enemy to Attempt to Assassinate You

... strike down the shepherd, and the sheep of the flock shall be scattered

Matthew 26:31 (NASB)

"Strike the shepherd and the sheep will scatter" is an instruction to assassinate the leader so that his followers become disillusioned and vulnerable. The shepherd, the king or the principal leader is of great interest to the enemy. If you can knock out the king, you can win the war quickly. Long protracted wars can be avoided if one person can be assassinated.

A good general, therefore, expects his enemy to attempt to assassinate him. The concept of assassinating the leader is so common that almost every great nation has experienced an assassination attempt on its leader.

Four American presidents Abraham Lincoln, James Garfield, William McKinley and John F. Kennedy have died at the hands of assassins in the last one hundred years. There have been at least twenty known attempts on US presidents' lives.

India's father of the nation, Mahatma Ghandi, was assassinated in 1948, whilst prime ministers Indira Ghandi and her son Rajiv Ghandi were also assassinated in 1984 and 1991 respectively. Lia Quat Ali Khan, the first Prime Minister of Pakistan was also assassinated in 1951. In Israel, Prime Minister Yitzak Rabin was assassinated in 1995.

Adolf Hitler the head of state of Germany had forty-two known assassination attempts on his life whilst Winston Churchill, the Prime Minister of England had at least two major attempts on his life. In the same season, Charles de Gaulle, the premier of France, endured 32 attempts on his life.

Africa has not been left out of the assassination line up. In Guinea Bissau, President Joao Brenado Bieira was assassinated in March 2009 in the capital Bissau. In Mozambique, Samora Machel was assassinated in 1986. The presidents of Burundi and Rwanda were assassinated together in 1994, opening the floodgates for a genocide.

In Congo, President Laurent Kabila was assassinated in 2001 by his aide. Jonas Savimbi of Angola was finally assassinated in 2002 after surviving more than a dozen assassination attempts.

As you can see from the list above, the elimination of the leader is of great importance to the enemy. A good general must therefore see himself as a potential assassination target. You must guard yourself and take many precautions to prevent the enemy from eliminating you. This is where time, expense and effort should not be spared. If your enemy knows your value you must also know your own value. If you are eliminated, everything will change. You must fight against assassination attempts on your life. I have experienced several assassination attempts on my life. Satan has tried to take my life on many occasions but the Lord delivered me from them all.

1.　　In 1997, whilst driving to Tamale in the northern part of Ghana, we had a terrible accident in which our car somersaulted off the road. We escaped death with our very lives.

2.　　Once, I was on board a KLM flight to Heathrow airport. Just as we were about to touch down, the pilot pulled the plane up steeply. Everyone was silent. Then the announcement came – there was another plane on the runway and we were about to collide with this plane. The pilot had pulled the plane up suddenly to avoid the collision.

3.　　On another occasion, our plane, a KLM flight almost collided with a car on the runway at the Accra international airport. When our wheels were almost on the ground, the pilot pulled the plane up steeply and we shot up into the sky again. Everyone on board was terrified but the pilot said nothing. When he eventually spoke, he explained that there had been a car on the runway which he would have collided with.

4.   On 22 of December 2011, a tipper truck almost ran over me at top speed. To avoid driving over me, the driver climbed over the curb, drove over a man who was walking on the island in between the two roads and drove into the oncoming traffic on the other side of the road.

5.   In Nigeria, after a church service one Sunday afternoon, armed robbers stormed the church premises, disarmed the policeman on duty and began shooting wildly and indiscriminately. Bullets were flying everywhere as we lay on the ground for cover. That week several people had been killed during rampant armed robbery incidents in Lagos.

6.   One Sunday morning, whilst preaching in the church, a man rushed out of the congregation and attacked me head-on. If he had had a knife, he would have killed me instantly.

7.   I have experienced attacks on my health when I sensed the devil trying to kill me.

All these were efforts by Satan to eliminate me before my time. Most people who are used by God notice satanic attacks and attempts to eliminate them. You must defend yourself against attempts to assassinate you.

Defend yourself against assassination attempts through prayer. In the spirit, bind the devil and all evil powers that are arrayed against you.

Defend yourself from assassination by looking after your health. I once knew a poor man who was chosen through his family lineage to become an important king. After he was chosen, he decided to play golf regularly. Now that his life was important, he decided to do something that would prolong it and give him health and strength for many years. You must do the same for yourself when you realise that you are a precious life chosen by God to work for him.

Defend yourself against assassination attempts by taking all forms of threats to your life seriously. Do not dismiss warnings and advice from doctors, advisers and other wise people. God uses them to deliver you from assassination attempts of the devil.

Do not dismiss advice on your diet, exercise, rest, lifestyle and sexual health. You may be dismissing a word of wisdom coming to you from the Holy Spirit. I have watched as ministers of the gospel dismissed advice on sexual health, only to become homosexuals. I have watched as ministers of the gospel dismissed advice on lifestyle, only to become invalids with back pain.

Defend yourself against assassination attempts by accepting that you are now an important person. Martin Luther King became important because of his civil rights protests. Perhaps he did not realise how important he had become. He was warned about threats to his life. Perhaps, he dismissed these threats, not realising how important and significant his work had become. Unfortunately, he died from an assassin's bullet, as the warnings had predicted.

Expect the enemy to plan to assassinate you. Satan wants to wipe you out. He would love for you to be dead so that you shut up forever. Satan does not like your voice and does not want to hear you speaking. Satanic forces are restricted by the angels and the power of God. Give no place to the devil and do not open the door of your life to assassination. You must not be the subject of a successful assassination attempt.

CHAPTER 44

Actively Attack the Hidden Agendas and Motives That Are Not the Goal of the Army

And Achan answered Joshua, and said, Indeed I have sinned against the Lord God of Israel, and thus and thus have I done: WHEN I SAW AMONG THE SPOILS A GOODLY BABYLONISH GARMENT, AND TWO HUNDRED SHEKELS OF SILVER, AND A WEDGE OF GOLD OF FIFTY SHEKELS WEIGHT, THEN I COVETED THEM, and took them; and, behold, they are hid in the earth in the midst of my tent, and the silver under it.

And Joshua said, Why hast thou troubled us? the Lord shall trouble thee this day. And all Israel stoned him with stones, and burned them with fire, after they had stoned them with stones.

Joshua 7:20-21, 25

The main mission of the church of Jesus Christ is the Great Commission to go into all the world and preach the gospel to every man on this earth. Today, there are many other reasons why the church exists. Some churches exist to provide humanitarian care. Some churches exist to provide a centre for funerals. Other churches exist for political and social activities.

People inevitably develop their own agenda, which is different from the original vision. You must be aware of this. You must crush the hidden and unspoken agenda in the followers by addressing them openly. Attack other subtle ideas and plans that develop in people's hearts as they claim to be following you.

Joshua, the great Israeli general, had one thing in mind – to conquer Jericho and enter the Promised Land. Achan was one of Joshua's soldiers but he had a hidden agenda to get wealthy through the war. This hidden agenda caused a curse to descend on God's people. The children of Israel were defeated in the war because of one person's private agenda to be rich. This is what is happening in the church today. The hidden agenda that we nurture in our hearts is different from God's agenda to win the whole world and preach the gospel to every creature.

Some soldiers may have a mind to become rich through the war. Others may have a hidden agenda to escape at the next possible opportunity. Other soldiers may have no intention of fighting at all.

The ministry of the Lord Jesus Christ is a boiling pot for many hidden agendas. People join the ministry for varied reasons. In my book, *The Art of Ministry*, I address many of the hidden agendas that people have when they come into full-time ministry.

Some people come into full-time ministry because they did not qualify for any other profession.

Others come into full-time ministry with a mind to be rich. They do this because those ahead of them in ministry seem prosperous.

Some people are in ministry because they want to travel often.

Others go into full-time ministry because they are unemployed.

Some people use the ministry as a stepping-stone to a better career.

Some pastors are in the ministry because of pressure from their wives.

Others are in the ministry because they are too lazy to look for another job and feel that ministry gives them a lighter schedule.

These are not good reasons for coming into full-time ministry. The only good reason for coming into the ministry is that God has called you and you want to please Him. You cannot use the ministry of Jesus Christ as an alternative source of employment. Anytime private visions grow within people, they undermine the original vision of the mission.

Alexander and His Troops

Alexander the Great set out to invade Persia and extend the authority of his father's kingdom into the East. He sought to reach the ends of the world and the great outer sea. He invaded India in 326BC and wanted to continue expanding into the rest of Asia. But after ten years of fighting, his soldiers developed another agenda different from the original agenda of going "to the ends of the world".

At the Hyphasis River, Alexander's men mutinied and refused to march any further east. This river thus marks the easternmost extent of Alexander's conquest. Alexander tried to persuade his soldiers to march further but his general, Coenus, pleaded with him to change his mind.

He explained, "The men long to see their parents, their wives, their children and their homeland." Alexander the Great eventually agreed to turn back to Greece and give up his campaign.

Notice how the private agenda of these soldiers to see their wives and children brought an end to Alexander the Great's vision of going to the "ends of the world".

This is exactly how the personal, domestic, financial vision that we have can quench God's vision and God's work. This is why Jesus said, "If any man come to me, and hate not his father, and mother, and wife, and children, and brethren, and sisters, yea, and his own life also, he cannot be my disciple" (Luke 14:26). Looking after your wife, children and family are important but it is not the same as building the church and doing the work of God.

Some people are surprised that a verse like Luke 14:26 can be found in the Bible.

Attack the hidden agenda of the people who live and work around you. Ensure that everyone has the same agenda and the same reason for being around. You must not receive people into the ministry who have a desire to earn a lot of money and be rich.

The church and ministry do not exist to provide good jobs for people. The ministry should not be an alternative source of employment. If you want a really good job, you must go to the bank or any other secular organisation, which can give you a really good job. Leave the ministry for those who love God and really want to serve Him! It is time to root out all those with a hidden agenda that is different from the original agenda.

One day, a lady applied for a job in the ministry. She wanted to receive as much money as she was receiving in the bank. When she mentioned the salary she expected to receive, I almost burst out laughing. The amount she mentioned was about twenty times the amount the highest person in the ministry was being paid. We obviously did not accept her in the ministry. The aim of the ministry is not to provide good jobs that are comparable to those in the secular world. The aim of the ministry is to minister the Word of God. We are to use every means; to go everywhere we can and convert the heathen!

CHAPTER 45

A Good General Continues to Fight in the Midst of Terror and Panic

And there went out a champion out of the camp of the Philistines, named Goliath, of Gath, whose height was six cubits and a span. And he had an helmet of brass upon his head, and he was armed with a coat of mail; and the weight of the coat was five thousand shekels of brass.

And he had greaves of brass upon his legs, and a target of brass between his shoulders. And the staff of his spear was like a weaver's beam; and his spear's head weighed six hundred shekels of iron: and one bearing a shield went before him.

And he stood and cried unto the armies of Israel, and said unto them, Why are ye come out to set your battle in array? am not I a Philistine, and ye servants to Saul? choose you a man for you, and let him come down to me. If he be able to fight with me, and to kill me, then will we be your servants: but if I prevail against him, and kill him, then shall ye be our servants, and serve us. And the Philistine said, I defy the armies of Israel this day; give me a man, that we may fight together. When Saul and all Israel heard those words of the Philistine, THEY WERE DISMAYED, AND GREATLY AFRAID.

1 Samuel 17:4-11

When war erupts, expect to be gripped with terror and panic. A good general cannot be moved by the enemy's campaign of terror and panic. A good general knows he will experience terror, fear and panic. This is because war is a terrifying experience. But a good general continues to function in the midst of terror, fear and panic.

Imagine having people you know dying all around you. Imagine people sitting by people you know whose heads are blown off. Imagine flying out on a bomber raid every night knowing that only a percentage of you are gong to come back. This is what the average soldier experiences.

The sound of gunfire alone is terrifying. The sound of a gunshot is so frightening that you can virtually jump out of your skin. Imagine having to live with this all the time. This is the reason why many soldiers become unstable when they return home from war. They have seen so much suffering, pain and terror that they are hardly the same again.

Why is it that people are so affected by war? Sometimes the soldiers return from war without a scratch. Yet, they still become disoriented and sometimes go mad. The soul of man is very tender and not comfortable with frightening, terrorising experiences. Near-death experiences are very traumatic and most people are changed forever after a near-death experience. Soldiers suffer from what is called the Post Traumatic Stress Disorder. Post Traumatic Stress Disorder is common because war has been proven to be a highly traumatic experience for many soldiers. Seeing close friends die and narrowly escaping death yourself is a terrifying experience.

Many soldiers will remember and re-experience the specific events of the war. This happens when they think, when they close their eyes or when they dream. Some soldiers react strongly to anything that reminds them of the war.

Soldiers can become reluctant to relate socially because loud noises and crowds remind them of bombs. Many soldiers are never emotionally the same again. Perhaps, the most severe effect of war on soldiers is that they are unable to form close bonds with loved ones because of the experience of a close friend dying. They fear that it will happen again. They fear that they will have to leave someone behind again. It has been said that the emotional effects of war on soldiers hinder their future achievements as they find it impossible to imagine or plan. As you can see, those who experience war suffer terribly.

Fear and Terror in the Ministry

There is also fear and terror in the ministry. When you see frightening things happening to those who have served the Lord, it ministers fear to you. Many people are put off the ministry because they see men of God experiencing failure, disgrace, humiliation, poverty and ridicule.

When a soldier sees his friend's head, arm or leg blown off, he knows that it could have been him. He was six inches away from being a dismembered piece of meat. How would he not be frightened?

When a pastor sees his mentor being humiliated, sent to prison, ridiculed, accused of many terrible sins, he will definitely be filled with terror and fear. When a minister of the gospel sees his friend falling into a difficulty that he himself is being tempted with, he is gripped with fear because he know he is under similar pressure.

When gripped with fear and terror, people react differently. Some give up. Some run away. Some are simply paralysed with fear and do nothing any more. When you hear certain news that terrifies you, you must realise that you are experiencing a terror attack. When you hear of pastors going on a journey and perishing in an accident, you become frightened because you recently embarked on a similar journey.

The Pressure of a Terror Attack

This is why medals, awards and decorations are handed out to soldiers for functioning in the midst of terror and panic. For instance, there are medals for "bravery under fire" and medals are given for "being an escaped prisoner of war". These two medals are rewards for persisting in the fight in spite of great danger, terror and panic.

What must I do? It is important that you have a good response under fire. When under fire and filled with terror, you must not stop travelling and preaching the Word of God. It is important that you do not change your message when you are terrified. You will be under pressure to stop preaching about long life because of the deaths of people around you whom you expected to live longer.

You will be under pressure to stop preaching about a good marriage because of marital failures you see all around you.

You will be under pressure to stop preaching about fornication because you can see how common it is.

You will be under pressure to stop preaching about homosexuality because you see the world accepting it as a normal thing.

Remember that a good general continues to function in the midst of terror and panic. When war erupts, expect to experience terror, fear and panic. But you must continue to function, to pray, to preach, to travel, to minister in the midst of terror and panic. You will receive a medal for your ability to function under fire!

CHAPTER 46

A Good General Fights to Win But Knows That He Will Have Some Losses

Jesus answered them, Have not I chosen you twelve, and one of you is a devil?

John 6:70

J esus Christ was well prepared to lose one of His favourite disciples. He knew he had done everything to save the soul of Judas Iscariot. But in a real war, there are casualties. The casualties must not confuse the general. Your victory can be defined as a summary of your gains and losses. When you put everything together, you must have gained more than you lost.

If you do not understand the realities of war, you will be discouraged and think of yourself as a failure when you are actually victorious. Did you know that many people drop out of the ministry thinking they are failures? Many people consider the ministry to be a waste of time. They see it as something with little fruit.

A sower went out to sow! The sower had very little response from his seeds. Only twenty-five per cent of the people responded. Out of the twenty-five percent, only a third responded completely. In other words, the sower lost 92.5 per cent of his seeds. That is the nature of ministry!

A good general must understand how the ministry works. A good general must understand what failure is and what success is. No matter how much you preach, a large number of people are going to make you think your preaching is useless. That is just the way it is in the kingdom of God.

Some people are going to fall to immorality, no matter what you do or say. The kingdom of God is going to have some losses in this battle. Some marriages will be lost no matter the amount of marriage counselling that is done. No matter how much you preach on loyalty and faithfulness, some people will be disloyal. No matter how good your leadership style is, some people will attack and accuse you of being a bad leader. No matter how kind and loving you are to some people, there will always be ungrateful and forgetful people. A good general knows that he will have losses in spite of all that he does. I have experienced all these losses as I have tried to build the church. There are sons and daughters I weep over today. How I wish they were with me! But there are losses in every campaign and you just have to accept them.

Ultimately, God will give you the victory and when you sum up the gains and the losses, you can see the increase of the Lord. John Wesley founded the Methodist Church. Through his strong leadership, a great movement was released into the earth. But this was not without losses along the way. We never hear much about the people John Wesley lost.

John Wesley's Losses - James Wheatley

John Wesley was not without loss. For instance, one of their lay preachers, James Wheatley was a very successful evangelist but was found to be committing some kind of sexual sin with a string of female Methodists. When James Wheatley was eventually suspended from preaching, he refused to stop. Instead, he preached against the Wesleys and other Methodist preachers.

Most of the Methodist preachers were successful ministers. John Wesley appointed 541 itinerant preachers in his lifetime but not all of them turned out to be successful preachers. For instance, his brother Charles Wesley, finding some of the preachers lacking, tried to remove some of these preachers from the list. On one occasion, he said that his brother, John Wesley had without God's counsel, "Made a preacher of a tailor; I with God's help shall make a tailor of him again." He even spent money setting up some of the preachers in business for the express purpose of making them less dependent on John Wesley.

John Wesley's Losses – John Bennett

A painful loss to John Wesley was through a man called John Bennett. John Bennet was one of John Wesley's most valued and successful lay preachers. When John Bennet married Grace Murray, the lady whom John Wesley had also intended to marry, he fell out with John Wesley. John Bennet became a rebel and loudly denounced John Wesley saying many bitter things about him. John Bennet spread out his arms in front of the congregation and cried, "Popery! Popery! Popery!" By this, he was accusing John Wesley of raising himself up to be another pope.

John Wesley's Losses – William Darney

A good general fights to win but knows that he will have some losses. John Wesley established many preachers but was also forced to dismiss a number of wayward preachers. For instance, he dismissed William Darney for persisting in preaching predestination.

John Wesley's Losses – John Edwards

Another pastor, John Edwards was expelled after he refused to give up the Leeds house and chapel. John Wesley managed to successfully repossess the house and the chapel from Edwards. Meanwhile Edwards set up another separate independent congregation with a large number of the Methodist members.

John Wesley's Losses – Thomas Marxfield

John Wesley had many faithful followers but some people broke away. One such painful loss was Thomas Marxfield. Thomas Marxfield was one of the first ever lay preachers and he worked with John Wesley for over twenty years. When John Wesley corrected him on his extremism with regard to perfectionism, he did not listen or submit to John Wesley's authority. Perhaps, he was too big and too familiar after twenty years of working with John Wesley. Thomas Marxfield broke away from the church with about two hundred members.

John Wesley's Losses – Charles Wesley

As you read these stories that reveal losses in a great general's ministry, you can see why a good general fights but knows that he will have some losses. John Wesley had many great relationships but also had some great losses. For instance, his relationship with his brother Charles Wesley was greatly affected by Charles' role in preventing his marriage to a lady called Grace Murray.

John Wesley was so hurt by what his brother had done. The rift between Charles and John was bitter and Charles said to his brother, "I renounce all intercourse with you but what I would have with a heathen man, or a publican."

John Wesley's Losses – William Fletcher

Another terrible loss came to John Wesley through the death of his appointed successor. John Wesley chose a man called William Fletcher. In 1757 Fletcher was ordained as a deacon in the Church of England. In addition to this he sometimes preached with John Wesley and assisted him with clerical duties in Wesley's London chapels. Fletcher was devoted to the Methodist concern for spiritual renewal and revival, and committed himself to the Wesleys. John Fletcher believed greatly in the Methodist movement and he was the best choice that John Wesley had. But then he died suddenly and John Wesley was left without a successor.

In spite of all these losses John Wesley chalked significant advances for the kingdom of God and built the foundation for the Methodist Church. Today, we hardly know about any of the terrible losses that John Wesley experienced as he fought the good fight.

A good general is fully aware that he may have to take some personal losses but he presses on for the ultimate victory. Personal losses are part of a good general's life. Jesus said, "He that loses his life will gain it and he that saves his life will lose it." Expect to have some personal losses as you follow the Lord. Indeed, I would have liked to be a specialist doctor and strut around proudly, knowing that no one knows it better than I do. But I had to lose that honour so that I could gain the Lord and the ministry of Jesus Christ.

What it Costs to Win a War

The Second World War was fought between Germany and the allied countries. It is true that the Second World War was won by the allies. The victory of the Second World War came with several losses. Many losses may be encountered but there is an overall victory. It is the overall victory that really matters.

The fact that a great general will have losses as he strives for victory is best depicted by the statistics of the Second World War.

Twenty-five million people from the Soviet Union died in the Second World War.

Fifteen million Chinese people died in the Second World War.

Six million Polish people died in the Second World War.

Two million people from British India died.

One million people from Yugoslavia died in the Second World War.

Half a million British troops died in the Second World War.

Half a million American troops died in the Second World War.

Half a million French troops died in the Second World War.

Romanians, Hungarians, Italians, Koreans, Greeks, Latvians, Austrians and even Ethiopians died in the Second World War.

Indeed, Adolf Hitler was crushed in the end. Germany was defeated. But a good general knows that there will be losses on his road to the overall victory. Do not be sad about some of the losses you have experienced as you have endeavoured to follow the Lord all the way.

CHAPTER 47

A Good General Knows That Death Can Happen But Does Not Throw Himself at Death

... but truly as the Lord liveth, and as thy soul liveth, there is but a step between me and death.

1 Samuel 20:3

King David was a good general. He believed in God and even wrote the wonderful promise of Scripture, "With long life will I satisfy him and show him my salvation" (Psalm 91:16). Even though David believed that God would satisfy him with long life, he knew that there was just a step between him and death. A good general knows that death can happen. But he does not throw himself at death because he knows that God will also satisfy him with long life.

A good general knows about the reality of death. He knows that death is something that happens when you fight. He knows that death is something that happens when there is a war. You cannot be a good general if you do not accept the reality of death. You can die in the midst of the battle! Your friends and associates can die fighting by your side! Your spouse can die! Your children can die!

You can receive a phone call with the devastating news of the death of a loved one. All these are part of the war we are called to fight in. If you read the story of the life of Adoniram Judson, the missionary to Burma, you will gasp at the tragedies that he experienced. He recorded death upon death of his children, his wives and his friends. He was a great man of faith. He was a good general.

What are your plans in the event of death? What are your plans for and in the event of someone else's death? Most people do not like to think about the possibility of their deaths. People are superstitious and do not like even the mention of the subject. But a good general knows that death is part of war. Death is part of life. A good general knows that he can die and others can also die. What type of escape plan do you have in the event of death? What type of escape plan do you have when death strikes in your life and ministry? What will happen to your church if you die? Have you thought it through?

A good general prepares for the reality of death. Preparing for death is done only by mature people who face realities as good soldiers. If you ignore the reality that death can happen, you open yourself up to a very deep crisis. I once met a soldier who showed me a chain tied around his neck. This crude chain had his name and number inscribed on it. He told me, "This chain was given to me to identify my body in case I die in battle." He continued, "All the soldiers have to wear this chain. Without it we may not be able to identify you when you are killed or wounded."

A good general must prepare for death. Escape plans come into play when the worst is happening or has happened. Most people do not want to think of the worst possible scenario. When death strikes what are your options? Do you have an escape plan? An escape plan is a way out of great difficulty! An escape plan is a plan to get out of a bad situation and somehow survive in spite of the worst scenario having happened.

A Good General Has a Will

A good general must have a will because he is conscious of how possible death is. Through your will, you will continue to fight even though you are dead. Do you have a will? Most spiritual people do not have wills. They do not believe in even thinking about the possibility of death. Just look around you and see the souls which part each day. People just like you pass into eternity, leaving everyone in shock. Why do you think that it can never be you? A good general must have a will. Do not leave your family in confusion. I once suggested to a pastor that he make a will. This pastor was ill and the doctors had told him that he had an incurable disease. Unfortunately, the pastor did not like my suggestion. I was seen as someone who was not walking in faith, anointing and power. The long and short of this story is that he did not make his will before he died. When he died, his family was left in confusion and difficulty. His family lived in difficulty for many years because he did not write a Will.

Julius Caesar's Will

Julius Caesar, Rome's most famous general, died suddenly from an assassination by his close friends and senators. Upon his death, there was confusion in Rome. But Julius Caesar continued to fight in Rome through his will. Mark Anthony, his closest friend and associate, assumed that he would succeed Julius Caesar. But Julius Caesar had other plans. And through his will, he implemented those plans even though he was dead.

After the funeral of Julius Caesar, and to everyone's surprise, Julius Caesar's will was produced. Julius Caesar had surprisingly named a successor and his successor was not Mark Anthony but rather an unknown nephew called Octavian. In his will, Julius Caesar left all his wealth to Octavian. He also left his name "Caesar" to be inherited by this young man called Octavian.

Julius Caesar's will shocked everyone in Rome and opened the door for the young Octavian to arrive on the scene and claim his position. The young man, Octavian, travelled to Rome and entered the city of Rome quietly to claim his inheritance. Obviously, there was a lot of tension between Mark Anthony, Julius Caesar's right hand man and Octavian. The tension between the older Mark Anthony and the young Octavian led to various conflicts and wars over the years. But Julius Caesar had left his great wealth to Octavian and Octavian used the money to raise armies to fight against Mark Anthony. In the end, Octavian prevailed and became the next Caesar. His name was later changed from Octavian to Augustus Caesar.

The history of the world was changed because Julius Caesar made a Will. It was during the time of Augustus Caesar that Jesus was born.

Perhaps, the future of your church depends on you making a will. A good general makes a will. A good general knows that death is a reality you will have to deal with.

Hitler's Will

Even Adolf Hitler wrote a will. He wrote his will the day before he died. Hitler's will was a short document signed on 29th April at 4.00am.

- It acknowledged his marriage – but does not name Eva Braun – and that they choose death over disgrace of deposition or capitulation; and that their bodies were to be cremated.

- His art collection was left to "A gallery in my home town of Linz on Donau".

- Objects of "Sentimental value or necessary for the maintenance of a modest simple life" went to his relatives and his "faithful co-workers" such as his secretary Mrs. Winter.

- Whatever else of value he possessed went to the National Socialist German Workers Party.

- Martin Bormann was nominated as the will's executor.

His will was witnessed by other wicked Nazi soldiers: Dr Joseph Goebbels, Martin Bormann and Colonel Nicholaus von Below.

"To the Strongest"

Apart from a will, you must have people who can take your place. There are many large churches today that have one great pastor who has ministered successfully and powerfully for many years. If that pastor were to die, the church would be plunged into confusion. No one else would be able to step up into that great pastor's shoes. A good general thinks about bearing fruit that abides. What is coming after you? Who will be able to do what you are doing as well as you are doing it now? Are you going to leave your ministry to the strongest, loudest and boldest associate?

Alexander the Great

Alexander the Great died when he was only thirty-three years old. His death was so sudden that reports of his death were not immediately believed. He had no obvious or legitimate heir. On his deathbed, Alexander the Great was asked who should succeed him and inherit his vast kingdom. His laconic reply was, "To the strongest."

Indeed, many pastors leave their ministries and estates to the strongest, the loudest and the most forceful. Instead of the kingdom falling into the hands of the most qualified and the most appropriate, it is the strongest, the loudest, the boldest and the most impudent that take over everything.

When Alexander the Great died, one party said he had passed his signet ring to Perdiccas, his bodyguard, thereby nominating him. Another group felt that as his wife Roxanne was pregnant they should wait to see if his child would be a boy or a girl. This child turned out to be a boy, Alexander IV. A third party also supported Alexander's half brother called Philip Arrhidaeus. In the end, Alexander IV, the baby, and Philip Arrhidaeus were appointed as joint kings.

However, confusion soon broke out and forty years of war between these different successors ensued. In the process, the three possible successors Perdiccas, Philip Arrhidaeus and Alexander IV were all murdered. In the end, Alexander the Great's kingdom was divided into four blocks and ruled by four of Alexander's generals. As you can see, it is not such a good idea to leave everything "to the strongest".

Do you not want your ministry to grow from strength to strength even when you are gone? Then do not leave all you have achieved "to the strongest". Make a will and make things clear. God will anoint the person you choose so that your ministry will carry on long after you are gone.

CHAPTER 48

A Good General Expects Attacks at His Weak Points

Remember what Amalek did unto thee by the way, when ye were come forth out of Egypt;

How he met thee by the way, and SMOTE THE HINDMOST OF THEE, even ALL THAT WERE FEEBLE behind thee, WHEN THOU WAST FAINT and weary; and he feared not God.

Therefore it shall be, when the Lord thy God hath given thee rest from all thine enemies round about, in the land which the Lord thy God giveth thee for an inheritance to possess it, that thou shalt blot out the remembrance of Amalek from under heaven; thou shalt not forget it

Deuteronomy 25:17-19

Everybody has weak points. Everybody has blind sides. Your weak points are of interest to your enemy. Your weak point is where you are more vulnerable. Defend them well because they will be attacked there. Every good general attacks what is weak and leaves what is strong. Therefore, brace yourself for attacks at your weak points.

Amalek was one such enemy who attacked the Israelites from their weaker backside when they were escaping from Egypt. Amalek was simply attacking what was easier. Your enemy will always look for your weak spot and attack you there.

Germany's Weak Spot

During the Second World War, Germany had an iron grip on the whole of Europe. In order to get to Germany and overthrow Hitler, the allies (British, American, Canadian and French forces) had to cross the sea from Britain and land in France. After landing in France, they would drive through Europe and enter Germany to defeat Adolf Hitler.

Now, the allies had to choose an appropriate weak spot on the coast of France where they could land their troops, tanks, trucks and cars. Where would they choose to do this massive invasion? Where would be most appropriate to land all these forces?

Something had happened earlier, which had taught the allies an important lesson. In 1942, the British and Canadians had raided a port city on the French coast. This raid was a disaster because the Germans had very heavy defences at the port. Through this, the allies learnt that the Germans had heavy fortifications in every port city. Invading a port city was going to be very difficult. The allies therefore decided to choose an area which was not a port and that would be thinly defended. They searched along the cost for a weak spot and they found Normandy.

Normandy was not a port city and it was not as heavily defended as real port cities. The British decided to tow an artificial harbour to Normandy and use it temporarily till the battle was over. Eventually, the day of invasion (D-day) came and the British and their allies were successful in establishing themselves in this relatively thinly defended coastal town called Normandy. Always remember that your enemy is looking for a weak spot. Your weak spots are of great interest to the enemy. He will invade you at your weak spot.

Weak Points Are Your Vulnerable Sides

Every minister has weak areas, which can be attacked. Every church also has weak areas that need strengthening. In these areas, you are more vulnerable to attack. The most common weak area in a minister's defences is his family. Your spouse and your children are often weak points through which attacks take place. Many of the terrible crises that ministers have endured have come through their families. In a family, everyone has a different level of spirituality. Some family members are more spiritual than others. Your great spirituality and convictions cannot cover all members of the family. People have to believe God for themselves especially when they are adults.

If your wife is less spiritual than you are, she becomes a weak point through which an attack can come. If your wife is beautiful, but quarrelsome, it becomes a weak point through which contention and confusion can enter. If your wife is stubborn and unyielding, it becomes a door through which witchcraft can enter your life.

Why a Spouse Can Be a Weak Point

A spouse can be a weak point in the ministry and open up the door to many potential evils. Why do I say this? Is marriage not supposed to provide you with a help meet for you? Is the helper you get not going to assist you to do better? The answer is "Yes" and "No!" Through marriage you can be helped greatly. But the same thing that is a blessing to you can be a weakness.

I believe all the books you have read, teach you why marriage is helpful for your ministry. The following points may explain why your spouse can be a weak spot and an entry point for Satan.

1. Marriage and having children must be a weak point because Jesus avoided it altogether. When heading towards the cross, Jesus could not be accused of irresponsibility towards His wife. He could not be accused of leaving his wife in the midst of her years to fend for herself. He had no woman to dissuade Him from dying on the cross.

    If even Peter tried to stop Him from dying on the cross, can you imagine what a wife would have done? She would have gone wild and opposed Him. She would have gone to the police and told them that her husband had become suicidal.

    She would have held up the children to Jesus, shaken them in his face and cried, "How do you expect us to survive? What will happen to us? Think of your family as well!" She would have wailed and wailed until Jesus changed His mind about His suicidal mission.

    But He had no wife or child in his life. He had no hindrance and no weak point. Jesus said, "Hereafter I will not talk much with you: for the prince of this world cometh, and hath nothing in me."

2. Your spouse can be a weak point because the Scripture says they that marry will have tribulation. "But and if thou marry, thou hast not sinned; and if a virgin marry, she hath not sinned. Nevertheless such shall have trouble in the flesh..." (1 Corinthians 7:28). The word trouble is the Greek work *thlipsis*. It means to be pressured, burdened, anguished and to have trouble and tribulation. This means that married people are going to have anguish, pressure, burdens, troubles and tribulations.

3. It is difficult to maintain unity between any two living human beings. When you are on your own, you do not have to maintain unity with anyone. You just flow along at your level. Being married, therefore opens the door to disunity. Many spouses disagree on most issues!

4. Your spouse can open the door to conflicts and quarrelling. When you are not married you do not have any conflicts over any issue. You just have your opinion and you move along with it. After marriage, the door to conflict and quarrelling is opened to you.

5. Your spouse can open the door to the problem of unforgiveness. Because you have expectations from your spouse, his or her failures to perform can lead you to bitterness. Many ministers are full of bitterness because they have unfulfilled expectations.

6. Your spouse can be a stumbling block of ingratitude. One party in the marriage is usually higher performing and the other party is usually lower performing. The high performer is usually subject to feelings of ingratitude. He wonders why the low performing partner does not show gratitude by performing well.

7. Your spouse can open you up to the danger of sexual temptation. Your spouse can open you up to sexual confusion and sexual frustration. Infrequent or discouraging sexual performances by a spouse can provoke the other spouse to seek happier times outside the marriage. You can be turned into an adulterer without realising what is happening to you.

8. Your spouse can force you into divorce. You may never have expected yourself to become a divorcee in this life. I know people who have been forced to divorce because their wives insisted on it. How could you become a divorcee if you had never been married?

9. Being married opens you to the dangers of sorrow, shock and death. Your spouse may die and leave you behind in sorrow, shock and death. If you are not married you will never receive a shocking message that your spouse is dead. Can you imagine how that message will change your life and lead you into depression and anguish?

10. Marriage opens you up to the possibility of being linked to someone with a personality defect or even a mental defect. Once your life is linked to this weakened person, a door is opened to many difficulties and possible attacks.

Why Children Can Be a Weak Point

1. Having children is also a weak point because your children make you more vulnerable to attack. We all know about the blessings of having children. To have many children is to have your quiver full of arrows and defenders. But children also open many doors to the enemy. Your children may not be as spiritual as you are. Their lives can be open doors to your enemy. The devil knows that if he attacks your children, he will get your attention. The more children you have, the more weak points you have!

2. Having children opens the door to potential disgrace. Your child can be a disgrace to you spiritually, academically, socially and in almost every other way.

3. Having children opens the door to potential financial difficulties. Children are the greatest expense that parents sometimes experience. There are many parents who steal money so they can look after their children. The more children you have, the more weak points you have. I know people who decided not to have children so they could focus on the ministry.

4. Having children opens the door to marital conflict. Many
    times children are the reason why parents have conflict.
    There are arguments about children and what should be
    done for them.

CHAPTER 49

A Good General Must Be Aware of the Long-Term and Short-Term Plans of the Enemy

Lest Satan should get an advantage of us: for WE ARE NOT IGNORANT of his devices.

2 Corinthians 2:11

There are many attacks of the enemy on the church of God. Unknown to most of us, there is a sinister long-term element to many of these attacks. Indeed, most of Satan's plans, schemes and devices are long-term.

You must consider each move that the enemy makes against you and ask yourself, "What is the long-term goal of this attack?" What are the real intentions of my enemy?

The Plans of an Enemy

In 1941, Adolf Hitler decided to invade the Soviet Union. The planned invasion was called Operation Barbarossa. On the surface, it looked like a simple invasion by one aggressive country against another. But that was not the case. There was much more to the invasion of Russia by Germany. Adolf Hitler had many long-term plans for the Soviet Union. These are some of the plans he had for the Soviet people.

1. A war of annihilation should be waged against the Soviet Union, which would violate all standards of civilized warfare and would be waged in the most inhumane way possible.

2. Germany would have all of Russia's oil, especially the rich Baku oil fields.

3. When the Soviet Union is defeated, labour shortage in German industries could be relieved. In other words, he saw the Soviets as a source of labour for his industries.

4. The Soviet people would be a vast source of forced labour under German rule.

5. When the Soviet Union is defeated, Ukraine would be a reliable source of agricultural products.

6. Entire urban populations of the invaded land (cities of the Soviet Union) were to be starved to death, thus creating an agricultural surplus to feed Germany.

7.   The urban populations of the Soviet Union would be replaced by the superior German upper class.

You can see from all these stated goals that Hitler's long-term plans for the Soviet Union were more terrible than the invasion itself. He had plans to turn the entire Soviet Union into a labour force, to starve entire cities to death and replace them with Germans.

So it is in every war! You must ask yourself, "What are the real long-term intentions of the invasion."

The Sex Attacks

What is a "sex attack"? A sex attack is an attack on your life and ministry through sex. A sex attack can happen to a man or a woman. Sex attacks are some of the commonest types of attacks on ministers. Sex attacks take many forms but the long-term goal of sex attacks are a hundred times more devastating than the short-term effects. You may not know that sex attacks are spiritual attacks, but they are! Sex is a very spiritual thing and the sex organs are portals through which spirits enter the human body (Revelation 18). Most Christians have been tempted at one time or the other to do something wrong sexually. On the surface, these attacks look like sexual mistakes that have no long-term consequences. We all assume that if confessed, God will forgive these sexual sins and the matter will be over. However, there are many long-term goals behind a sexual attack. These long-term plans of the enemy are not easy to discern. Indeed, when they materialise, you can hardly link what is happening to the sexual deed of yesteryear. There are three types of sex attacks that exist. "Fornication attacks", "low frequency and quality sex" attacks and "zero sex" attacks.

Fornication Attack

A certain smooth young man who had the attention of many girls thought that he was the king of kings and lord of lords as he went around from hen to hen. Initially, he thought he was just having a good time with all the different girls. When this brother finished university, he wanted to get married and found a nice Christian virgin whom he married.

However, after being married for some time, the brother realised that he was simply unable to faithfully stay with only one girl. He had grown up having sex with absolutely every girl he ever interacted with. Remember that this is not unusual for many young men. Most guys take a hundred women to bed, but one to the altar.

One day, the young man came to see the pastors. He was desperate because his marriage was breaking down as he was unable to remain faithful. When I spoke to him, he was a broken man. "I want to stop committing fornication, but I can't stop." His wife did not want to stay with him any longer.

I explained to him that few women would accept to stay with someone who sleeps with everyone they ever meet. The wife of this young man was faced with a difficult decision: Stay on in the marriage and risk catching HIV from the husband's uncontrollable sex life? The other option for the lady was to divorce her husband. Unfortunately for this brother, there was no woman who was willing to accept his helpless fornication lifestyle.

I remember another situation in which a brother who had lived a life of multiple and indiscriminate fornication, although married to a very beautiful girl, was unable to enjoy sex with her. Somehow, she never matched up to some of the exotic and energetic young ladies he had had sex with. Having sex with his wife even produced a guilt feeling for him.

Soon, this brother was having very little sex with his wife until he became a self-declared impotent and non-sexual man. His wife never knew why he was not aggressive or interested in having sex with her. In the long term, this brother's life of multiple and indiscriminate fornication had destroyed his ability to dwell normally with one woman. It had given rise to premature impotence and an abnormally low sex drive.

In yet another situation, a brother who lived continually in fornication simply developed HIV and began to die slowly. Unfortunately, his response to the HIV virus was poor and he succumbed quickly to the illness.

As you can see, there are many different ways in which a simple act of fornication plays out. You must always be aware of the long-term intentions and plans of the enemy. The long-term goal of the sex attack is actually the destruction of marriage, the destruction of normal living, the destruction of marital harmony and making it impossible for a couple to live together. Other long-term goals of a sex attack is sickness, disease and death. A good general engages in a campaign to foil the long-term plots of his enemy. Long-term plots are sometimes not easy to see or understand.

Low Frequency, Low Quality Sex Attacks

Your sexual needs are determined by how God created you – male or female. Christians have a lot of sexual problems.

The sexual life of pastors is a context for many of the long-term and short-term plans of the enemy. In my book, *Model Marriage*, I devised a "sex-o-meter", which measures the frequency of sex between couples. Some people mocked the existence of such a meter. Why mock me? Don't you realise that Satan also has a "sex-o-meter"? He is the one who watches the frequency and quality of your sexual life. If it were not so, how would he be able to know when you have not had sex for some time, so that he can tempt you? Is that not what Paul said? "Defraud ye not one the other, except it be with consent for a time, that ye may give yourselves to fasting and prayer; and come together again, that Satan tempt you not for your incontinency" (1 Corinthians 7:5). Satan tempts you based on your sexual frequency and quality. You can expect Satan or one of his agents to be in the bedroom with you to monitor the frequency and quality of your sex life.

A certain brother married to a Christian sister struggled to have sex often. There is always a reason why sex does not happen and cannot happen often. For some people, if it does happen, it is of the lowest quality in the world. This is called "hard-to-get" sex. Many people suffer from "hard to get" sex. This is a sex attack and it is spiritual in its nature. It is also called a "low frequency and quality" sex attack. In this case, sex is technically available to the man. But in reality, it is of the lowest frequency and of the lowest quality you can imagine. The quality of sex is so poor that it is undesirable.

The next step in this cleverly, thought-through sex attack is for the brother to find an eager, willing, beautiful young girl who does not have the grumpiness and bad attitude of his Christian wife who is always in church working for God. One of the cheapest things to find is a willing and eager girl who is ready to sleep with an important person.

Soon, this Christian husband is committing adultery with frisky, cheerful, chirping and energetic ladies. He has turned away from his "low frequency and quality" sex life and found many delightful alternatives. He has turned away from the "hard to get sex" to the "easy to get" sex.

He now says, "I like these young girls. They are like toy cars; when you press a button, they start moving!"

One lady said to me, "I have slept with so many married men whom I did not love. I did many fantastic and exotic things to them because I knew I would get a lot of money afterwards."

The Christian man is now enjoying fantastic and exotic things as compared to the hard to get, cold shoulder, busy chorister, grumpy old lady option in his bedroom.

What has been the long-term outcome of this type of sex attack? Adultery and unfaithfulness! But it may not end there. This situation may get worse and lead to divorce. Hatred for each other may develop in the marriage. The hatred could also lead to murder. As you can see, the sex attack has many long-term effects.

Zero Sex – Sex Attack

"Zero sex" is a situation where a man does not have sex at all. This can come about because he is unable to find someone he loves. He proposes to one girl after another but no one likes him. Some male students we interviewed in the university explained why they were engaged in sex with other boys in the school. They said, "The girls are very hard to get. They make fun of you and it is difficult to enter a relationship with them. Fellow brothers are much easier to get along with."

As a result, these young men in the university have become homosexually active. Recently, a man went on a rampage in the United States of America. He killed six people and eventually killed himself. He left a note saying that all the girls he tried to befriend refused him. No one liked him and he developed a hatred for anyone he felt was having sex.

When a young man is unable to get a wife, for whatever reason, the "zero sex" attack can turn him into a homosexual, a rapist or a pornographer. Some people also become rapists because they are unable to have a sexual release. Many young people, unable to have sex when they want, turn to pornography and become serial expert pornography students.

Perhaps, one of the saddest effects of the "zero sex" attack is when a husband or a father is turned towards other men for his sexual needs. A normal husband becomes someone who now has homosexual relationship with boys and men.

Many priests have been forced into a "zero sex" mode. This "zero sex" mode attack resulted in the priests becoming homosexuals and abusers of their power. As you can see, "zero sex" is also a spiritual attack with devastating spiritual consequences. It is only when you look at the long-term effects of "zero sex" or little sex and poor quality sex that you realise that it was actually an attack of the devil on your life. A good general must be aware of the long-term and short-term plans of the enemy!

Do you want to eventually become a rapist?

Do you want to eventually become a pornographer?

Do you want to eventually become an adulterer?

Do you want to eventually not have a home or family?

Do you want to be someone who can never get married?

Do you want to become a divorcee?

Do you want to eventually become homosexual?

Do you want to become someone who sleeps with both boys and girls?

If not, do not take any of these sex attacks lightly. Do not see fornication as something that just passes and goes away.

Do not see the absence of sex as a short-term, temporary problem.

Do not see "zero sex" as something with no long-term effect on you. A good general is very conscious of the long-term goals of his enemy. Brace yourself against all forms of sexual attacks. They all have long-term components, which will be activated against you. A good general must be aware of the long-term and short-term plans of his enemy!

CHAPTER 50

A Good General Must Judge by Actions

And David and all Israel went to Jerusalem, which is Jebus; where the Jebusites were, the inhabitants of the land.

And the inhabitants of Jebus said to David, Thou shalt not come hither. Nevertheless David took the castle of Zion, which is the city of David. AND DAVID SAID, WHOSOEVER SMITETH THE JEBUSITES FIRST SHALL BE CHIEF AND CAPTAIN. SO JOAB THE SON OF ZERUIAH WENT FIRST UP, AND WAS CHIEF. And David dwelt in the castle; therefore they called it the city of David.

1 Chronicles 11:4-7

King David judged Joab to be worthy of the position of commander of the armies based on his actions in the war against the Jebusites. "Whoever goes first will be the chief." Joab went first and became the chief commander of Israel's armies.

If a general has led his troops into destruction, he must be judged as a destroyer. What people say about themselves does not matter.

Who people say they are does not matter.

Look at their deeds. Their deeds do not lie.

A hard line of assessment is important in war. Assess pastors by the fruits they produce. Most ministers don't know and don't accept their faults.

YE SHALL KNOW THEM BY THEIR FRUITS. Do men gather grapes of thorns, or figs of thistles?

Matthew 7:16

Jesus taught us to know people by their fruits and not by what they say. Everyone says good things about himself and everyone has explanations for what they did not do. "Most men will proclaim every one his own goodness: but a faithful man who can find?" (Proverbs 20:6).

Over the years, I have come to think less and less of what people say. Sometimes, I know the exact explanation that would be given and I have learnt that they are all not true. The only thing that is true is the evidence and the actions that speak clearly and loudly.

In war you cannot afford to make the childish mistake of trusting what people say. You must trust what they do. What they do is who they are! In court, the judges have the mature task of ignoring the explanations that criminals give for their actions. They are taught to focus on the evidence because that is what really matters.

A Good General Must Judge by Actions

You cannot employ someone to work with you who has been disloyal to your fellow minister. This person comes to you with a thousand excuses and reasons why things went the way they did. But the evidence that stares at you is the fact that he has not been loyal to his former leader.

Why do you take this person on when you have evidence of treacherous behaviour in his previous position? You are getting married to a beautiful lady who has nice words and beautiful smiles, but quarrels with everyone she works with? Why do you marry this lady who is unable to maintain a good relationship with anyone?

Why do you believe her explanations?

Why do you believe in her beauty?

Why do you believe you will receive nice things when you marry her?

The evidence is there and if you are going to war, you cannot afford to ignore evidence, actions and hard facts. If the young lady is stubborn at home, why do you believe she is going to be submissive and yielding when she is your wife.

If you are going into the ministry, you are going to war. You cannot put your life and everyone's life into jeopardy by taking childish decisions that are based on what you see and hear.

Watch out for how people treat their husbands. That is who they really are!

If they are nasty, stubborn, rude and wicked to their husbands, that is who they really are. Do not believe their beautiful appearance and nice dressing. It is just outward paint! When you are going to war, depend more on the evidence and the actions of people. You must trust evidence more than nice words.

The Rubicon River

In the days of the Roman Empire, Roman generals would go out on great campaigns and conquer nations and territories, which they added to the empire. There was a time when there were three great generals, all operating at the same time and conquering territories for their empire.

Crassus, one of the generals, conquered lands and territories in the east but was killed when he tried to go as far as Alexander the Great did in Persia.

Pompey the Great also conquered great territories in the east but was an older statesman who had settled in Rome.

Julius Caesar, our most famous Roman general conquered lands and territories in Gaul (France). He also invaded Britain and took those territories for the empire.

These generals had great armies at their command and were so powerful that they threatened the peace and stability of the Roman Empire when they returned home. The generals would be welcomed in Rome and be celebrated for their great conquests. But they were asked to please not come to Rome with their armies. The presence of these powerful generals with their armies threatened the senate and the government in Rome. The generals were therefore given a marker beyond which they should not cross with their armies when they were on the way back to Rome. This marker was the Rubicon River. The Rubicon River is a small river in the northern part of Italy. Anyone coming home was not to cross the Rubicon River with troops.

Unfortunately, when Julius Caesar was returning from the Battle of Alesia he crossed the Rubicon River with his troops. When the news got to Rome that Julius Caesar had crossed the Rubicon River, the experienced and wise men in Rome knew that trouble was coming. Crossing the Rubicon River was enough evidence of looming war. What else do you want to see? What else do you want to discover? The crossing of the Rubicon River was enough evidence.

Pompey and most of the members of the senate needed no further evidence that Julius Caesar meant harm. They knew he was not just returning home for a party. Pompey and most of the members of the senate ran away from Rome. Pompey and the members of the senate were wise to leave Rome because Julius Caesar had said privately that, "I'd rather be the head of a village than number two in Rome."

As I have said, the evidence and the actions are the main thing. The crossing the Rubicon River was more than enough to show the intentions of Julius Caesar. Indeed, Julius Caesar pursued Pompey to Spain and finally defeated him in the battle of Pharsalus. Pompey escaped to Egypt but Julius Caesar pursued him there. Upon his arrival in Egypt, the citizens of Egypt handed the head of Pompey in a sack to him because they had assassinated him in advance for Julius Caesar. Julius Caesar was intent on eliminating any threat to his power base in Rome.

Pompey always knew that Julius Caesar was a very dangerous person. He probably envisaged that Julius Caesar would kill him. I am sure he was not surprised that he was eventually killed. The people in Egypt also had enough evidence that Julius Caesar was a ruthless man. They had no intention of fighting with Julius Caesar over Pompey.

Remember that a wise person lives by the evidence of the actions that people have taken. He does not trust what people say about themselves. Trust what they do and remember what they have done!

Everybody has a Rubicon River. Watch out for people who have crossed the Rubicon River! Don't take it lightly when somebody crosses the Rubicon River of your life! You have enough evidence.

CHAPTER 51

Identify Dangerous Enemies and Declare War on Them

And a man's foes shall be they of his own household.

Matthew 10:36

T o win a war, you must declare war. To win a war you must become war. First of all, you must identify men who are dangerous enemies. Secondly, you must identify behaviour that signals aggression and danger.

Thirdly, you must declare war on identified enemies. To win a war you must declare war and become war! As long as you have not declared war, forces will not mobilize themselves. The enemy is always happy that you have not declared war. The enemy always hopes that you will not notice that he is an enemy.

Many Christians believe that a man cannot be an enemy. This is because of the Scripture which says, "...we wrestle not against flesh and blood..." (Ephesians 6:12). In other words, "flesh and blood" can never be an enemy. But this is not true because Jesus told us that a man's enemies would even come from his own household.

There are many human beings who are as much your enemies as evil spirits are! Many human beings are enemies on whom you must declare war! It is time to grow up and mature in spiritual warfare. We are in a war and you must stop thinking like a child. You must know your enemy even if he comes all dressed in a suit and a tie! You must know your enemy even if he is your schoolmate!

You must know your enemy even if it is your best friend!

You must know your enemy even if it is your wife!

You must know your enemy even if he is a pastor!

You must know your enemy and declare war no matter what he looks like. If Jesus says your enemies are men in your own household, then so it is. Paul the apostle encountered several different men who were enemies of the gospel. You yourself as a human being were once an enemy of the gospel. Certainly, it is not only spirits that can be enemies. Human beings, flesh and blood can also be enemies. Here is a list of human enemies from the Bible.

1. You, yourself as a human being, were an enemy to the gospel and therefore to all those who preach the gospel. Remember that you are not a spirit but a human being. You are flesh and blood.

And YOU, that were sometime alienated and ENEMIES in your mind by wicked works, yet now hath he reconciled
                                                    Colossians 1:21

2. Men living in your own household can be enemies. A foe is an enemy.

And A MAN'S FOES shall be they of his own HOUSEHOLD.
                                                    Matthew 10:36

3. People that hate you are your enemies.

That we should be saved from OUR ENEMIES, and from the hand of all that hate us;
                                                    Luke 1:71

4. There are men (not spirits) who are your enemies and whom you are supposed to love and even lend money to. You cannot lend money to a spirit. You can only lend money to human beings.

But LOVE YE YOUR ENEMIES, and do good, and LEND, hoping for nothing again; and your reward shall be great, and ye shall be the children of the Highest: for he is kind unto the unthankful and to the evil.
                                                    Luke 6:35

5.   There are earthly-minded and fleshly men who are your enemies. These earthly-minded men who love their bellies so much are obviously not spirits. They are flesh and blood.

For many walk, of whom I have told you often, and now tell you even weeping, that they are THE ENEMIES OF THE CROSS OF CHRIST:

Whose end is destruction, whose God is their belly, and whose glory is in their shame, who mind earthly things.

Philippians 3:18-19

Enemies of Church Growth

There are also men who fight against the churches we are building. Building a church is a great effort to win souls, to gather them to the house of God and to teach them all things Jesus has entrusted to us. As we try to build the work of God, there are men who rise up as enemies of church growth. I certainly believe that there are spirits that are assigned to fight churches and to prevent church growth.

But there are also men who are spiritually empowered to cause stagnation and decline in church attendance. Who are these men and how do they operate? How do they spoil churches? What are they like? How come they are enemies of the church? This is what you must endeavour to find out.

When I first began to teach on these things people made fun of me. They said I did not have revelation and I was only teaching childish things. With time, however, many have realised that the enemies of the church were having a field day, as no one knew who they were. Satan was not happy when I mentioned their names and asked people to beware of them. Here is a shortlist of some of the top enemies of the church. These people are enemies of pastors. The works, manoeuvres and activities of these people are well laid out in some of my books. I have written a book about each of them so that people will know who they are and be ware of them.

Enemy No. 1: Those who leave you
   (*See my book "Those Who Leave You"*)

Enemy No. 2: Those who are disloyal
   (*See my book "Loyalty and Disloyalty"*)

Enemy No. 3: Those who accuse you
   (*See my book "Those Who Accuse You"*)

Enemy No. 4: Those who pretend
   (*See my book "Those Who Pretend"*)

Enemy No. 5: Those who forget
   (*See my book "Those Who Forget"*)

Enemy No. 6: Those who are dangerous sons
   (*See my book "Those Who Are Dangerous Sons"*)

Enemy No. 7: Those who are ignorant
   (*See my book "Those Who Are Ignorant"*)

You may ask why I wrote a book about each of them. Because I do not want them to roam about freely in churches! I want people to know that those who pretend, those who forget and those who accuse are dangerous people. I do not want those who leave to be considered innocent, when in fact they are destroyers of entire ministries and churches. I want people to beware of sons who are dangerous sons. I do not want you to go around ordaining and anointing dangerous enemies. If you anoint your enemy he will become an anointed enemy and will be even more effective in his campaign against you. It is time to declare war on all enemies whether they are spirits or men.

The Mistake of Not Identifying Adolf Hitler as a Dangerous Person

Adolf Hitler caused the deaths of fifty million people. Adolf Hitler was allowed to roam free and develop into the monster that he became. Instead of stopping this dangerous person, several negotiations and meetings were held with Hitler to appease him and grant him his wishes.

On the 29th of September 1938, Neville Chamberlain, Prime Minister of Britain, Edouard Daladier, Prime Minister of France, Benito Mussolini, Prime Minister of Italy and Adolf Hitler held a historic one-day conference in Munich. This Munich Conference was to discuss Hitler's aggression towards Czechoslovakia. Hitler strongly desired to invade Czechoslovakia under the pretext that lots of Germans were living in sections of the country. But the Munich Conference led to the Munich Agreement, which handed over a part of Czechoslovakia to Germany. This Munich agreement was supposed to appease Hitler and calm him down.

The Munich agreement seemed to be successful and Neville Chamberlain, the Prime Minister of Britain, was satisfied with the outcome and described it as "peace for our time". This particular phrase spoken by the British Prime Minister is primarily remembered for its irony because in less than a year, Europe was plunged into a world war. Hitler, on the other hand, was actually disappointed that a diplomatic solution had been found for the Czechoslovakia crisis. As a result of this Munich Conference and agreement, Adolf Hitler was selected to be *Time Magazine's Man of the Year in 1938*.

Instead of identifying and restricting a dangerous enemy, Adolf Hitler was being made Man of the Year! Little did they know the kind of firestorm Hitler was about to unleash onto the world.

This is what many Christians do. Instead of restricting, limiting, dismissing, stopping, marking and identifying dangerous people, we admire them, ordain them, elevate them and present them as honourable people to the congregation. When you ordain a devil he will be anointed to fight you.

CHAPTER 52

A Good General Is Visible

And Saul was afraid of David, because the Lord was with him, and was departed from Saul. Therefore Saul removed him from him, and made him his captain over a thousand; and HE WENT OUT AND CAME IN BEFORE THE PEOPLE. And David behaved himself wisely in all his ways; and the LORD was with him. Wherefore when Saul saw that he behaved himself very wisely, he was afraid of him. But all Israel and Judah loved David, because he went out and came in before them.

1 Samuel 18:12-16

King David, the great general, was seen going in and out in front of the people. A good general must be seen by his troops. War is messy and scary. Many people die horrible deaths on the battlefield. Perhaps the greatest inspiration for the troops is to see their leader in the thick of the battle and the danger with them. All the great generals were seen in the thick of the battle. They were seen risking their lives and fighting alongside their men.

This is why God does not send angels to be our pastors or shepherds. He uses ordinary people who live here on earth and experience the trials and tribulations that every normal human being on this earth does. When ordinary Christians who are struggling to live the Christian life look around and see their pastor wading through the same kind of mud, they are encouraged to press on.

Do not be discouraged when God allows you to experience trials, temptations and struggles in this life. Being a minister of the gospel is not the same as being an angel.

To be a minister is to be a struggler! A struggler in this difficult life of darkness, temptation and deception! I will say it again: To be a minister is to be a struggler! God wants the people to see that you are obeying Him even though you are struggling just like they are.

A good general is involved practically in the real fight for victory. People who are traditionally known as poor leaders, sit in armchairs and never get involved in the real problems. Such people cannot lead properly and have destroyed the nations that are subject to their kind of leadership. Look around at nations that are ruled by armchair leaders who sit at the back and never roll up their sleeves or get involved.

Many wars are truly foolish wars fought because of the lunacy of evil rulers. Many soldiers know they are fighting a foolish war for no good purpose. Many soldiers are aware that they are fighting to satisfy one person's grandiose delusions. For instance, the Second World War, which caused the deaths of fifty million people was fought to achieve the delusions of Adolf Hitler who wanted to build a superior German kingdom.

Famous Generals Fight from the Front

Alexander the Great was admired by his troops because he fought from the front. He rode his horse and walked ahead of his troops. Alexander the Great did not hide at the back in a golden luxurious carriage. He ate the same food and drank the same water that his troops did. Because he was with his troops, he knew their physical and emotional state and would not require something of them that was unreasonable or impossible.

Julius Caesar was also known to be close to the frontline, communicating constantly and encouraging his troops. Julius Caesar put himself in as much danger as his troops were. This raised the morale of the soldiers who fought alongside Julius Caesar.

CHAPTER 53

A Good General Knows How to Overcome Superior Enemies and Stalemates

And Saul and the men of Israel were gathered together, and pitched by the valley of Elah, and set the battle in array against the Philistines. And the Philistines stood on a mountain on the one side, and Israel stood on a mountain on the other side: and there was a valley between them.

And there went out a champion out of the camp of the Philistines, named Goliath, of Gath, whose height was six cubits and a span.

And he had an helmet of brass upon his head, and he was armed with a coat of mail; and the weight of the coat was five thousand shekels of brass.

And he had greaves of brass upon his legs, and a target of brass between his shoulders. And the staff of his spear was like a weaver's beam; and his spear's head weighed six hundred shekels of iron: and one bearing a shield went before him. And he stood and cried unto the armies of Israel, and said unto them, Why are ye come out to set your battle in array? am not I a Philistine, and ye servants to Saul? choose you a man for you, and let him come down to me.

If he be able to fight with me, and to kill me, then will we be your servants: but if I prevail against him, and kill him, then shall ye be our servants, and serve us.

And the Philistine said, I defy the armies of Israel this day; give me a man, that we may fight together.

1 Samuel 17:2-10

And it came to pass, when the Philistine arose, and came and drew nigh to meet David, that David hasted, and ran toward the army to meet the Philistine.

And David put his hand in his bag, and took thence a stone, and slang it, and smote the Philistine in his forehead, that the stone sunk into his forehead; and he fell upon his face to the earth.

SO DAVID PREVAILED OVER THE PHILISTINE WITH A SLING AND WITH A STONE, AND SMOTE THE PHILISTINE, AND SLEW HIM; BUT THERE WAS NO SWORD IN THE HAND OF DAVID.

Therefore David ran, and stood upon the Philistine, and took his sword, and drew it out of the sheath thereof, and slew him, and cut off his head therewith. And when the Philistines saw their champion was dead, they fled.

1 Samuel 17:48-51

The Philistines and the Israelites were engaged in a long battle in which neither could gain the upper hand. The Philistines had presented Goliath as the man to beat. If you were able to defeat Goliath then you won the war. The two sides stood across the valley looking at each other with neither being able to gain the upper hand.

There are many situations like that in the ministry, where old problems remain for years and you are not able to break out into the next level.

The new idea that broke the stalemate was a new and unknown warrior called David. This new warrior had a new weapon – a catapult. No one had used this weapon in a war and no one was expecting it. Goliath certainly was not expecting a little boy with six pebbles to approach him. He was taken off-guard and that was the end of the stalemate.

In church growth it is often difficult to cross the hundred barrier, the 200 barrier, the 500 barrier and the 1000 barrier. Your church may hover around a certain size for many years. Most pastors are locked in a stalemate. You cannot go forward and you cannot go backwards. To break stalemates, you need to be led by the Holy Spirit to introduce new ideas that you have not used before. In my book, *Church Growth,* I have eighteen different ideas that may break the stalemate in your quest for church growth.

If you are engaged in a power struggle with your associate, you may have to deploy a new idea different from your old ideas. The old ways have not worked that is why you are in your situation.

Continuing to do the same thing in the same way with the same intensity and expecting a change is madness. If you have been experiencing marital turmoil and conflict for many years, you need to think of a new approach to fight an old problem.

Sometimes the key you need is in a book. In that book you will find a new idea that may break the stalemate. That is why real leaders love books. They know that there could be a secret on a page that would make a difference to their whole lives and ministries. The story below is a story of a 1000-year long stalemate that was broken by a young man with some new ideas.

Siege of Constantinople

Constantinople (Istanbul) had been attacked many times over the centuries. For one thousand years no one had been able to overcome it. Indeed, new ideas were needed. Constantinople (present day Istanbul) was a great, fortified city that was once the headquarters of the Roman Empire. The Roman emperor Constantine established the city which remained an imperial capital from the time it was created in AD 330. Constantinople had special walls built by Constantine the Great. These walls later had numerous additions and modifications over the centuries and were one of the most complex and elaborate systems ever built.

The walls of Constantinople surrounded the city on all sides, protecting it against attack from both sea and land. A famous double line of walls was built by King Theodosius who lived in the 5th century. When well manned, the walls were virtually impregnable. Even when cannon technology was used, the walls could be repaired between reloading.

For one thousand years, Constantinople was a veritable fortress with impregnable walls. For ten centuries the city had been attacked and besieged many times but no one had been able to really conquer it. It had fended off attacks from the Latins, the Arabs, the Serbians, the Bulgarians and the Ottoman Turks.

But a good general knows how to overcome stalemates and superior enemies. For one thousand years, Constantinople stood undefeated and impregnable. But when Sultan Mehmed II became the new ruler of the Ottoman Empire, Constantinople was threatened again. Sultan Mehmed was a young man, only nineteen years old but he had new ideas. It is only with new ideas that you can overcome superior enemies.

His first step was to build an Ottoman fortress set directly across the straits from an older fortress built by his grandfather. These twin fortresses gained full control of the sea traffic for the Turks. Most of all, it cut off access to all ships that would want to come to the rescue of Constantinople.

Another new idea that the Ottomans introduced to the war on Constantinople was its ability to cast cannons. This was new technology and the men of Constantinople had no idea of the extent and power of the Ottoman's cannon.

A third new factor was a secret weapon called the Basilica, which was sold to the Ottoman Empire by an arms dealer called Orban (a Hungarian). Orban had boasted to Mehmed II that his cannon could "blast the walls of Babylon itself". This basilica created by Orban was 8.2 metres long, and able to hurl a 272 kilogram stone ball over a distance of 1.6km. Earlier on, Orban had tried to sell this weapon to the occupiers of Constantinople but they had been unable to secure the funds to pay for this special weapon.

Given abundant funds and materials, the Hungarian engineer built the gun within three months at Adrianople, from which it was dragged by sixty oxen to Constantinople. Orban's giant cannon was said to have been accompanied by a crew of over 400 men. Orban's cannon had some drawbacks. For instance, it took three hours to reload.

Mehmed planned to attack the Theodosian Walls of Constantinople, which were the intricate series of walls and ditches protecting Constantinople from an attack from the West, the only part of the city not surrounded by water.

Even if Constantinople was being attacked by one hundred and twenty-six ships, they were confident that the 20km of high walls around the city would hold out. In addition, they had a relatively well-equipped fleet of twenty-six ships that would help to protect the city till help came. Indeed it was claimed that Constantinople was "the best-defended city in Europe" at that time.

At the beginning of the siege, Mehmed's massive cannon fired on the walls for weeks, but due to its imprecision and extremely slow rate of reloading, the Byzantines were able to repair most of the damage after each shot, limiting the cannon's effect.

Constantinople had an internal harbour that was also protected. Emperor Constantine XI had ordered a huge chain to be placed at the mouth of the harbour. This chain, which floated on wooden logs, was strong enough to prevent any Turkish ship from entering the harbour. The Ottoman fleet, like other ships in the past, could not enter the harbour of Constantinople.

Mehmed came up with yet another new idea. He pulled his ships out of the sea and hauled them across the land to avoid the long chain that was blocking the harbour. Imagine rolling a fleet of ships across the land! The sudden appearance of the Ottoman fleet in the harbour demoralized the defenders of Constantinople greatly. From then on, the siege advanced with several frontal assaults on the land wall.

Shortly after midnight, successive waves of attackers breached sections of the walls and entered the city. A Venetian eyewitness to the siege, wrote in his diary that it was said that Constantine hanged himself at the moment when the Turks broke in at the San Romano gate, although his ultimate fate remains unknown.

Mehmed II allowed his troops to plunder the city for three days as it was customary. Soldiers fought over the possession of some of the spoils of war and all through the day the Turks made a great slaughter of Christians through the city. Thousands of civilians were killed and 30,000 civilians were enslaved or deported. Someone described blood flowing in the city like rainwater in the gutters after a sudden storm, and bodies of the Turks and Christians floating in the sea like melons along a canal.

After one thousand years, the stalemate was broken. The superior and mighty city of Constantinople was finally overcome by a young commander with new ideas. Your key to resolving stalemates lies in your imagination. Think outside the box! Use unexpected, flexible and unconventional methods. Sometimes you must deliberately act in a way that is contrary to normal expectations. It is time to break all longstanding stalemates in your life!

CHAPTER 54

A Good General Is Unpredictable

The wind bloweth where it listeth, and thou hearest the sound thereof, **BUT CANST NOT TELL WHENCE IT COMETH, AND WHITHER IT GOETH:** so is every one that is born of the Spirit.

John 3:8

The Holy Spirit is the mysterious and powerful third member of the Trinity. You cannot tell when He is coming and where He is going. All this adds to the mysterious power of the Holy Spirit. Many of us have tried to determine where and when the presence and power of God will manifest. Some have said, " If we pray in tongues for five hours the presence of God will appear." Others have said, "If we fast for seven days we will feel the glory of God." Others have thought, "If we hold our peace without chatting and jesting, the power of God will not leak away and we will experience a mighty move of the Spirit." And yet you and I have experienced the presence of God when we did not fast, when we did not pray and when we were chatting with our friends.

We have also fasted, prayed and waited on God without feeling anything at all. Indeed, the Holy Spirit is unpredictable in His ways, His plans and His presence. The wind blows and you cannot tell where it is coming from. That is how the Holy Spirit is. You can never tell when or how He is going to flow in our midst. A person who is born of the Spirit is as unpredictable as the wind. A good general will follow the Spirit's leading and become unpredictable in a good way. I am not talking about failing to turn up for your appointments or programmes. I am talking about not being predictable in your style, your moves, your plans and your activities. It is time to overcome familiarity by learning to be unpredictable.

Having a programme in the same way, at the same place every year and doing exactly the same things will cause your church members to glance at each other knowingly. They know what to expect and they know what is coming next. They begin to yawn and to sleep whilst you do exactly what they expected you to do. Repeating yourself in a very predictable way makes people familiar with you. And familiarity will stop the power of God from flowing in your ministry.

When Jesus went to His hometown, He could not perform miracles because of familiarity. He wanted to do great things but

He could not! (Mark 6:2). Why was the greatest power on earth prevented from flowing and blessing the people? Familiarity! Familiarity is the only thing that could stop the power of the Holy Spirit from working in the ministry of Jesus.

The presence of thousands of evil spirits in the mad man of Gadara were unable to stop the power from flowing. But familiarity was able to stop the flow of the Holy Spirit in the ministry of Jesus. In your ministry, those who are familiar can inhibit the move of God.

When you start to prophesy and move in the Spirit, questions will arise in their hearts. They will say, "But we know you! We know when you started! We know where you are from! We know everything about you! You are too predictable for us!" As soon as this attitude descends on the people they are unable to receive and the power of God is blocked. That is why a prophet is not accepted in his own home. In his home, they know everything about him. But outside his home, they know little. Learn this great quality of unpredictability so that you can escape the traps of familiarity and despisement that have been set for you. Have you ever wondered why human beings are able to catch wild animals? It is because they are very predictable. They always do the same things in the same way and at the same time. You should watch a snake trapper hunting for snakes. You will be amazed at how he will go to specific locations and uncover a snake to your amazement. When you are predictable you are easy to monitor and easy to trap. When a minister of the gospel is very predictable, the anointing and the power of God are neutralized by the spirit of familiarity.

Most people expect your behaviour to follow a known pattern. Your duty is to disappoint them. You must upset their expectations. Do ordinary and expected things sometimes, but combine it with unusual and unconventional decisions. Your ordinary ministry can become extra powerful when you are not so predictable.

German Predictability

Germans fought many winning battles in Europe. Their chief strategy was blitzkrieg. This was a lightning strike in which the German military would invade at top speed covering several miles in a short while. During the invasion of the southern part of Russia by the Germans, under what was known as Operation Blue, the blitz krieg strategy was not as successful as it had been a year earlier. One year earlier, the Germans had invaded Russia in what was known as Operation Barbarossa. During that operation, they had used the strategy of blitz krieg successfully. Through lightning strikes, the Germans had taken so much land in a short time.

Germans are known for their precision, their time keeping and their regimental behaviour. By the next year, the Russians had gotten used to the predictable style of a blitzkrieg attack and would simply outpace the invading Germans avoiding confrontation. This would allow the Soviets to strike back at the Germans who were now deep in their territory.

The Russians knew that the German planes would come at a particular time, followed by the tanks, etc., in a very regimented way. Their predictable pattern of attack allowed the Russians to predict exactly when the Germans would implement their blitz krieg strategy. This time, the Russians were ready and eventually defeated the Germans, driving them out of Russia. A good general must be unpredictable. Your strategy may be good, but too predictable to be successful!

CHAPTER 55

A Good General Is Worth Ten Thousand Men

But the people answered, Thou shalt not go forth: for if we flee away, they will not care for us; neither if half of us die, will they care for us: but now THOU ART WORTH TEN THOUSAND OF US: therefore now it is better that thou succour us out of the city.

2 Samuel 18:3

A good general is worth ten thousand men! Really? Is a good leader really worth ten thousand men? On the surface, it may not seem as though a good leader is worth ten thousand men. Truly, the value of a good leader is not understood by ignorant men.

Why do people study courses on valuation for several years at the university? Because it takes intelligence, deep thinking and excellent analysis to truly determine the value of something.

What then is the value of a good general? Is he worth two men, five men, ten men or a hundred men? The Bible says that he is worth ten thousand men. This is the value of a good leader.

Let us try to understand why a good general is worth ten thousand men.

Evidence That a Good General Is Worth Ten Thousand Men

1. Every outstanding victory in a war is attributed to the general and not to the masses that actually fought the war. Wars are remembered in the light of the great generals who actually commanded the troops. Sometimes a general could command up to three million men. Yet there is no mention of any of the men who actually fought. Only the general who commanded the troops is remembered.

2. Banks and multinationals give their good leaders value by paying them salaries and bonuses which are ten thousand times more than a clerk in the bank. Today, banks and multi-national corporations pay millions of dollars as bonuses to their chief executives. There are many protests about the bonuses of chief executives of banks. Here are a few examples:

    According to Forbes, the top three bonuses of 2013; a total of $84million, was paid to three top Wall Street executives; Michael Farrell, Ian Cumming and Leslie

Moonves. A former CEO of a real estate investment trust Annaly Capital Management, Michael Farrell received $29 million. Ian Cumming, CEO of Leucadia National Corp. and Leslie Moonves, CEO of CBS received $27.5 each.

The CEO of Nabors Industries received a bonus of $17.5 million.

The former CEO of Strategic Hotels & Resorts, Inc, also earned $16.5 million dollars whilst the CEO of GAMCO Investors earned $37million.

3.   Nations spend millions of dollars to choose one person to lead them. The great fuss that is made over elections is actually the great fuss that is being made over the selection of a good general.

4.   Every outstanding achievement of mankind such as going to the moon (Neil Armstrong), flying aeroplanes for the first time (the Wright brothers), creating electricity (Michael Faraday), heart transplants (Norman Shumway), creating of personal computers (Bill Gates), creating of new technology such as iPads and iPhones (Steve Jobs) are all attributed to particular men.

5.   Successful soccer teams that are worth millions of dollars and have won trophy after trophy have their successes usually attributed to one man – the coach. These teams have several players, reservists and thousands of fans. But over time the coach of the team is the one who is recognized as the real key to the success of the team.

6.   The absence of a good general is seen in the devastation, loss and death that comes to an army which is commandeered by a fool. All the men under his command are doomed.

7.   Perhaps, the greatest evidence that a good general is worth ten thousand men is seen in nations, where the

absence of good leaders has turned rich continents into a wilderness of backwardness, poverty and deprivation.

After over fifty years of self-rule, there is clear evidence that some nations have been led by fatally deficient and hopelessly incompetent leaders. Each new group of leaders that come into power have excuses of why they cannot succeed. Over time, their excuses for non-performance no longer work. We all know that they simply cannot lead. One good general in certain countries would transform the nation completely.

What to Do with a Valuable General

Protection is the key thing that must be done for a valuable general. He must be protected in all seven dimensions. In the account above, King David was not allowed to be exposed to too much danger. They called him the light of Israel. They said to David, "If you die, a darkness will descend on all our people. We must protect you at all costs."

1. A good and valuable general must be protected spiritually.

2. A good and valuable general must be protected from financial temptations and worries.

3. A good and valuable general must be protected from physical attack.

4. A good and valuable general must be protected from stress.

5. A good and valuable general must be protected from the public eye.

6. A good and valuable general must be protected from sexual attacks.

7. A good and valuable general must be protected from accusations.

CHAPTER 56

Expect Your Enemy
to Send A Woman

… I will give him her, that she may be a snare to him…

1 Samuel 18:21

Expect your enemy to send a woman. On three occasions we see women clearly being used as weapons to fight against the people of God.

1.   The Philistines sent Delilah as a weapon to fight against Samson and the Israelites.   Samson's openness to Delilah was a good opportunity for the enemy to use her. All of Delilah's softness, tenderness, sexuality and delightfulness were motivated by a reward. Many women are unmotivated to be pleasant.   They are ill natured unless there is a clear reward for their pleasantness.

And it came to pass afterward, that he loved a woman in the valley of Sorek, whose name was Delilah.

And the lords of THE PHILISTINES CAME UP UNTO HER, AND SAID UNTO HER, ENTICE HIM, and see wherein his great strength lieth, and by what means we may prevail against him, that we may bind him to afflict him: and we will give thee every one of us eleven hundred pieces of silver

Judges 16:4-5

2.   King Saul sent Michal as a weapon to fight against David. Saul perceived that David would eventually take his throne. He was agitated and wanted to destroy David. He thought of a plan to use his daughter, Michal, as a weapon against David. Michal was sent as a snare and a trap to lock David into a situation that he could never escape from. Many men of God are locked in; unable to escape from a marriage they have contracted. Because of their commitment to a life-long marriage without divorce they are truly trapped with a beast whose name is beauty.

And Michal Saul's daughter loved David: and they told Saul, and the thing pleased him. And Saul said, I WILL

GIVE HIM HER, THAT SHE MAY BE A SNARE TO HIM, and that the hand of the Philistines may be against him...

1 Samuel 18:20-21

3.   Antiochus the great sent a woman to destroy and corrupt his enemy. This woman was specifically sent to ruin the enemy. How many people's ministries have been ruined by women?

He will set his face to come with the power of his whole kingdom, bringing with him a proposal of peace which he will put into effect; HE WILL ALSO GIVE HIM THE DAUGHTER OF WOMEN TO RUIN IT. But she will not take a stand for him or be on his side.

Daniel 11:17 (NASB)

This use of women as weapons is standard practice by almost every enemy. Because we are fighting a war, you can expect all these strategies to be used against you. Dear pastor, expect women to be used against you. A woman can be used against you to destroy you. A normal man is attracted to women. A normal man is gentler and kinder towards women.

How can you know when a woman has been sent to you by an enemy? It is not so difficult if you really want to know! You must watch out for the signs of a motivated lady operating in and around you.

Many married women are highly unmotivated to be nice, soft, sexual or delightful. It takes a highly motivated woman to be used as a weapon of war against you. This very motivated woman will display unusual niceness, softness and sexuality. She will be full of softness, comforts and delights that will charm the average man. What he does not get from his unmotivated, disgruntled wife will be laid before him on a silver platter. The average man is taken in by pleasantness, cheerfulness and subtle sexual undertones.

Because of the beauty and charm of women, a man rarely thinks of a woman as an enemy.

This delightful creature cannot be a liar. This delightful creature cannot be a murderer or a killer. This is how men think. It is time to realize that you are at war. In war, women are used as spies and as secret agents.

Women are used by the enemy because they are beautiful and deceptive. Women are often used as weapons of deception, espionage, camouflage, forgery, and sabotage. Women are used for these things because they are good at lying and stubbornly concealing their lies. Look around and arm yourself in preparation to uncover delightful but deceptive agents sent into your life to have sex with you, to influence you and to confuse you.

The End of Genghis Khan

Genghis Khan was the conqueror of one of the largest empires in the world. His kingdom was the largest kingdom ever and extended across most of Europe and Asia. Genghis Khan had a strong appetite for women, choosing women of the highest rank.

He loved women with small noses, red lips, rounded hips, long silky hair and melodious voices.

When the women were not to his taste, he would send them to his officers' tents while he ravished several women at the same time.

It is said that he fathered more children than any one else in history. This is according to geneticists who have found some sixteen million people to be sharing similar genes with Genghis Khan.

His death came through a Tangut princess who went to bed

with him and killed him. She is said to have castrated him with a hidden dagger from which he never recovered.

Once again, we see the enemy coming in the form of a woman. This great warrior who conquered more territories than any other kingdom, including the Roman Empire, was brought to his end by the castrating knife of a princess. He was not killed in battle but in bed!

Make sure that your natural appetite and interest in women does not bring your life and ministry to an end. May you be delivered from the spirit of Genghis Khan. May you be delivered from the spirit of a Tangut princess who is sent to castrate you with a hidden spiritual dagger. The power of God is released to give you the upper hand in the battle against every woman that is sent into your life as a weapon.

CHAPTER 57

Fight with Technology

I wisdom dwell with prudence, and find out knowledge
of witty inventions.

Proverbs 8:12

Technology is the wisdom of witty inventions. A mobile phone, an iPad, a computer, an air conditioner, a television, a satellite, a video player are all witty inventions. To wage a good warfare, you must deploy every single witty invention that exists. Do not think that you do not need witty inventions to do well. Have you ever heard of the arms race? The arms race is a race for witty inventions.

The Great Mistake

The great mistake, when it comes to technology, is the assumption that it will come to you naturally and that you will find yourself using it anyway.

The great mistake is to sit and wait for technology to come to you. The great mistake is to assume that technology will find a way of finding you.

The great mistake is to think that you will not have to intentionally learn how to use technology. All nations that have used technology to fight and to win wars did so intentionally. Whilst they used their current technology, they assigned people to invent things in the hope that they would lay hands on something better than what they already had. It is time to do just that.

You must ask yourself, "What technologies exist that I do not use in my ministry?" Whilst everyone is using a tablet or an iPad you may still be using the printed page. You must decide to move ahead and actively acquire new technologies in your life so that you are not bereft of new inventions.

One day, whilst in Israel I noticed certain hi-tech gadgets that were being used commonly. The Holy Spirit impressed on me that that technology could be used in the church. I could not figure out what such a gadget could do in the house of God. I intentionally and consciously decided that this gadget should exist somewhere in my ministry. Today, it is one of the key instruments that we use in the ministry and has brought about many great improvements.

Uzziah was the king who used technology in his warfare. In the day he lived, he used engines invented by cunning men. Every invention you use will help you war a good warfare. Think about the internet. Sixty percent of traffic on the internet is pornography. Why would you not fight a good fight on the internet? The devil has already taken over sixty percent of the internet. The Bible is supportive of your use of technology to fight a good fight of faith. Notice the technology of king Uzziah.

The Technology of Uzziah

Moreover Uzziah had an host of fighting men, that went out to war by bands, according to the number of their account by the hand of Jeiel the scribe and Maaseiah the ruler, under the hand of Hananiah, one of the king's captains.

The whole number of the chief of the fathers of the mighty men of valour were two thousand and six hundred.

And under their hand was an army, three hundred thousand and seven thousand and five hundred, that made war with mighty power, to help the king against the enemy.

And Uzziah prepared for them throughout all the host shields, and spears, and helmets, and habergeons, and bows, and slings to cast stones. And HE MADE IN JERUSALEM ENGINES, INVENTED BY CUNNING MEN, to be on the towers and upon the bulwarks, to shoot arrows and great stones withal. And his name spread far abroad; for he was marvellously helped, till he was strong.

2 Chronicles 26:11-15

There was a time when military men felt that wars could be won by having more men fighting. In fact, by the end of the First World War it was believed that you should outnumber your enemy by a ratio of three to one.

These theories were about to be dispensed with as new technologies would change the very nature of war. Germany lost the First World War that ended in 1918. The Germans realised that their defeat had come about due to new inventions like the tank and aeroplanes. The Germans, therefore, invested heavily in developing these ideas. The British who had won the First World War, largely with manpower, felt confident that good leadership and large numbers of committed soldiers would win the day, any day.

By 1939, the Germans had developed tanks (panzers) and had large armoured divisions of tanks whereas the British did not have even one armoured division.

The Germans had also introduced newer, faster military aircraft such as fighters and dive bombers.

When the Second World War started, Germany invaded Poland who were completely bereft of technology. Poland had a sizeable army of one million men, with which they hoped to withstand Germany.

Poland was still using a horseback cavalry! When the Germans came out with their tanks, the Poles charged on them with their horses.

This was to be the last time horses would be used to fight a war in our modern world. The Polish army were quickly defeated by the modern mechanized German army of tanks and planes. What good are soldiers on horseback in a modern hi-tech world?

Perhaps, they thought they were still in the days of Robin Hood! Within a few days, Poland was completely subject to the highly developed technological force of Germany.

Dear Christian friend, perhaps you are just like the Polish army in 1939. You believe strongly in your old ways. You are fighting the war of ministry with horses whilst others are fighting with tanks and planes. Where is technology in your life? How aggressively do you acquire new technologies? Do you want to be Robin Hood in a modern world? Do you want to fight with manpower when no one does that any more? Fight with technology!

CHAPTER 58

Fight by Building

There was a little city, and few men within it; and there came a great king against it, and BESIEGED IT, AND BUILT GREAT BULWARKS against it:

Ecclesiastes 9:14

Building is an act of war! One of the ways to fight a war is to build things. War is about land, space and buildings. The devil is trying to take over the earth and God has sent us to win territories for Jesus. A good general will build when he has to, knowing that construction is an important part of war. The Scripture above shows us that a conqueror knows all about building.

Buildings solidify your gains and stabilize you for the future. Buildings can be a defence in time of difficulty and need. Many denominations are still in existence because of their buildings. Churches tend to disappear into thin air after some years. Without buildings many of the great churches you and I know would not exist today.

Defend yourself against future attacks by building structures and constructing things to the glory of God.

Have you ever wondered why the Israelis keep building in certain occupied territories? Have you ever wondered why there is so much resistance to this construction? It is because the building of concrete structures makes victory permanent and brings even more stability to the conqueror. The lack of a building makes it more difficult for churches to thrive. It is not that easy to lead people out of an established building and into an open space. You may convince some people to follow you but many will not be convinced because you are not leading them into a higher level of establishment.

Many Christians are carnally oriented and respond to carnal leadership. Carnal people need to see natural and human power. Natural human power is based on what you see.

Carnal Christians are stabilized by the church buildings in which they worship. You can stabilize many people with a church building. Real buildings give the outward impression of permanence and stability.

Get ready to lose all your members one day if you do not build something! Don't be surprised if you are left with nothing in the future. If you are a good general you must know how to build. Building is an act of war! Building is an act of defence! Building and construction is the art of sealing your victory with a stamp of permanence.

Julius Caesar

Julius Caesar is the name we all remember when we think about the Roman emperors. He was the most famous of the Roman Emperors and the month of July is named after him. Each of the Roman generals became powerful by going abroad and conquering new lands and territories for the empire.

The Roman general most famous for fighting with the Gauls was Julius Caesar.

Julius Caesar in particular conquered many territories in Gaul, modern-day France. I am sure that you have read some comic stories from the Asterix series. In that comic series, Asterix, Obelix, Getafix, Geriatrix, etc. are fighters from Gaul who fought against the Roman armies of Julius Caesar.

One battle of note between the Gauls and the Romans was the Battle of Alesia. The battle of Alesia was also Julius Caesar's greatest military triumph. Julius Caesar won this war by creating a super siege.

The siege of Alesia came about because the Gauls, led by Vercingetorix had revolted against Roman rule and Julius Caesar was in hot pursuit of them. He caught up with them at Alesia, a fortified Gallic city. Alesia was on a hill and surrounded by rivers and valleys, and therefore offered a strong defensive position. Arriving with his army, Caesar decided to lay siege to the town.

Caesar expected the siege to be brief. To ensure that Alesia was fully cut off from aid, Julius Caesar instructed his men to build an encircling set of fortifications. Julius Caesar set about to build an eleven mile long set of walls, ditches, watchtowers, and traps. This first wall was to prevent the people of Alesia from escaping.

Vercingetorix, the Gallic general, launched several attacks to prevent the completion of this eleven mile long wall. During one of these attacks, a small force of a Gallic army escaped to bring reinforcements to help the army in Alesia.

Julius Caesar promptly set about to build a second set of identical walls, ditches and traps. This second wall was thirteen miles long. This second wall was to prevent any army from coming to rescue the people within Alesia. Now the city of Alesia was surrounded by two rows of walls.

Julius Caesar himself occupied the space between the two walls. Through his determination and ability to build two sets of walls and traps, the city of Alesia was isolated and conditions quickly deteriorated as food became scarce.

Hoping to alleviate the crisis, the Gauls sent out their women and children with the hope that Caesar would have pity on them and allow them to leave. But Julius Caesar, the builder of the super siege had no mercy on the women and children and left them to starve outside the walls. As the women and children starved, the morale of the soldiers in the town was destroyed.

The Gauls within the city did receive help from an external Gallic army that came to their aid. They launched an attack on Julius Caesar from outside while the besieged forces forced an attack from the inside. Through the leadership of Julius Caesar and Mark Anthony, the Gauls were defeated on both sides.

With the Gauls unable to break out of Julius Caesar's siege, their leader, Vercingetorix, surrendered himself to the victorious Caesar who promptly executed him.

Indeed, Julius Caesar defeated the Gauls through his super construction efforts in building two sets of walls, one eleven miles long and another thirteen miles long. Building is an act of war!

Become a builder and you will be a successful fighter.

Through building, you will overcome many enemies and secure yourself for the future.

CHAPTER 59

Encircle Your Enemy

The Philistines made yet another raid in the valley.

David inquired again of God, and God said to him, "YOU SHALL NOT GO UP AFTER THEM; CIRCLE AROUND BEHIND THEM AND COME AT THEM IN FRONT OF THE BALSAM TREES.

It shall be when you hear the sound of marching in the tops of the balsam trees, then you shall go out to battle, for God will have gone out before you to strike the army of the Philistines."

David did just as God had commanded him, and they struck down the army of the Philistines from Gibeon even as far as Gezer.

1 Chronicles 14:13-16 (NASB)

Encirclement is a military strategy that has been used throughout the centuries by military leaders, including generals such as Alexander the Great, Hannibal, Sun Tzu, Shaka Zulu, Napoleon, Zhukov and King David of Israel.

Encirclement is a military term for the situation where an enemy is isolated and completely surrounded by enemy forces.

This situation is highly dangerous for the encircled enemy. The encircled enemy cannot receive supplies, help or reinforcement. This gradually weakens the enemy who is not happy to be within the circle. The encircled enemy becomes desperate because he cannot escape from any side. On the other hand, an encircled enemy can be very dangerous because he is desperate.

Encirclement of Stalingrad

Germany started the Second World War by invading Poland and other western countries. After successfully overpowering these nations, they made the mistake of invading the Soviet Union. In 1941, Germany attempted to take Moscow but were stopped by the stubborn resistance of the Soviet army. It seemed Adolf Hitler had not learnt anything from his failure to capture Moscow so he decided in 1942 to stage another invasion, this time towards Stalingrad.

Stalingrad was a very important city in the southern part of Russia. This invasion of Stalingrad was called "Operation Blue". At Stalingrad, Hitler failed again. The entire army that he had sent into Russia was encircled and crushed. This is how it happened.

The Germans started their attack on Stalingrad, Operation Blue, on 28 June 1942 under the command of General Friedrich von Paulus. The Germans were fully expecting a quick victory as they pushed the Soviet forces back and penetrated the Soviet Union until they got to the Volga River where Stalingrad is situated. They sang patriotic songs, even taking time off to visit Mount Elbus, planted a Nazi flag and claimed it for Germany.

The swift German advance alarmed Stalin (Russia's Premier) so much that he issued his infamous "not one step back" directive of 28 July, ordering execution for the slightest sign of defeatism. Behind the Soviet frontlines roamed a second Soviet line ready to shoot any retreating "cowards" or "traitors of the Motherland". As Georgy Zhukov, one of Stalin's top generals said, "In the Red Army it takes a very brave man to be a coward."

By 23 August 1942, the German advance had reached the outskirts of Stalingrad and, with 600 planes, unleashed a devastating aerial bombardment. Entering the city, the Germans, along with units from Italy, Romania and Hungary fought the Russians street to street, house to house and sometimes, room to room. This, as the Germans called it, was rat warfare, where a strategic stronghold would change sides many times. The frontlines of the war were so close that one could throw back a grenade before it exploded. A soldier's life expectancy in Stalingrad was three days.

But the Soviet army led by General Zhukov launched a well-planned counter attack to encircle the Germans who had invaded Stalingrad. The Soviets came sweeping in from two different directions and within four days they had totally encircled the German forces in Stalingrad. The encirclement was so swift that the Soviet camera crews missed the moment and battalions of soldiers had to re-enact the essential moves for the benefit of the cameras. The Soviets squeezed the 250,000 Germans tighter and tighter. As the feared Russian winter set in the temperatures dropped to the minus forties. The German army was cut off and began to perish from starvation, frostbite, disease and suicide.

The German air force, promised Hitler that their planes could drop 500 tons of supplies each day into Stalingrad to supply the encircled Germans with their needs. But the Soviet anti-aircraft guns and poor weather prevented most of these supplies from getting to the encircled German army.

Meanwhile the frozen bodies of German soldiers and horses were piled up and used as sandbags. The remaining starving Germans resorted to eating rats and raw horse flesh.

By January 24th, the encirclement of the German forces was complete and airtight. General Paulus requested permission to surrender. He was completely encircled. General Zhukov of the Russian army had completely surrounded General Paulus. General Paulus sent a message to Adolf Hitler, "Troops without ammunition or food. Effective command no longer possible. 18,000 wounded without any supplies or dressings or drugs. Further defence senseless. Collapse inevitable. Army requests immediate permission to surrender in order to save lives of remaining troops." Hitler refused to give permission for the German surrender saying they should stand fast to the last man even though they were encircled.

By 26 January 1943, the encircled German army was trapped in two small pockets of the city.

Despite the hopeless situation, Hitler still refused to give permission to surrender. Instead, he promoted General Paulus to the rank of Field Marshal on the 30th of January. Hitler followed this by bestowing over a hundred field promotions, hoping it would inspire Paulus and his command staff not to surrender. Adolf Hitler was hoping that General Paulus would not surrender because no German Field Marshal had ever surrendered. However, on 31st January 1943, General Paulus surrendered. General Paulus later explained that being a strong Catholic, he had no intention of committing suicide. He is quoted to have said, "I [had] no intention of shooting myself for this Bohemian corporal" (referring to Hitler).

Thus the Battle of Stalingrad ended on Sunday, January 31, 1943.

Out of an original force of 285,000 soldiers, 165,000 had died in Stalingrad, while some 29,000 wounded had been air lifted out.

The 91,000 survivors, including 24 generals and 2,500 officers, hobbled off in the snow to begin years of captivity in Russian prisoner of war camps in Siberia.

Only five thousand would survive the ordeal and return home. The Germans knew how badly they would be treated in captivity because they had not treated Russian prisoners of war well. Russian casualties at Stalingrad are estimated at a million dead.

After the defeat of Stalingrad, embittered General Paulus, who had been encircled by the Russians, turned against his country.

Encircle Disloyal Enemies

To encircle the enemy is to give the enemy no option and to wipe him out. The strategy of encircling your enemy must be used to crush difficult enemies who have invaded your territory. Just as Hitler's invading army was encircled, you must encircle invading disloyal forces that penetrate the church. Hitler regretted sending his army all the way to Stalingrad only to be encircled and wiped out. Your enemy will regret invading your space when you use this strategy.

Today, disloyalty, treachery, confusion, forgetfulness, ungratefulness have invaded the church.

These enemies have come to take away love, unity and harmony, which are needed to build churches. These enemies are those who are disloyal, those who forget, those who leave you, those who pretend, those who accuse and those who are dangerous sons. It is time to encircle these characters and give them no more options to operate and manoeuvre within our church space.

How can you encircle the enemies of unity and loyalty? You can encircle the enemy by repeatedly teaching on loyalty and disloyalty. Teach it on Sundays, teach it on Tuesdays, teach it on Fridays and teach it on any day possible!

Encircle the enemy of disloyalty by teaching against it in large conferences, in medium-sized meetings, in small groups, and even to individuals.

Encircle the enemy of disloyalty by teaching against disloyalty and confusion at all times. You can preach against it in the morning, at midday and in the evening. Don't restrict the teachings against disloyalty to any particular time.

Encircle the enemy of disloyalty by teaching against accusations and disloyalty yourself, or by inviting others to teach on them. You can even ask disloyal people within your church to teach sessions on loyalty. This sometimes causes the person to self-correct.

Encircle the enemy of disloyalty by filling your church with books, videos, documentaries and other programs that fight against disloyalty.

Encircle the enemy of disloyalty and crush disloyalty by sacking rebellious people and not welcoming disloyal people to come around any longer after they leave.

The enemy of disloyalty will not flourish when you take such measures. He will be surrounded, encircled, crushed and eliminated.

Just like General Zhukov who captured twenty-four generals and one field marshal in his encirclement of Stalingrad, you will also capture the accusers, the opinion leaders, the proud men and conspirators of your ministry.

CHAPTER 60

Fight with All Your Weapons

Put on THE WHOLE ARMOUR of God, that ye may be able to stand against the wiles of the devil.

Ephesians 6:11

To fight a war you must be well equipped. An ordinary civilian need not be armed and clothed in heavy metallic armour. He is not going to be attacked by anyone. But a soldier fighting in a war needs all these equipment. Are you in a war or not? Are you fighting or are you playing games?

The Lord has honoured us by placing us in the last battle. God knows the dangers we are in. That is why we are told to use all the necessary equipment and armour. The spiritual war we are in requires wide-ranging defensive armour. The Bible describes the armour of God but most ministers take it lightly. Most ministers of the gospel take no notice of this list of powerful life-saving equipment. Indeed, the armour of God seems vague in its ability to protect a minister from attacks of the devil.

But the armour of God only looks weak and ineffective to you because you are not experienced in long-term spiritual warfare with the kingdom of darkness. All ministers who are lacking in this armour are doomed to destruction. Destruction is what happened to secular generals who did not take their weapons seriously. "For the weapons of our warfare are not carnal, but mighty through God to the pulling down of strong holds." (2 Corinthians 10:4).

All good generals ensured that their soldiers were well-equipped with specific and intentionally designed armour. The success of their campaigns depended on the equipping of each soldier with a set of war-winning equipment. You must ensure that all soldiers are well equipped for the fight that lies ahead. Notice how each of the well-known generals had specially designed equipment for their armies.

Shaka Zulu and the Iklwa

Shaka, the famous Zulu general, felt that the longer throwing spears were not helpful in winning wars. He decided to introduce a new variant of the commonly used Zulu spear. He invented a shorter spear used more for stabbing which had a larger and broader blade. This weapon was known as iklwa after the sound that was heard as it was withdrawn from its victim. Amazingly, this new weapon gave them a terrifying advantage over their opponents who were used to throwing spears but avoided hand to hand conflict. Shaka Zulu also introduced a larger heavier shield made of cowhide and taught his soldiers how to use the left side of the shield to hook and draw their enemy's shield to the right, exposing their ribs for a fatal spear stab. This equipment greatly transformed Shaka Zulu's soldiers into an unbeatable force in the South African realm. Indeed, if you want to win a war, you must equip your soldiers with effective and powerful weapons.

Hannibal and the Elephants

Hannibal also supplied his army with elephants and took them along with him through the icy Italian Alps. Hannibal considered his elephants so vital that he refused to leave them behind in Africa. Every good general knows what equipping an army will do for him. Hannibal terrified his enemies by charging on them with the elephants. The elephants trampled down and crushed their terrified enemies before they knew what happened.

Hitler and the Winter Clothing

The invasion of Russia by Germany during the Second World War ended up in disaster for the Germans. The German armed forces marched up to the gates of Moscow but were neither able to enter Moscow nor were they able to defeat the Soviet army. This was the first time that Adolf Hitler's lightning wars had not worked according to plan. The Germans had started this invasion in June and expected to subdue Russia within a few weeks. Due to several miscalculations the invasion ended in disaster. One of the miscalculations by Germany was that the war would be over in six weeks.

This over-estimation of the speed with which they would conquer Russia caused the German army to be poorly equipped to fight this war. It was basically the lack of supplies, lack of food and lack of equipment that caused the defeat of the Germans.

The Germans lacked tanks that could drive through snow and mud. The Germans lacked food supplies to keep them going. The Germans lacked the chemicals that would keep their fuel from freezing. They had to light fires under the fuel tanks to melt the frozen fuel. The Germans lacked winter clothing to keep them warm and alive in the terrible Russian winter. Most of their soldiers froze to death on the field. They were not expecting to be out in the open at that time of the year.

In a dramatic way, the undefeated and seemingly invincible German army was crushed in Russia because of a lack of equipment.

The Romans and the Ballista, the Polybolos and the Scorpio

The Romans equipped their armies with catapult type weapons that were able to throw missiles at the enemy. Three common ones were the ballista, the scorpio and the polybolos which were capable of launching large missiles at the enemy.

The ballista was an ancient missile-throwing weapon. It could throw large objects at a distant target. Julius Caesar was known to have used this weapon in the siege of Alesia. These projectiles could break the walls of cities and punch giant holes in the defences of the enemy.

The scorpio was a smaller catapult type weapon which could be operated by one man. This catapult used a system of torsion springs and was basically a giant crossbow capable of cutting down any enemy within a distance of a hundred metres.

The polybolos was a special ballista or catapult which could fire again and again without needing to re-load (a kind of ancient machine gun). With this terrifying array of killer catapults, the Romans were a terrifying army to encounter.

Today, the absence of military equipment is showing in the church. It seems as though all is well because there are many mega churches and many pastors on television. But if you look closely at the statistics, you will find that the church is not really growing. Other religions are having a field day and expanding into territories that were once Christian strongholds. The basic reason for this is the lack of military spiritual equipment. An army where many of the soldiers do not have guns is going to be mowed down and annihilated.

Would you like to be sent out on the battlefield without a gun? Are you going to use your bare hands to fight the machine guns of your enemy?

The Effect of the Absence of Weapons

1. **The absence of the helmet of salvation (Ephesians 6:17)**: The helmet of salvation is the consciousness of salvation in your ministry. Today, many ministers are not conscious of salvation. Sermons are preached without salvation altar calls. Many pastors cannot preach extensively about salvation. Salvation is a little known subject in charismatic circles today. It is considered a basic topic. Someone described me as a pastor without revelation because I preach about salvation. He said, "He preaches the basics and lacks revelation." The absence of the helmet of salvation has opened up the church to seek out other fields of endeavour. Many ministers are therefore proudly engaged in business, politics and secular education. Instead of becoming anointed pastors and evangelists, ministers of the gospel are proudly becoming chief executive officers of multi-national companies. Evil spirits have happily invaded the church because of the lack of consciousness of salvation.

2. **The absence of the breastplate of righteousness (Ephesians 6:14)**: The breastplate of righteousness is the second piece of equipment. Righteousness is a broad defence against powerful accusations. In the ministry, you will be accused of almost every imaginable sin. The longer you stay in ministry, the more varied and extensive your accusations will be. What will you do

to defend yourself against the stories and ideas that are peddled about you? Your biggest defence against wicked accusations is the fact that you have not done any of the things that you are being accused of. This is why righteousness is called the breastplate of righteousness. Righteousness is a broad defence against your wicked and hateful enemy. Without the breastplate of righteousness you are done for. All the things your enemy says about you are true and you will pay the price for your sins. Mercies upon mercies!

3. **The absence of the belt of truth (Ephesians 6:14)**: The third and critical piece of the armour is the belt of truth. The belt of truth holds everything in place. When truth and sincerity are set aside, things fall apart. It takes the belt of truth to engage in self-analysis, self-criticism and self-judgment. The church is failing because the foundation of truth telling is not there. I once encountered a demon which had entered a Christian, causing him to fall away into various sins. The evil spirit said plainly that he had been able to enter this individual because the belt of truth was loose. What a shock! Demons can see when truth, honesty and sincerity are missing or lacking in your life. You better tighten your belt of truth.

One minister of the gospel was invited to preach in a church. He was unwell and unable to make the commitment. He called the pastor who had invited him and asked him to lie to the congregation that he had had to travel urgently to Europe. This was an unnecessary lie because the pastor had not done anything wrong by not going for that programme. He was genuinely unwell and unable to preach. A minister of the gospel can become used to telling lies but this is a dangerous practice. Lies open up the door to Satan. Satan is the father of lies. Anytime you notice a lie or a liar, there will be evil spirits somewhere in the vicinity.

4. **The absence of the soldier's shoes (Ephesians 6:15)**: The fourth piece of equipment that can be dangerously absent are the shoes of the preparation of the gospel. The preaching of the gospel involves movement, travelling and preaching about salvation.

   When the church retires from travelling to preach the gospel, it opens itself up to a host of evils. Today, the church of God is weak and blind because great men of God no longer travel to conduct evangelistic crusades in the nations of the world. It is assumed that Christianity has spread everywhere. But that is not the case! Christianity has not spread everywhere.

   A church on the move that preaches the gospel is different from a stagnating church which is just celebrating anniversaries, renovating its old buildings, re-carpeting and re-air conditioning its facilities whilst multitudes go to Hell! When your feet are shod with the gospel, a new life and new favour will come into the church. Expect danger in your life as you sit at home. You can expect to be struck with sudden fear as you neglect to move around and preach the Word of God.

5. **The absence of the shield (Ephesians 6:16)**: The shield of faith is another important piece of defensive equipment. The absence of faith is catastrophic. Without faith the church no longer pleases God. Without faith you no longer love God and you no longer obey Him.

6. **The absence of the sword (Ephesians 6:17)**: The absence of the sixth piece of equipment - the sword of the Spirit, is suicidal, to say the least. The sword of the spirit is the only offensive weapon we have. Most people see the Word of God as a weak and ineffectual weapon, but it is actually very powerful. It takes one out of forty million sperms to achieve a pregnancy, but it takes only one out of four doses of the Word of God to produce a

result. The Word of God is a very effective seed. It is a sword that cuts away nonsense and gets to the bottom of the issues in our lives.

The Bible contains the word of God that you need. It is essential for the war.

Certain books contain the word of God for your life. These books are essential equipment for you.

Certain conferences will have the word of God that you need in your life and ministry. The videos of these conferences are essential equipment for your war. Certain preaching messages contain vital truths and nuggets of wisdom. The audio CDs of these messages are essential equipment for your life.

Certain TV broadcasts contain the word of God that you need. Having access to that TV station is essential equipment for your ministry.

Certain radio broadcasts contain the word of God that you need. Having access to that radio station is essential equipment for you.

Certain websites contain keys of wisdom, knowledge, understanding and counsel for your life and ministry.

Certain podcasts will lead you on the road to humility, love, holiness and faith.

To leave any of these out of your life is like Hannibal leaving his elephants behind. To forget to take your books, your tapes and your Bibles is like a Roman soldier who leaves his ballista, scorpio and polybolos behind.

7. **The absence of prayer (Ephesians 6:18)**: The absence of prayer is the absence of the mighty two-way weapon. Prayer is both defensive and offensive. Prayer is a mighty defence against the onslaught of the enemy. Prayer is also the key that makes God involved in a

practical way in your life. Whatever you ask God will
be answered. Whatever you request will be given to you.
Why not spend time in prayer! Prayer is your best two-
way weapon. You can attack with it and you can defend
yourself with it.

CHAPTER 61

As Long As the Enemy is Not Completely Defeated, He May Defeat You

And when the devil had ended all the temptation, he departed from him for a season.

Luke 4:13

Satan is well known for his repetitive attacks. Anyone fighting the good fight of faith must expect repeated attacks of the same kind. As long as your enemy is not completely defeated, he may defeat you. Satan has been defeated but is not completely defeated and eliminated. When Jesus encountered the devil in the wilderness, He defeated him but the devil was not completely wiped out. This same devil re-appeared in Jesus' ministry on several occasions tempting Him, testing Him and even accusing Him. Even on the cross, Jesus was tempted with the exact same temptation He experienced at the beginning in the wilderness. Because your enemy is not totally defeated, you must expect him to return again and again. You must expect your enemy who is not totally defeated to try many times to destroy you. No matter how old you are and no matter how long you have been fighting the enemy, you cannot rest in this world.

I once saw a man of God who had served the Lord for almost eighty years being attacked by the elders in his church. These people had been pastored, taught and loved for more than fifty years. And yet they rose up to destroy their pastor in his old age. It was unbelievable but real. Satan is not yet defeated. He may be quietened and subdued, but he is alive and planning another onslaught.

Never think that you have won the fight. There is a demon spirit standing in your room that looks like half human, half goat. That entity is seeking a way to get at you. Satan considers your triumphs as fleeting victories.

There is clear evidence that the devil is not totally defeated today. Let me give you some scriptural reasons that prove this reality.

1. The devils said to Jesus, "Have you come to torment us before the time?" There seems to be a time that has been set for the punishment of the devil. Since God is fair and just, He seems to be keeping to that timetable. The evil

spirits know that they have a time when their punishment will be due. This reality makes them desperate but also allows them to exist in our world.

2. After the showdown on the cross when Jesus defeated death, hell and purchased our salvation, demons seem to be roaming freely on this earth. If all the devils had been totally defeated at the cross there would have been no evil spirit operating in the book of Acts. But apostle Paul cast out devils from the girl in Thyatira (Acts 16:16). The seven sons of Sceva were also beaten by a man possessed with devils (Acts 19:14-16). The devils in this mad man apparently knew both Paul and Jesus.

3. At the end of the book of Revelation, the devil is bound on two occasions. On one occasion he is bound for a thousand years (Revelation 20:2-3). Yet again, he is released and causes havoc in the world. It is indeed puzzling to understand why Satan would be bound for only a thousand years and be released again. But that is what happened according to the book of Revelation.

4. Finally, in the book of Revelation, the devil is bound and dealt with permanently. The final and absolute defeat of the devil is recorded in the book of Revelation. "And the devil that deceived them was cast into the lake of fire and brimstone, where the beast and the false prophet are, and shall be tormented day and night for ever and ever" (Revelation 20:10).

Never forget; as long as the enemy is not completely defeated, he may defeat you and you will no longer be your own master. Your enemy will then dictate to you as you did to him. Fight on whilst on earth. Rest when you get to Heaven. Don't allow people to feed you with the delusion that you have "arrived". You are not yet successful. It is not yet over.

The Return of Napoleon

The defeat and imprisonment of Napoleon on an island and his escape from that island, returning from prison to the throne, is like a story out of a fairy-tale. But it illustrates the point that "as long as your enemy is not completely defeated, he may defeat you and you will no longer be your own master".

Napoleon is considered to be one of the greatest generals who ever lived. He was a French military and political leader who started his career as a very young man. He fought several wars and even invaded Russia. He was very successful in most of his campaigns. However, by 1813, Napoleon was running out of luck and was defeated by a coalition that included countries like Austria, Sweden, Prussia, Britain, Spain and Portugal. After France's capital, Paris, surrendered to the coalition, Napoleon was at the mercy of the coalition of nations. These allies decided to exile Napoleon to the Island of Elba.

Elba was just twenty kilometres off the Tuscan coast. Napoleon was given this island of twelve thousand inhabitants where he would retain his title Emperor. Napoleon, who was not forty-five years old, worked hard to improve the island. To all observers, it seemed as though Napoleon was content to live a life of peace and retirement. Whilst he was on the island, Napoleon was under the constant watch of the Austrian and French guards. He also received thousands of letters and read major newspapers from all over Europe that kept him abreast of events all over the world.

After some months of apparent defeat, Napoleon somehow escaped from the island, slipped past a British ship and returned to France. He arrived on the French mainland two days after he escaped. But there was a new government in France which did not want Napoleon back. The government of France, hearing of his escape, sent the army to intercept him.

When Napoleon saw the approaching regiment, he dismounted his horse when he was within gunshot range and shouted, "Here I am, kill your emperor if you wish."

The soldiers responded, "Vive l'empereur." The French police forces and military, upon arriving in his presence, kneeled before him and troops rallied and hailed the returned emperor. Triumphantly, Napoleon marched into Paris and the king, Louis XVIII fled to Belgium.

Amazingly, Napoleon was back in power in Paris. Napoleon had been defeated in war, he had been captured but he had not been executed.

Remember, that if your enemy is not completely defeated he may rise up and defeat you!

When the coalition of nations which had fought against Napoleon received the news of his escape, they were intensely shocked. They instantly declared Napoleon an outlaw and pledged 150,000 soldiers each to fight to recapture Napoleon and put him out of business once and for all.

After a hundred days, Napoleon was finally defeated at the Battle of Waterloo. Napoleon was defeated because he had to fight two armies with one. When Napoleon heard that Prussian troops were sent to capture him dead or alive, he fled, intending to escape to the United States.

However, British ships blocked every port, preventing his escape and he was finally captured and imprisoned. This time, he was sent to the island of St Helena, 1,780 km nearer the west coast of Africa. From this place, Napoleon had little chance of escape and remained a captive until his death in 1821. He spent only six depressed years on this island before he died. His body was brought back to France in 1840 where a state funeral was held for him.

Your Conquered Enemy Sees Defeat as a Passing Evil

Afterward the prophet said to King Ahab, "GET READY FOR ANOTHER ATTACK. BEGIN MAKING PLANS NOW, FOR THE KING OF ARAM WILL COME BACK NEXT SPRING."

After their defeat, Ben-hadad's officers said to him, "The Israelite gods are gods of the hills; that is why they won. But we can beat them easily on the plains.

Only this time replace the kings with field commanders!

Recruit another army like the one you lost. Give us the same number of horses, chariots, and men, and we will fight against them on the plains. There's no doubt that we will beat them." So King Ben-hadad did as they suggested.

The following spring he called up the Aramean army and marched out against Israel, this time at Aphek.

1 Kings 20:22-26 (NLT)

All enemies think this way. Your conquered enemy sees his defeat as a passing evil, which may be repaired after a time. You must beware of your conquered enemy. We have all watched films in which the conquered enemy escapes and rises up to regain control.

An equilibrium only leads to the suspension of war but always expect war when there is a favourable opportunity for one party! Always expect your enemy to come back if he is not completely defeated.

CHAPTER 62

War Does Not Spring Up Quite Suddenly, It Does Not Spread to the Full in a Moment

A prudent man foreseeth the evil, and hideth himself: but the simple pass on, and are punished.

Proverbs 22:3

There is no war that springs up quickly. There will always be signs of looming war. The Second World War took many years to develop into a full-scale war. The Second World War did not spread to the full in a moment. The Second World War actually started in 1939 but there were many signs indicating the coming conflict. Even after the war began in 1939, there was a very long lull period in which nothing happened. Several months later, Germany invaded France and it kicked up into a full-scale war.

War does not spring up suddenly! There were many signs for the coming Second World War in which fifty million people would die. None of these events happened suddenly. Notice a series of events that occurred prior to the Second World War. A discerning eye would have seen the beginning of the build-up towards a big conflict.

Hitler became the chancellor of Germany in 1933.

Adolf Hitler gained full control over the government and the police of Germany. Adolf Hitler suppressed all other political parties and groups in Germany and sent them to concentration camps.

Adolf Hitler merged his chancellorship position with the presidency and became the supreme head of the government with control over the military. Hitler began to oppress the Jewish community in Germany. Germany withdrew from the League of Nations (United Nations) in October 1933.

Germany expanded its army in spite of treaties that prevented increasing the size of the army. Hitler re-occupied a de-militarized zone in a part of Germany called the Rhineland. Germany was not supposed to do this, according to the treaty they had signed after the First World War.

In 1938, Hitler declared unification of Austria with Germany and annexed the entire country of Austria. How can you annex an entire nation? Hitler annexed a part of Czechoslovakia in which Germans lived and promised not to go any further. This area was called the Sudeten land.

In March 1939, however, Hitler took over the rest of Czechoslovakia, even though he had said he would not, and divided it into two: Bohemia and Moravia.

A treaty of non-aggression between Germany and the Soviet Union was signed in Moscow on 23 August 1935. This agreement gave Hitler the go-ahead to invade Poland and a guarantee that the Soviets would not fight with Germany.

On the 1st of September 1939 Hitler invaded Poland, which started the Second World War. From September 1939 to May 1940 there was hardly any military activity. But after that, all hell broke loose. War does not spread to a full in a moment!

Your Future Battles

Your future battles can be seen looming in the future. No war springs upon you suddenly and the signs of the fight you are going to be involved with are already there. This principle that, war does not spring up suddenly, teaches you to anticipate battles and conflicts that lie ahead. Let us look at several examples of future battles.

If your fiancé whom you are engaged to does not talk much, you are looking at a future conflict in the area of communication. Several misunderstandings and conflicts are likely to erupt because he does not speak much. If he did not speak much during the relationship, then it is likely he will not talk much when you are married.

If during your relationship you have a lot of pre-marital sex, you can expect certain battles in the future. Years later, you may be wondering if your spouse is faithful to you because you used to commit fornication with him. You know his secret ways and his ability to have a "quick dip".

If during your relationship you demonstrate that you do not obey the Word of God when you are in a secret place, you are showing that in the future you may not obey the Word of God when you are in secret. War does not spring up suddenly but shows many signs that it is coming.

If your future mother-in-law warns you about the laziness and slowness of her daughter towards housework, you must take it seriously. You are likely to have many battles in the future, trying to get your pretty wife to line up and do some housework. In your youthful days, you could not see anything wrong even when it was pointed out. The war of your marriage does not spring up suddenly. You were warned about the nature of the girl you were marrying.

If the young man you are going to get married to enjoyed anal sex with other men before marrying you, you must be concerned. War does not spring up suddenly. In the future, the man that you have married may turn his sexual interest to other men instead of you. A young married lady once showed me the homosexual videos that her husband was addicted to. She was embroiled in a battle for the soul of her husband who was leaving her for other men. But war does not spring up suddenly. Most of these things have indicators that they are going to be future problems.

If you are in a tumultuous relationship with somebody and are experiencing constant conflict, you must look to the future and see war. You will have numerous conflicts in your marriage. The wars of your marriage will be similar to the ones you have had in your relationship. Indeed, you can even predict the things you will quarrel about when you do get married. War does not spring up suddenly. There are many signs that lead to the eventual outbreak of war.

CHAPTER 63

Primarily Operations of War Are Carried Out in Danger, So the Foremost Quality Required in a General is Courage!

BE STRONG AND OF A GOOD COURAGE: for unto this people shalt thou divide for an inheritance the land, which I sware unto their fathers to give them.

Only BE THOU STRONG AND VERY COURAGEOUS, that thou mayest observe to do according to all the law, which Moses my servant commanded thee: turn not from it to the right hand or to the left, that thou mayest prosper whithersoever thou goest.

Have not I commanded thee? BE STRONG AND OF A GOOD COURAGE; be not afraid, neither be thou dismayed: for the Lord thy God is with thee whithersoever thou goest.

Joshua 1:6-7, 9

J oshua was charged three times to be strong and courageous. It was very important for him to be courageous.

A general who is not courageous will find many excuses to back out from his calling.

There are many dangers in war. There is every good reason to be afraid in a war. Fear and terror are normal emotions experienced by warriors. A good general must know how to operate even though he senses and feels terror. You need courage to make war. There are many dangers for someone who decides to serve the Lord.

You need to become a man of great courage. We are all in danger as we do the ministry. There are dangers on all fronts that are as real as you are. Perhaps, it is time to rise up and honestly address the fact that you are a coward. You are a coward because you are running away from the danger. Instead of running towards the will of God, you are running away from God's plan. God says to you today, "Be courageous. Be strong. Put away your cowardice and do the work of God." Stop running away from the will of God and start running to the will of God!

There are rewards given for bravery under fire. Bravery under fire is different from bravery when there is no fire. Several dangers are encountered by those who decide to serve the Lord: you can be attacked by evil spirits because of the work that you do!

You can be attacked by men who hate God's servants!

You can die in an attack of the enemy against you!

In the ministry, you are in danger of falling into temptation!

In the ministry, you are in danger of financial difficulty!

In the ministry, you are in danger of disgrace!

In the ministry, you are in danger of sin!

The ability to wage war in spite of the danger reveals your courage and for this you will receive awards. These are many awards that secular soldiers receive for their bravery and courage. Each of these awards reveals how important bravery and courage are to a soldier.

Courage is shown when you risk your life above and beyond the call of duty. In the ministry, you may be called upon to do things that are beyond the call of duty. When you show extraordinary heroism whilst in action, you qualify for a medal. Are you ready to show extraordinary heroism in the ministry? There is even a medal for fighting in the frontline. Many people do not want to fight in the front. It is much safer in the middle and at the back of the line. In the ministry, there are people who are at the front of everything. They are in danger all the time. They are the ones who make advances for the kingdom.

Here are some of the medals you can have if you fight in human earthly wars. Remember that your medals for courage on earth will be valid only for as long as you live on this earth. In the movie, Rambo probably received many of these medals for his courage. In eternity, you will need a different set of medals. I hope you will have earned some eternal medals for bravery and courage in the ministry.

Medals

1. *You can receive the United States Army Medal of Honor:* This is conferred on members of the United States Armed Forces who distinguish themselves through conspicuous gallantry and intrepidity AT THE RISK OF HIS LIFE ABOVE AND BEYOND THE CALL OF DUTY: while in action against an enemy of the United States; while engaged in military operations involving conflict with an opposing foreign force or while serving with friendly forces engaged in armed conflict against an opposing armed force in which the United States is not a belligerent party.

2.   *You can receive the United States Distinguished Service Cross:* It is awarded for EXTRAORDINARY HEROISM WHILE IN ACTION against an enemy of the United States; while engaged in military operations involving conflict with an opposing foreign force or while serving with friendly forces engaged in armed conflict against an opposing armed force in which the United States is not a belligerent party.

3.   *You can receive the British Queen's Medal for saving life at sea.*

4.   *You can receive the British Queen's Commendation for Brave Conduct.*

5.   *You can receive the British Queen's Commendation for bravery in the air.*

6.   *You can receive the French Medal for Escaped Prisoners of War.* This medal was awarded to military personnel as well as civilians who ESCAPED THROUGH ENEMY LINES and put themselves at the disposal of the French military authorities.

7.   *You can receive the French Combatant's Cross:* This cross was awarded to all military personnel that FOUGHT ON THE FRONTLINE.

Men of Courage

David's mighty men were all mighty men of great valour. All these men of courage did great acts in spite of the danger to themselves. They are remembered in the Bible because of their courage. You will also be remembered because of your courage.

1.   Jashobeam is remembered because he was in great danger as he courageously fought and killed 300 men.

And this is the number of the mighty men whom David had; Jashobeam, an Hachmonite, the chief of the captains:

he lifted up his spear against three hundred slain by him at one time.

1 Chronicles 11: 11

2. Eleazar is remembered because he was in danger of death by the hand of the Philistines.

And after him was Eleazar the son of Dodo, the Ahohite, who was one of the three mighties. He was with David at Pasdammim, and there the Philistines were gathered together to battle, where was a parcel of ground full of barley; and the people fled from before the Philistines. And they set themselves in the midst of that parcel, and delivered it, and slew the Philistines; and the Lord saved them by a great deliverance.

1 Chronicles 11:12-14

3. Three of David's mighty men were remembered because they were in danger of death at the well of Bethlehem. They fought courageously and broke through the host of the Philistines.

Now three of the thirty captains went down to the rock to David, into the cave of Adullam; and the host of the Philistines encamped in the valley of Rephaim. And David was then in the hold, and the Philistines' garrison was then at Bethlehem. And David longed, and said, Oh that one would give me drink of the water of the well of Bethlehem, that is at the gate! And THE THREE BRAKE THROUGH THE HOST OF THE PHILISTINES, and drew water out of the well of Bethlehem, that was by the gate, and took it, and brought it to David: but David would not drink of it, but poured it out to the Lord, And said, My God forbid it me, that I should do this thing: shall I drink the blood of these men that have put their lives in jeopardy? For with the jeopardy of their lives they brought it. Therefore he would not drink it. These things did these three mightiest.

1 Chronicles 11:15-19

4.   Abishai is remembered because he was in danger as he fought alone against three hundred men. He is mentioned because of his great courage.

And Abishai the brother of Joab, he was chief of the three: for lifting up his spear against three hundred, he slew them, and had a name among the three. Of the three, he was more honourable than the two; for he was their captain: howbeit he attained not to the first three.

1 Chronicles 11:20-21

5.   Benaiah is remembered because he fought with lion-like men and giants. He was in great danger of being killed by ferocious lions and oversized giants.

Benaiah the son of Jehoiada, the son of a valiant man of Kabzeel, who had done many acts; he slew two lionlike men of Moab: also he went down and slew a lion in a pit in a snowy day.

And he slew an Egyptian, a man of great stature, five cubits high; and in the Egyptian's hand was a spear like a weaver's beam; and he went down to him with a staff, and plucked the spear out of the Egyptian's hand, and slew him with his own spear.

1 Chronicles 11:22-23

Today, a new list of mighty men is being written in Heaven! Will you be in that list? When we get to Heaven, will you receive any awards for extraordinary heroism? Will you receive any awards for risking your life above and beyond the call of duty? Will you be pushed aside into the outer darkness of Heaven because of your cowardice and refusal to do the will of God? How many people are going to perish because of your cowardice? God is looking for brave and courageous generals today!

CHAPTER 64

A Good General Fights to Capture the Minds and Hearts of People

Then the king of Assyria sent Tartan and Rab-saris and Rabshakeh from Lachish to King Hezekiah with a large army to Jerusalem. So they went up and came to Jerusalem. And when they went up, they came and stood by the conduit of the upper pool, which is on the highway of the fuller's field.

When they called to the king, Eliakim the son of Hilkiah, who was over the household, and Shebnah the scribe and Joah the son of Asaph the recorder, came out to them.

Then Rabshakeh said to them, "Say now to Hezekiah, 'Thus says the great king, the king of Assyria, " What is this confidence that you have?

You say (but they are only empty words), ' I have counsel and strength for the war. ' Now on whom do you rely, that you have rebelled against me? Now behold, you rely on the staff of this crushed reed, even on Egypt; on which if a man leans, it will go into his hand and pierce it. So is Pharaoh king of Egypt to all who rely on him.

But if you say to me, 'We trust in the Lord our God,' is it not He whose high places and whose altars Hezekiah has taken away, and has said to Judah and to Jerusalem, 'You shall worship before this altar in Jerusalem'? Now therefore, come, make a bargain with my master the king of Assyria, and I will give you two thousand horses, if you are able on your part to set riders on them. How then can you repulse one official of the least of my master's servants, and rely on Egypt for chariots and for horsemen?

Have I now come up without the Lord's approval against this place to destroy it? The Lord said to me, 'Go up against this land and destroy it. '"''
Then Eliakim the son of Hilkiah, and Shebnah and Joah, said to Rabshakeh, "SPEAK NOW TO YOUR SERVANTS IN ARAMAIC, FOR WE UNDERSTAND IT; AND DO NOT SPEAK WITH US IN JUDEAN IN THE HEARING OF THE PEOPLE WHO ARE ON THE WALL."

But Rabshakeh said to them, "HAS MY MASTER SENT ME ONLY TO YOUR MASTER AND TO YOU TO SPEAK THESE WORDS, AND NOT TO THE MEN WHO SIT ON THE WALL, DOOMED TO EAT THEIR OWN DUNG AND DRINK THEIR OWN URINE WITH YOU?"

Then Rabshakeh stood and cried with a loud voice in Judean, saying, "Hear the word of the great king, the king of Assyria.

Thus says the king, ' Do not let Hezekiah deceive you, for he will not be able to deliver you from my hand; nor let Hezekiah make you trust in the Lord, saying, "The Lord will surely deliver us, and this city will not be given into the hand of the king of Assyria." Do not listen to Hezekiah, for thus says the king of Assyria, " MAKE YOUR PEACE WITH ME AND COME OUT TO ME, AND EAT EACH OF HIS VINE AND EACH OF HIS FIG TREE AND DRINK EACH OF THE WATERS OF HIS OWN CISTERN, UNTIL I COME

AND TAKE YOU AWAY TO A LAND LIKE YOUR OWN LAND, A LAND OF GRAIN AND NEW WINE, A LAND OF BREAD AND VINEYARDS,

A LAND OF OLIVE TREES AND HONEY, THAT YOU MAY LIVE AND NOT DIE." But do not listen to Hezekiah when he misleads you, saying, "The Lord will deliver us." Has any one of the gods of the nations delivered his land from the hand of the king of Assyria?

Where are the gods of Hamath and Arpad? Where are the gods of Sepharvaim, Hena and Ivvah? Have they delivered Samaria from my hand? Who among all the gods of the lands have delivered their land from my hand, that the Lord should deliver Jerusalem from my hand? "'

But the people were silent and answered him not a word, for the king's commandment was, "Do not answer him."

Then Eliakim the son of Hilkiah, who was over the household, and Shebna the scribe and Joah the son of Asaph, the recorder, came to Hezekiah with their clothes torn and told him the words of Rabshakeh.

2 Kings 18:17-37 (NASB)

Rabshakeh was sent by the king of Assyria to capture the hearts and minds of the people of Israel and to make them believe that they were going to perish. Eliakim, the messenger of Hezekiah sensed that Rabshakeh was winning the hearts and minds of the people by speaking to them in the Jewish language. So he shouted out to him that there was no need to speak to them in the Jewish language. He wanted them to speak in Aramaic so that the ordinary Jews listening would not understand the threats and dangers they were in. Every general knows the need to convince the masses of certain things. A good general therefore knows the importance of information dissemination. Through the information that is put out, you can control the population and make them believe almost anything.

Many evil regimes were thought of as good governments during their reign. After these governments were overthrown, the real picture came out. Today, many useless politicians maintain their deceptions and power by propaganda and lies on television, radio and the internet. This is how they win elections and gain control of the masses. With time, it is seen that they were really a useless government. Everyone comes to know the truth about that government. In the same way, the devil has fed this world with lies and deceptions. Unfortunately, most of the people in this world have believed it. Many evil governments, which are heavily inspired by the devil, were very good at propaganda, lies and deception.

How Adolf Hitler Won the Hearts of Germany

Adolf Hitler did not come into power because he was popular or liked. He and his Nazi party never actually won the majority of votes at an election. He was the leader of the largest party but they still did not have the majority support in the country. When Adolf Hitler did come into power, he knew that he had to convince those who opposed him that it was pointless to continue with their opposition. He also wanted those who had chosen him to be informed about how correct their decision was.

To do this, Adolf Hitler appointed a Minister of Public Enlightenment and Propaganda. As the Minister of Enlightenment, it was his job to ensure that no one in Germany ever produced or read any negative material about the Nazi party. He was also to ensure that the views of the Nazi party were put out in as persuasive a way as possible. They then set about to work with the secret service to hunt out those who might produce negative materials and eliminate them.

In order to censor everything that was produced in the country, Goebbels, the Propaganda Minister, set up a chamber of commerce which was an organisation to deal with literature, music, radio, film and newspapers. Everything that was published or produced in the country had to pass through this chamber of commerce. From then on, you could only read, see or hear what the government wanted you to. Goebbels organized book burning episodes. Books that did not match the Nazi doctrine were burnt in public. Libraries were raided and offending books were brought out and burnt.

Films were also controlled and only films that centred on the Jews or the greatness of Hitler were produced. Two films of note were made. *Hitlerjunge Quex* was made in 1933. This film told the story of a boy brought up in a communist family in Germany who broke away from this background, joined the Hitler Youth and was murdered by the Communists in Germany for doing so. *The Eternal Jew* was a film that vilified the Jews comparing the Jews in Europe to a hoard of rats spreading disease. As the World War approached, the films produced centered on how badly Germans were being treated in other countries – a way of preparing people for war with nations that were not treating Germans nicely.

To ensure that everybody could hear Hitler speak, Goebbels organized the sale of cheap radios. These were called the "People's Receiver" and they cost only 76 marks. A smaller version cost just 35 marks. Goebbels believed that if Hitler was to give speeches, the people should be able to hear him. Loud speakers were put up in streets so that people could not avoid any speeches by Hitler. Cafes and other such properties were ordered to play in public the speeches by Hitler.

Goebbels, the man of propaganda and public enlightenment, organized spectacular night time displays at Nuremberg, the headquarters of the Nazi party. Here, he organized massive rallies and parades that were designed to show the world the might of the Nazi party. Huge arenas to hold 400,000 people were built, 150 search lights that could be seen from about a hundred kilometers away, surrounded the whole area and were lit up vertically into the night sky.

Initially, Goebbels did not believe in anti-semitism, but turned around completely and organized attacks on the Jews. Goebbels' hatred for Jews was propagated through a systematic campaign to turn the entire nation of Germany against Jews. He said, "The Jews must get out of Germany, indeed out of Europe altogether. That will take some time, but it must and will happen." By 1938, Goebbels was working on requiring all Jews to wear an identifiable mark and confining them to a ghetto. He wrote, "Our aim is to drive the Jews out of Berlin and that without any sentimentality."

With his propaganda, he drove everyone to hate Jews, to kill them and to eliminate them from the world, even making people believe that it was the Jews who had started the Second World War.

He wrote, "Our state's security requires that we take whatever measures seem necessary to protect the German community from the Jewish threat."

Goebbels developed ten commandments of propaganda for his hearers.

1. Your Fatherland is called Germany. Love it above all and more through action than through words.

2. Germany's enemies are your enemies. Hate them with your whole heart.

3. Every national comrade, even the poorest, is a piece of Germany. Love him as yourself.

4. Demand only duties for yourself. Then Germany will get justice.

5. Be proud of Germany. You ought to be proud of a Fatherland for which millions have sacrificed their lives.

6. He who abuses Germany, abuses you and your dead. Strike your fist against him.

7. Hit a rogue more than once. When one takes away your good rights, remember that you can only fight him physically.

8. Don't be an anti-Semitic knave. But be careful of the "Berliner Tageblatt".

9. Make your actions such that you need no blush when the New Germany is mentioned.

10. Believe in the future. Only then can you be the victor.

Goebbels controlled the minds and the hearts of Germany till the very end. He made the people of Germany believe in all that Hitler was doing. The Second World War lasted from 1939 to 1945. In June 1941, Adolf Hitler invaded Russia where his army was defeated. That was the beginning of his downfall and the downfall of Germany and the Nazi party. But all through the decline of Germany, from 1941 up to 1945, Goebbels maintained a strong control on the hearts and minds of the people convincing them that Germany was a mighty power, successful in all that it did when in actual fact it was declining from as early as 1941. Through intensified propaganda on radio, television and the print media, Goebbels ensured that Adolf Hitler looked good until the very end.

When the war was clearly lost in the east, he continued his campaign of deception and lies; writing in the newspaper, "Our soldiers in the east will do their part. They will stop the storm from the steppes and ultimately break it. They fight under unimaginable conditions. But they are fighting a good fight. They are fighting not only for our security but also for Europe's future.

Sadly, he believed the very lie that he created and said it was not worth living if Adolf Hitler and the Nazi party were not in power. After Hitler committed suicide, he killed his six children and then killed himself and his wife.

Satanic Propaganda

Today, large sections of the world have fallen to captivity through propaganda. Today, ordinary young men are made to believe that they are homosexual because of the onslaught of lies and deception. Today, the most unnatural sexual practices are promoted by respectable-looking politicians and other dignified leaders. It is not about understanding homosexuals or giving them rights but the fact that the world is being forced to believe that it is a normal thing rather than seeing it as something that needs compassion and help to correct. The point I am making is that deception is very pervasive and over time, some untruths can become the main truths. Today, people in Europe have decided that there is no God. They have decided that they made themselves and came into the world through a big bang. With time, the entire continent of Europe will be overwhelmed with the absurd idea that there is no God.

A Good General Must Launch His Own Campaign

A good general knows that the enemy will launch a campaign to capture the minds and hearts of the people. A good general, therefore, launches his own campaign of propaganda to counter the deceptions of the enemy. There are many arguments against the insanity of atheism. These arguments must be sought out and disseminated so that our children will not believe that there is no God. There are also many arguments against the depravity of homosexuality; perhaps, the greatest being that there are no homosexual animals. The arguments against accepting homosexuality as an orientation and a normal lifestyle must be disseminated strongly, lest half of the church falls to this deception and becomes a homosexual community.

A strong campaign to capture the hearts and the minds of people must be launched through camp meetings, church services, the internet, radio and television. You cannot leave the enemy to have a field day with his campaign of lies and deception. During the Second World War, the British fought against the deception of the Nazi Germans by throwing leaflets on them. Some of these leaflets had no words but simply showed a picture of a large open field with thousands of graves of German soldiers. This effort was to demoralize the German soldiers and to discourage them from continuing to fight.

CHAPTER 65

War Moves in an Atmosphere of Risk, Danger, Uncertainty, Physical Effort, Energy and Change

For every battle of the warrior is with confused noise, and garments rolled in blood; but this shall be with burning and fuel of fire.

Isaiah 9:5

Six Atmospheres of War

The atmosphere of war is coloured by six things: *risk, danger, uncertainty, energy, physical effort* and *change*. The ability to function, to think and to operate in the midst of such difficulty is the most needed ability of the warrior.

A pastor will experience all these atmospheres at different times and will have to be level-headed and do what is right even under pressure. In the ministry, there is the need to change, to use energy, to be conscious of danger, to ignore the uncertainties and to make the effort to move on.

Are you ready to risk something for God? You cannot fight the good fight of faith if you are not prepared for danger and uncertainty. You will exert energy. You must exert great effort to fight a war successfully. Laziness, dullness, sleepiness are not compatible with being a good general. Your lack of energy will destroy your ministry. This is why God calls people when they are young. By the time you are older, you are disillusioned, disappointed and discouraged about what life really holds. You are not prepared to espouse certain great ideals any more. You just want peace and calm.

I once observed a set of politicians in a country. They organised a revolution and rose up to bring great changes to the nation. They executed people who had been corrupt and tried very zealously to wipe out stealing and dishonesty. Thirty-five years later, I noted how calm these same people were towards the same kind of corruption and wickedness. They seemed listless, disillusioned and too discouraged to attempt another revolution.

The ministry is no different. A sower went out to sow and what did he experience? A hundred percent success rate? Certainly not! Most of the seeds that the sower sowed did not bring back a good result. Very few of the sower's seeds yielded a positive response.

Only one-twelfth of the seeds yielded a hundredfold return.

Three quarters of the seeds yielded nothing at all.

Out of the one-quarter which yielded something, a third gave thirtyfold and a third gave sixtyfold and another third gave a hundredfold.

The sower was therefore left with only a third of a quarter which gave a hundred percent return. Only one-twelfth of the people you minister to will truly give you a good feedback. The results of ministering to men are indeed very low and discouraging. This is why God calls you when you are young, ready to exert all the physical effort you need, ready to take risks, ready to experience danger and ready do His will.

Are you ready for war? War brings change! War beings uncertainty! War brings death! War brings risks! All these are part of war. No one can take part of the good fight without experiencing these things. No one can war a good warfare without facing uncertainty and change!

Every good general has had to face danger, fear, risk, uncertainty and change.

Alexander the Great in Malli

Alexander the Great was known for his energy, youthfulness and speed. These are characteristics found in every great general.

Near the end of his short life, Alexander the Great was unable to convince his men to carry on fighting in India. His commanders explained to him that the men "longed to again see their parents, their wives and children, their homeland". Alexander, seeing the unwillingness of his men, agreed and turned back.

On the way back, Alexander encountered the city of Malli and besieged it. The Indians of Malli hid in their city but Alexander and his forces were able to force one of the gates and make their way into the outer parts of the citadel. At a point, Alexander became impatient at the pace of the siege, so he grabbed a ladder and went up and over the wall himself. Many of Alexander's men tried to prevent Alexander the Great from getting into that situation.

Alexander found himself alone inside the city of Malli where only two of his soldiers had been able to follow him. The rest of his soldiers tried to follow but as they crowded unto the ladder it collapsed.

Alexander the Great was now virtually alone in the city of Malli, surrounded by the enemies. When the Mallians realized that Alexander the Great was all alone within their walls, they focused their energies on him to try and kill him. Instead, Alexander leaped into the inner area of the citadel and killed the Mallians' leader. Alexander, however, was severely wounded when an arrow penetrated his lung.

The Greeks thought their king was dead and forced their way into the city of Malli to revenge the supposed death of Alexander the Great. The citizens of Malli, men, women and children were massacred. However, Alexander the Great survived due to the efforts of his surgeon.

As you can see, Alexander the Great was a man who was full of energy and physical effort. He moved, he jumped, he ran, he fought, he took risks and experienced much danger. This is the characteristic of a good general.

Dear friend, you cannot build a church with dullness and stillness. "Be still and know that I am Lord" is not the Scripture you must quote when you are doing battle for the Lord. "Be still and know that I am Lord" is not the Scripture you must think of when you are starting a church.

You cannot be still when you need to go out on outreach and follow up new converts.

You cannot be still when you need to organise people and mobilise the church into action.

It is time for war and not worship! The times of worship do not include danger, risk, physical effort and uncertainty. Fight the good fight of faith and be a good soldier!

CHAPTER 66

War Is No Leisure, No Mere Pastime, No Mere Hobby, No Work of a Free Enthusiast; War Is Serious Business with a Serious Object

No man that warreth entangleth himself with the affairs of this life; that he may please him who hath chosen him to be a soldier.

2 Timothy 2:4

Apostle Paul pointed out that a real soldier cannot be deeply involved in the affairs of this life. To please the one who called you, you must be fully dedicated to your work as a soldier.

Ministry is war! It is not a pastime or a mere passion. Nor is it the work of a free enthusiast who wants to work for God at his own convenience. Ministry is not something to do in the last two years of your life. The ministry is not something a free enthusiast can take up in the evenings and on some weekends. It is a full scale, full time, all out war. Ministry is a full-time job!

Ministry is War

War is no pastime, no mere passion, no work of a free enthusiast. War is a serious means for a serious object. In the same way the ministry is no pastime, no mere passion, no work of a free enthusiast. Ministry is serious business.

Real ministry is not a hobby or an evening activity. It is actually war. Many laymen do not understand what ministry is. They think it is something you can do on Sunday afternoons or Tuesday evenings. Ministry, just like war, must be attended to with all the forces you can muster.

When you consider the ministry as a war, you will rise up and fight in a professional way. The devil will see the difference in you and respect the fact that he is dealing with a soldier who knows what he is about. Perhaps it is time to stop seeing the ministry as a hobby and start seeing it as something that requires your full attention.

One of the greatest armies ever to operate on the surface of the earth came about when they put aside part-time voluntary services and became professional full-time soldiers. The Roman army is well known for its conversion from an army of laymen to a full-time army. The Roman army used to consist of farmers who would offer some of their time for any war that came up.

But then came a time when they realised that they needed a full-time army if they were to overcome the kinds of enemies that were coming against them. This is how it happened.

How the "Lay" Roman Army became a Full-Time Roman Army

In 113BC the Cimbri and the Teuton tribes invaded Rome and destroyed two Roman armies. General Marius, Rome's leading general was asked to re-organize the army to face this new menace. At that time, soldiers of the Roman army were basically farmers who owned land. It was actually a requirement to own land to belong to the army. The soldiers, basically, lived off their land and volunteered their services to fight for Rome when they were needed.

General Marius changed everything. He said it was no longer required to own land to be a soldier. He offered military service as a full-time employment where a soldier would serve for twenty years, after which he would be discharged and given a plot of land as his pay. This was attractive as fewer and fewer people owned land.

General Marius also standardized the Roman Army's arms and equipment. He changed the old structure where the newest recruits attacked first whilst the veterans stayed behind to rescue them. Marius mixed both veterans and new recruits on the front line.

General Marius also changed the system of supplying the troops with their needs. The Roman armies used to be followed by supply trains and wagons containing all the needs of the soldiers. However, these supply wagons would lag behind for many miles and slow the army down. General Marius had the soldiers carry most of their supplies. Each soldier would carry about 35kilos worth of arms, equipment and supplies. These soldiers were mockingly called Marius' Mules.

General Marius also rotated the battle lines frequently, putting fresh troops into the front all the time. He also increased their stamina by making them march around Italy with their supplies. These measures totally transformed the Roman army. The endurance, stamina and preparedness of the Roman soldiers were greatly heightened. When the Cimbri and Teuton tribes invaded again, they were slaughtered by this transformed Roman army.

Time for Change

Perhaps if our armies were transferred from volunteers and evening workers to all-out professional ministers who are ready to die on the job, there would be great growth in Christianity.

Perhaps it is time to restructure things along professional lines. Perhaps it is time to put aside voluntary work and be transformed into a full-time, all-out, chosen vessel.

Giving full attention to anything will transform it. You cannot say that the lay ministry is the same as full-time ministry. When the lay Roman army was transformed into a full-time Roman army, it accomplished great things and decisively destroyed the Cimbri and Teuton tribes.

Giving yourself all-out every day is different from working for God once in a while.

It is time for full-time ministry for you! Ministry is war! It is not a pastime or a mere passion. Nor is it the work of a free enthusiast who wants to work for God at his own convenience.

Real ministry is real war!

CHAPTER 67

The Stronger the Motive the Greater the War Effort

For the which cause I also suffer these things: nevertheless I am not ashamed: for I know whom I HAVE BELIEVED, AND AM PERSUADED that he is able to keep that which I have committed unto him against that day.

2 Timothy 1:12

The stronger the motive the greater the war effort! The apostle Paul was a highly motivated person. He served the Lord with great passion, travelling all over the world and ministering eternal words of life. Without strong motivation, the war effort is weak. What makes motivation strong? A number of things can drive and motivate the leader. Why was Paul so highly motivated?

1. **Paul had seen the Lord.** "I knew a man in Christ above fourteen years ago, (whether in the body, I cannot tell; or whether out of the body, I cannot tell: God knoweth;) such an one caught up to the third heaven" (2 Corinthians 12:2).

2. **Paul had been to Heaven and knew that Heaven was real**. Anyone who has been to Heaven and seen the reality of the glory that awaits us becomes confused on earth, realising that we are running around for nothing on this earth. "For to me to live is Christ, and to die is gain. But if I live in the flesh, this is the fruit of my labour: yet what I shall choose I wot not. For I am in a strait betwixt two, having a desire to depart, and to be with Christ; which is far better" (Philippians 1:21-23).

3. **Paul had received much mercy from the Lord.** This motivated Paul to never give up and to press on with the ministry. "Therefore seeing we have this ministry, as we have received mercy, we faint not" (2 Corinthians 4:1).

4. **Paul seemed to be in danger of divine judgment if he did not obey his call.** "...for necessity is laid upon me; yea, woe is unto me, if I preach not the gospel" (1 Corinthians 9:16).

I once met a soldier who was working for the UN in an African country. He was among the peacekeeping troops who had been sent to that nation to help maintain the peace. I asked how the morale was among the troops. He told me that many of the soldiers had become taxi drivers and some of the soldiers had moved into diamond mining. I was shocked and asked why soldiers would become taxi drivers and diamond miners in a war zone. He laughed and said, "No one wants to die a foolish death in this foolish war. The politicians, through their wickedness and ineptitude have created a foolish war.

Every soldier asked himself, "Why should I die a foolish death in a foolish war?" These soldiers were highly unmotivated to fight for peace in that country. These unmotivated soldiers were glad to find a few diamonds and do a little business.

The stronger the motivation, the stronger the war effort!

Many ministers are highly unmotivated. Money is a weak driver for ministry. Pleasing a human being cannot motivate you to war a good warfare. There must be an engine inside you that drives from within. The love of God at work within you must be your great motivation.

Why is your church not growing? Many times, the vision, the passion and the zeal for church growth is simply not there. Many pastors do not have growing churches because they do not have a strong drive or motivation for church growth. They simply do not love God enough. The number one factor that affects your ministry is your love for God. You cannot war a good warfare when you are not internally motivated.

Troy

There are different motives for fighting wars. To gain land and to acquire wealth are some of the common motives for war. Wars that have been fought out of strong motives have a greater effort and force applied.

One famous war, however, was fought out of an even greater motive: a kidnapped wife! The famous Trojan War was fought between Greece and Troy. According to the sources, a visiting prince of Troy, Paris, fell in love with Queen Helen of Sparta. Unfortunately, she was the wife of another man called Menelaus. In spite of being married to Menelaus, she eloped with her new lover, the visiting prince of Troy.

Queen Helen's husband was outraged that this prince of Troy had abducted his wife. He convinced his brother, who happened to be Agamemnon, the king of Mycenae to lead his armies to Troy to retrieve his wife. King Agamemnon summoned the best warriors such as the legendary Achilles, Odysseus, etc. and led a fleet of over one thousand ships across the Aegean Sea to recapture the Queen Helen. They besieged the city of Troy for ten years because of this woman and her lover, Paris.

The siege of Troy lasted for more than ten years and was punctuated by battles and skirmishes that resulted in the deaths of the Trojan prince Hector and Achilles. Finally, after 10 years, the Greek armies retreated from their camp, leaving a large wooden horse outside the gates of Troy. After much debate (and unheeded warnings) the people of Troy pulled the mysterious wooden horse into the city. But when night fell, the horse opened up and a group of Greek warriors, led by Odysseus, climbed out and destroyed the city of Troy from within. In the end, the Greeks slaughtered the Trojans (except for some of the women and children whom they kept or sold as slaves). After the Trojan defeat, only a few of the Greeks returned safely to their homes. Helen was returned to Sparta to be with her original husband, Menelaus.

The motive for this famous Trojan War was the stealing of Helen the wife of a Spartan king, Menelaus. One thousand ships and ten years of fighting was the result of this outrage. The Trojan War was fought between Troy and the Greeks over a man who felt cheated of his wife. Indeed, the stronger the motives the stronger the war effort. When people are not well motivated, they cannot fight properly.

Does Anyone Love God Today?

Today, the great motive for real ministry is missing. What is the great motive for ministry? The love of God, the love of our Saviour, Jesus Christ! How many people really love the Lord? People do not love God. Most people just want to prosper and have a good life. God is looking for people who really like Him and love Him.

Even I, am afraid of people who want to work for me for money. How nasty it is to relate to people who just want something from you. It is a far better thing to have people who do things out of love. That is the greatest motive you can have for doing anything. Would you like to marry someone who is just thinking of what financial benefits they can get when they marry you? Wouldn't you want to marry someone who is marrying you because of love?

Pray that God will touch you so that you develop a deep love for Him. Loving God is not the same as coming close to Him when you are in trouble. To love God is to come to Him and like Him because He is God. To love God is to want to be in His presence. To love God is to talk to Him every day. To love God is to be intimate with Jesus Christ. To love God is to have feelings about God, His kingdom and His work. To love God with all your heart is to cry when you speak to Him. To love God is to have deep feelings when you think about God. How many people really love the Lord? How many people even think about God? How many people even wonder how God really feels? If you love God, you will obey Him and serve Him with feeling, with zeal and with passion.

CHAPTER 68

When War Erupts, Find Out Who Is Financing Your Enemy; That Is Your Real Enemy!

And it came to pass afterward, that he loved a woman in the valley of Sorek, whose name was Delilah. And the lords of the Philistines came up unto her, and said unto her, Entice him, and SEE WHEREIN HIS GREAT STRENGTH LIETH, and by what means we may prevail against him, that we may bind him to afflict him: and we will give thee every one of us eleven hundred pieces of silver.

Judges 16:4-5

Y ou must always expect an attack on the source of your strength. Whatever makes you strong is of interest to your enemy. If he can take that away from you, he can destroy you. You must also attack your enemy's source of light, fuel and food. The reason why your financiers are under attack is because they are a source of strength for your ministry. The enemy is always interested in the source of your strength.

The financing of a war is the strength that keeps the parties fighting.

There is nothing like a war without a financier. The financier of a war is the power behind the war. Who is the powerful person behind your enemy? That is the real person you are dealing with. A good general knows that there is something powerful behind every war. Every war is fought by two parties and behind each party are the real makers of the war.

When war erupts, you must find out who is financing your enemy. That is your real enemy. War is no cheap activity. War is serious and expensive business. Do you know the cost of war? Ordinary people cannot wage a war in today's world. They need serious financial backing because the cost of equipment is so high that without a large amount of money, no one can wage a war.

The Cost of War

Did you know that a single bullet could cost as much as 30 dollars?

Did you know that one AK 47 machine gun costs at least 600 dollars?

Did you know that one medium-sized rocket launcher costs about 1,000 dollars?

Did you know that a battle tank costs 8.5 million dollars?

Did you know that a bomber costs 300 million dollars?

Did you know that a fighter jet costs as much as 211 million dollars?

Did you know that one air-to-air missile costs about 400,000 dollars?

Did you know that a one torpedo costs 900,000 dollars?

Did you know that a destroyer ship costs more than 800 million dollars?

Did you know that a submarine costs as much as 2.5 billion dollars?

Did you know that one submarine launched ballistic missile costs 65 million dollars?

Did you know that one inter-continental ballistic missile costs about 50 million dollars?

To have thousands of men bearing arms and shooting indiscriminately is a very expensive business indeed!

Your real enemy is therefore the person who is dishing out the money to those who are fighting you. A good general attacks the source of the strength of his enemy. The financier of your enemy is the main person who hates you and wants to eliminate you.

It is almost impossible to win a war against someone who has more money than you. The person who has endless sources of income has endless sources of strength. These mysterious financiers of wars are those who are behind rebel wars and insurgencies all over the world.

This is how come poor men who live in the village are able to possess tanks and other sophisticated weapons to wage wars with. The real enemy heavily finances them. In real life, these people would not have enough money to buy even one bullet. There is always a hidden power behind the war.

The Power behind the Angolan Civil War

In 1974, Angola became independent of Portugal. Soon after their independence, the country was plunged into war. The war was fought between two main group s: the MPLA (Marxist Popular Movement for the Liberation of Angola) and UNITA (Anti-Marxist National Union for the Total Independence of Angola) led by Jonas Savimbi. These two groups fought a vicious war but could never have sustained their war without support from outside.

Indeed, the MPLA, being a Marxist movement, was funded by the Soviet Union and Cuba. The UNITA on the other hand, was supported by the United States and South Africa. However, when the Soviet Union broke up and the Cold War ended, these major powers were no longer interested in financing such wars.

In 1992, elections were held and the MPLA won and formed a government. But the peace did not last and by 1998 the war had fully resumed.

Every time a war erupts, you must ask who is behind the war. So who was behind this war since America and the Soviet Union were no longer interested in sponsoring it? The answer is simple.

Since Angola was rich in diamonds and oil, multinational companies moved in and indirectly took over the financing of these wars.

UNITA's main source of income came from diamonds, whilst MPLA's main source of income was oil. UNITA controlled most of the diamond production in the country and earned at least 3.7 billion dollars between 1992 and 1997. MPLA on the other hand, had most of its funding from the oil riches of the nation.

As you can see, Angola's war was always financed by somebody. Initially, it was funded by powerful nations. Then after that, it was financed by powerful companies. When war erupts, find out who is financing the war. That is your real enemy!

Who Financed the War in Mozambique?

The independence of Mozambique and Angola by 1975 was a shock to the apartheid government in South Africa. It demonstrated that even with great resources and military might, it was virtually impossible for a small white minority government to maintain control over a large hostile black population. The downfall of the Portuguese in Mozambique gave great hope to the black people who were fighting for freedom in South Africa.

Mozambicans now offered South African and Rhodesian resistance movements a safe haven from where they could coordinate their operations and train new forces. Samora Machel of Mozambique said in a speech in 1975, "The struggle in Zimbabwe is our struggle." In other words, forces to destabilize South Africa were going to be nurtured in Mozambique.

It was therefore now in the interest of South Africa to destabilize the newly-independent countries of Mozambique and Angola. Once the governments of Mozambique and Angola were unstable, they would not be able to support anti-white movements in South Africa and Rhodesia (Zimbabwe). By these supports, the civil wars in Mozambique and Angola were fuelled for many years.

Indeed, there has never been a war without a financier. Rebel war after rebel war has been sponsored by rich powers who have other interests. The wickedness of man is seen by his sponsorship of war and death because of his selfish political ambition. Without these financiers there would be no war because there would be no money for bullets, guns, tanks and bombs.

Who Finances Your War?

There are hidden financial powers behind every spiritual war. These mysterious financial powers are necessary if you are going to wage war. The war that you will fight will be paid for by somebody. The ministry that God has given you will be financed by God-sent financiers.

- A good general is concerned about the financiers of his ministry.

- A good general is concerned about his relationship with his financiers.

- A good general is concerned about his integrity towards his financiers.

- A good general is concerned about the well being of his financiers.

- A good general fights off those who attack his financiers.

An attack on your financiers is an attack on your ministry.

You must identify who these financiers are and patiently nurture and protect them. That does not mean that you worship them and obey them. You must recognize whom God is using to pay for the wars He sends you to fight. I realised that God was using ordinary church members to pay for the crusades. I have always wanted to be able to point to some millionaires and say, "This is my financier. He pays for this and he pays for that." But somehow, it has not been any millionaires but ordinary people in the church whom God has used to pay for His work.

Your financial strength is of great interest to the devil. Whatever makes you strong financially is of interest to your enemy.

I watched as the marriage of a great man of God disintegrated. Initially it seemed that he was having marital problems and being de-housed. As time went by, I realised that it was actually an attack on his financial strength. Because of his divorce, most of his partners stopped supporting him. Soon, his crusades and outreaches came to an end. It became clear that the attack on his marriage was actually an attack on his finances.

Who is Behind the War?

Who is behind the conflicts in your life? Perhaps, you are wondering why you are always having conflict with your pastors, your wife and your children. It is time to grow up and know that there is always someone behind the war. There is someone behind the marital conflict that you are experiencing and it is Satan. Satan is the one behind every conflict, every war, and every fight. Notice, as soon as the devil is set free from the one thousand year imprisonment, he gathers people to fight against each other. Gathering people to fight against each other is Satan's work.

And when the thousand years are expired, Satan shall be loosed out of his prison, and shall go out to deceive the nations which are in the four quarters of the earth, Gog and Magog, to gather them together to battle: the number of whom is as the sand of the sea.

Revelation 20:7-8

It is time to recognise that there is always someone behind a war. The marital conflicts in your home, the confusion in your church, the enmity in your family are all demonically inspired. Satan is the one who gathers people to war against each other. You must rise up in the night and bind the devil. You must curse his operations. You must limit and weaken his access to your life. Through the power of God, you are destroying every hidden force fuelling conflicts in your life.

CHAPTER 69

You Cannot Force a Good General to Turn Away from Battle

HE THAT OVERCOMETH SHALL INHERIT ALL THINGS; and I will be his God, and he shall be my son. But the fearful, and unbelieving, and the abominable, and murderers, and whoremongers, and sorcerers, and idolaters, and all liars, shall have their part in the lake which burneth with fire and brimstone:which is the second death.

Revelation 21:7-8

In Heaven, rewards are offered to those who overcome. When you are on a mission, you can either overcome or be overcome. Everyone who is overcome by a problem is full of excuses. Actually, the song of the defeated is a string of excuses.

The people who live here are difficult! The people don't understand the Word of God! The people don't like going to church! The people are not educated! The people are poor! There is no money here! The people are backward! Nothing works here! The people don't understand the technology! The people do not understand the culture!

These are just some of the excuses of failing and defeated ministers.

To be successful in your ministry, you must be a leader who cannot be turned away from your vision or purpose. Why do you come up with all these excuses and obstacles? You must settle in your mind that you will accomplish what you have set out to accomplish.

You must not be turned back!

No matter how long it takes, you cannot come back home without victory in your hands. You cannot come back with a basketful of excuses.

A basketful of excuses is a sign that you have been defeated. Perhaps you were not told about all the problems you would encounter, but that does not matter. Just sort out all the problems and issues and you will be honoured as an overcomer.

Imagine standing outside your house and looking at the moon and saying to yourself, "I will go to the moon and walk on it one day." That is what some people did. Today, man has been to the moon and back several times. Can you imagine the problems they had to overcome in order to go to the moon and come back safely? Can you imagine the questions they had to answer?

Will the equipment work? Will the people be safe?

Will they get there? Will they come back?

Will the supplies of fuel, food, oxygen, etc. be enough? Every great mission has problems and questions that need solutions and answers.

When you are sent on a mission do not come back without results.

Has God put it in your heart to build a big church, to preach the gospel or to be a prophet?

Your mission contains many diverse problems. Overcome them! A good general does not turn back and give excuses for not accomplishing. Sit down and think about how you can overcome the problems you face.

The Determination of Alexander the Great

Alexander the Great was one of the most famous generals of all time. In his quest to conquer Asia, he came across an important island called Tyre. This island was located about a kilometre from the coast. In addition to being an island in the Mediterranean Sea, Tyre had very high walls that towered to a height of one hundred and fifty feet. Scaling these walls from the sea was going to be difficult. If the walls surrounded the city that was on the land, it would be a different thing.

Recognising that Alexander the Great was out to fight them, envoys from Tyre met with Alexander and declared their intention to honour his wishes. Alexander the Great explained to them that he just wanted to sacrifice to the Greek god Heracles on the island of Tyre. But the Tyrians refused that request saying that Alexander could make the sacrifice in old Tyre, which was on the mainland. Thus, Alexander was refused entry to the island of Tyre.

The people of Tyre now knew that Alexander the Great would attack them because they had refused to allow him onto the island. But they had survived several sieges in the past and knew that it was virtually impossible for anyone to break into the island from the sea.

But Alexander the Great refused to be turned away! He was determined to have that little island. He called for a meeting of his other leaders and explained to them the importance of capturing this island before advancing. He explained to them that the island of Tyre would become a stronghold for their enemies in the future.

In an attempt to avoid a long and exhaustive siege Alexander sent out further special envoys to Tyre. But the island of Tyre would have none of it. Alexander the Great's messengers were executed and their bodies thrown into the sea. This was a bad thing to do to someone like Alexander the Great.

Negotiations had failed, but Alexander the Great was not one to turn away from his purpose. He decided to overcome the problem of invading the island by building a "road" into the sea. He wanted to join the island to the mainland so that he could march onto Tyre and scale the walls. Imagine that! Filling the sea with rocks, timber and rubble until you link the main land to an island! Alexander the Great was determined to spend one year linking the island of Tyre to the mainland so that he could destroy it. Initially, the water between the mainland and the island was shallow but at a point the sea floor dropped to a depth of eighteen feet and more.

Also, periodically, the people of Tyre came out of their island to attack those building the walkway. On their first major attack, the men of Tyre destroyed the construction and burnt down the entire walkway. This initial attack against Alexander was a great success but Alexander the Great was not one to be turned away.

Alexander himself spent much time supervising the building of this walkway. On several occasions the men of Tyre attacked the walkway with ships and boats. To defend against these assaults, Alexander constructed two 150 feet tall towers with catapults to drive off enemy ships. These were positioned at the end of the walkway with a large screen stretched between them to protect the workers. But these towers were also attacked by a huge fire ship, which was launched by the island of Tyre. Whilst all this was going on, both sides were engaged in a long and bitter artillery fight.

Indeed, Alexander the Great, could not be turned back in spite of the many setbacks he had encountered. Alexander decided to fit several ships he had at his disposal with catapults and battering rams. With these, he broke through the wall on the southern part of the city. Alexander then prepared a massive assault with troops attacking through the broken walls. Despite fierce resistance from the Tyrians, Alexander's men were able to overwhelm the defenders and swarmed through the city. Tyre eventually fell to a commander who would not be turned back.

Can you be turned back? Do the problems you face overwhelm you? Do they make you turn around and go back home with reasons and excuses? Alexander the Great overcame the sea, the walls, the enemy ships, the enemy fighters and the fierce resistance of men who were fighting for their very lives. For every great victory there are many obstacles that you must not turn away from. Turning away from the mission is not an option. You must be more determined than Alexander the Great!

You must be determined to build roads into the sea, overcome fire, overcome attacks, overcome setbacks, spend a lot of time, overcome resistance, motivate your leaders and do everything necessary if you are to overcome in the ministry. Decide that you will be more determined than Alexander the Great in your ministry. Nothing will turn you back from the mission that God has sent you on.

CHAPTER 70

The Staunchness of a General is His Resistance to a *Series* of Blows

Wherefore take unto you the whole armour of God, that ye may be able to withstand in the evil day, and having done all, to stand.

Ephesians 6:13

You must be able to stand in an evil day. An evil day is a day when you receive a *series of blows*. After you have received a *series of blows*, will you still be standing? Do you have staunchness? Can you resist a series of blows? A series of blows is different from a single blow.

Your depth and latitude are what are tested in an evil day. How deep are you? How wide are you? How substantial are you? It is a series of blows that differentiates the boys from the men.

The Staunchness of the Soviet Union

When the German aggressors launched the Second World War with a series of strategic blows, most countries simply collapsed. But the Russian armies demonstrated staunchness when they fought with Adolf Hitler. They withstood onslaught after onslaught that was unleashed against them by the German Wehrmacht. Unlike nations like Poland, Ukraine, Holland, France and Belgium, which quickly succumbed to the German onslaught, the Soviet Union withstood a series of blows from the oncoming German forces.

The Soviet Union was led by Stalin, a man of steel. Stalin was not an easy enemy to crush. The staunchness of a general is his resistance to a series of blows. The Soviet Union endured a series of blows and battles from the invading German army but eventually overcame them.

In June 1941, the Russians withstood "Operation Barbarossa" in which over four million soldiers invaded the Soviet Union.

The first blows to the Russians were the frontier battles.

The Soviet Union received many blows in the battle for Minsk which they lost.

The Soviet Union received many blows in the battle for Smolensk.

The Soviet Union withstood a series of blows in the battle for Kiev.

The Soviet Union withstood a series of blows in the battle for Leningrad.

The Soviet Union withstood "Operation Northern Light", which was intended to finally destroy Leningrad.

The Soviet Union then withstood "Operation Typhoon" which was the march against Moscow itself.

The Soviet Union then endured "Operation Blue", which was intended to capture Stalingrad.

The Germans were soundly defeated in Stalingrad and this marked a turning point in the Second World War. The Germans were eventually defeated in the Soviet Union and driven back to their own country. The end of the story is simple.

The Soviet Union was able to withstand a series of blows from Operation Barbarossa, to Operation Typhoon, to Operation Blue to Operation Northern Light! The ability of the Soviet Union to withstand a series of hard blows from a very disciplined and wicked German army reveals staunchness of the highest order. The staunchness of a general is his resistance to a series of blows! Can you withstand a series of blows? Or will you faint at the first setback?

Your ministry will experience a series of blows and your ability to withstand it is called staunchness. People like John Wesley experienced a series of blows in their lives and yet were able to persist with the ministry of preaching, teaching and building the great Methodist Church. Lesser individuals would have succumbed to the persisting problems of his life.

John Wesley continued his preaching and pastoral duties, almost without pausing. John Wesley refused to change his preaching and his ministry in spite of the blows he was receiving in his life. John Wesley said, "I cannot understand how a Methodist preacher could answer to God to preach one sermon or travel one day less in a married than in a single state." He insisted, "It remaineth that they which have wives be as though they had none."

The summary of the blows to John Wesley through marriage is that John Wesley and his wife, Mary Vazeille (nicknamed Molly) were married in 1751, but stopped living together after seven years. They were reconciled for a short period in the 1770s, and then again separated from each other. On their 20th anniversary, Molly walked out and a year later she came back on her own. Again she travelled with her famous husband in his ministerial tours. When he was 73 and she was 67 they separated for the last time. From the beginning till the end, she always felt that people were placing John on a pedestal and her in the gutter. John wrote, "The water is spilt. It cannot be gathered up again." Two years later, he wrote his last letter to his wife that was a bitter note: *"If you were to live a thousand years, you could not undo the mischief you have done."*

A Series of Blows

John Wesley's wife complains: Molly complained about her husband's lack of sensitivity to her needs. Molly was starting to feel paranoid. She tried travelling with her husband on the roads. England's roads were not easy to travel; especially the way John Wesley travelled them. After a meeting, while John would exult about spiritual blessings, Molly would complain about the hard beds, the itchy blankets that were too small, and the bed bugs.

John Wesley's wife physically attacks him: According to one of Methodism's travelling preachers, he saw Molly trailing John Wesley by the hair of his head. She had in her hands venerable locks which she had plucked up by the roots.

John Wesley's wife accuses him: John Wesley naively encouraged Molly to open any letters that came to their home, when he was travelling. This kick-started another tantrum because John's intimate counselling of women through letters did not change after his marriage. Molly started to imagine the worst. In a particular letter to a woman named Sarah, John Wesley had told his problems with Molly. Molly misunderstood the language John had used in the letter.

John Wesley's wife attacks church members: In a public meeting, John Wesley's wife pointed to this lady called Sarah and called her a "whore."

John Wesley's wife tries to destroy John Wesley's reputation: John Wesley's wife gave some of Sarah's letters to John Wesley to the London newspapers to publish. John responded by listing ten major complaints against Molly.

John Wesley's wife becomes an evil presence in his house: John Wesley said he could not pray with his wife around because he felt that she was daily watching to do him hurt.

John Wesley's wife becomes stubborn and unyielding: Do not forget that stubbornness is the same as witchcraft. If you are married to a stubborn person you are married to a witch. Since Molly knew that she was not the wife she ought to be for John she did not want all the blame for their unhappy marriage. John could persuade most women, but he was unable to change Molly. And yet in spite of the series of blows that John Wesley experienced in his marriage, he staunchly pressed on and did the work of God. He set aside his sexual needs and his needs for comfort and pressed on to lay the foundation for the Methodist church.

You must ask yourself: Do I have staunchness? What is my resistance to a series of blows?

CHAPTER 71

Poor Communication Will Destroy the General

And they said unto him, From a very far country thy servants are come because of the name of the Lord thy God: for we have heard the fame of him, and all that he did in Egypt,

And all that he did to the two kings of the Amorites, that were beyond Jordan, to Sihon king of Heshbon, and to Og king of Bashan, which was at Ashtaroth.

Wherefore our elders and all the inhabitants of our country spake to us, saying, Take victuals with you for the journey, and go to meet them, and say unto them, We are your servants: therefore now make ye a league with us.

This our bread we took hot for our provision out of our houses on the day we came forth to go unto you; but now, behold, it is dry, and it is mouldy: And these bottles of wine, which we filled, were new; and, behold, they be rent: and these our garments and our shoes are become old by reason of the very long journey.

And the men took of their victuals, and ASKED NOT COUNSEL AT THE MOUTH OF THE LORD.

Joshua 9:9-14

In this chapter, you will learn the importance of clarifying issues. You will learn the importance of not jumping to conclusions too quickly. You will learn the importance of not attacking your own friends. I have lost wonderful pastors because there was a misunderstanding. I have lost life-long friends because they did not bother to clarify issues. It's time to communicate properly!

Poor communication will destroy a good general. In war, it is important to maintain communication with your superiors. It is also important to maintain very good communication with your colleagues and subordinates.

War takes place in an atmosphere of confusion, loud noises, poor visibility, misunderstanding and chaos. The war atmosphere is very prone to misunderstandings, offenses and hurts! Unless you communicate properly, you are going to get hurt and offended very soon. Every good general masters the art of communicating properly.

The commonest sign of a pastor who will not do well, is someone who does not stay in touch or someone who does not communicate properly. Through communication and dialogue you will understand what is happening and what is not happening. You can clarify things you do not understand and you can ask questions when you need to.

Real war is full of misunderstanding, miscommunication and confusion. A good general is very careful in situations that can lead to hurts and offences. A good general knows that he could mistakenly attack and accuse the very person he needs. A good general may not be able to avoid situations in which hurts and offenses develop but he fights to maintain communication and to avoid the worst. A good general does not break communication!

A good general does not break fellowship.

A good general does not break lifelong friendships.

A good general does not break contact with his spiritual family.

A good general does not break contact with fellow soldiers!

Not communicating with God means being prayerless.

Not communicating properly with your co-equals means you have an independent and separatist spirit.

You will soon become isolated. Isolation is a dangerous state to fall into. Isolation and non-communication will kill your ministry. We are to walk in the light as He is in the light and we are to have fellowship with one another. It is not easy to overcome hurts and injuries when they come from your own colleagues. Being hurt is the open door to evil spirits of unforgiveness and bitterness.

Evil spirits enter the church because of poor communication. Sometimes asking a question and getting a genuine answer will drive away all forms of misunderstanding.

A good general avoids situations in which hurts and offenses develop. A good general does not break communication! A good general does not break fellowship and lifelong friendships. A good general does not break contact with his spiritual family and fellow soldiers!

Miscommunication, Misunderstanding and War

In war, when miscommunication and misunderstanding take place you end up attacking your own forces and your best friends. Why would you attack or kill the one you need the most? Only miscommunication and misunderstanding lead to such unfortunate situations.

Sadly, you end up doing the enemy's work and shooting down your friends. How sad it is that the real enemy is left out of the picture whilst we fight one another in the church. History has shown us many examples of people attacking their loved ones and friends. You cannot imagine the level of confusion and destruction that can come about when there is poor communication and misunderstanding. There are several famous but tragic examples of the results of poor communication. The devil is hoping that you will misunderstand things and break off communication. He hopes that you will attack the person you need. The history of war shows how common it is for misunderstandings and miscommunication to happen. Let us look at a long list of friends attacking each other due to the misunderstanding and miscommunication of war.

1. In 1796, the French General Amade Lahap who commanded one of Napoleon's divisions, was killed by one of his own men while returning from reconnaissance.

2. On the 10th of June 1948, Mickey Marcus, Israel's first general was mistaken for an enemy and shot and killed by a sentry while returning at night to his headquarters.

3. On July 3, 1950, during the Korean War, eight Australian fighter jet pilots were misinformed that an area was in enemy hands. They attacked and destroyed a train carrying their own people. Thousands of American and South Korean soldiers who were mistaken for a North Korean convoy were on board the train. There were more than one thousand casualties.

4. During the First World War, an estimated 75,000 French soldiers were mistakenly killed by their own artillery.

5. During the Second World War, on the 10th of September 1939, the British submarine, Triton sunk another British submarine. After communicating with the other British submarine and receiving no response, they assumed they must have located a German submarine and fired two torpedoes, killing 50 people.

6. During the Second World War, on the 10th of May 1940, German bombers mistakenly bombed the German city of

Freiburg. They were actually on their way to France to bomb the French and were misdirected due to navigational errors.

7. On the 3rd May 1945, three days after Adolf Hitler had died, three German transport ships, Cap Arcona, Thielbek and Deutschland came under attack by the British Air Force. All three ships were sunk in the Baltic Sea by bombs, rockets and cannon fire. Unknown to the pilots, was the fact that the ships were full of British and allied prisoners of war and survivors from Hitler's concentration camps. Some of the German guards on board jumped off and were rescued but the prisoners were left on board the sinking ships. It is estimated that almost 10,000 concentration camp survivors were killed in the attack.

8. In the Burma campaign on 21st February 1942, American pilots shot retreating Commonwealth forces because they thought they were an advancing Japanese column. On the same day, retreating Commonwealth forces with about 300 vehicles were mistakenly bombed by the British Air Force, resulting in 159 vehicles being destroyed. The Air force killed over 200 of their own men on that day.

9. During "Operation Husky", United States ground and naval forces shot down 23 of their own planes and damaged 37 resulting in 318 casualties.

10. During "Operation Cottage", United States and Canadian forces mistook each other as Japanese although there were no Japanese on the island and engaged each other in a deadly fire fight. As a result, 28 Americans and 4 Canadians were killed. Is it not amazing that there were no Japanese troops on the island?

11. In 1944, a train carrying 800 British, American and South African prisoners was bombed by the British when it crossed a bridge. The prisoners were being transported to Germany in unmarked cattle cars and were padlocked within. The driver stopped the train on the bridge, leaving the prisoners

locked inside to their fate. Hundreds were killed because the British did not know that they were killing their own men.

12. On the 8th of August 1944, two battalions of the 77th Infantry exchanged prolonged fire in Guam. They did not realize they belonged to the same infantry division until they called for artillery to bombard and silence the other side. The mistake was realized when both sides called for help from the same artillery unit.

13. On 14 April 1994, US Army Blackhawk helicopters carrying 26 crew and passengers entered the no-fly zone headed for their military coordination centre. They were intercepted by two US fighter jets that were patrolling the no-fly zone. The identification Friend or Foe system aboard the helicopters failed, causing a failure in communication. The two US fighters decided to visually identify the helicopter. They mistakenly thought it was an Iraqi helicopter and shot down the helicopter with air to air missiles. There were no survivors. Many factors were blamed for this unfortunate incident, including misidentification of the helicopter as an Iraqi aircraft. How sad it is when you mistakenly identify your friend as an enemy!

14. In April 1944, a training exercise to harden soldiers to the battle conditions of the coming invasion of Europe was conducted in Lyme Bay. Live ammunition from a ship was therefore used to fire at a beach where soldiers were training. Unfortunately, the soldiers moved into the wrong areas of the beach where 308 of them were mistakenly killed.

15. On 19 February 1940, six German destroyer ships were sent to intercept a number of suspicious British fishing vessels off the Dogger Bank. When a German plane flew overhead, the German ships mistakenly fired on it. The German plane was convinced that the six German ships were British ships and began bombing them. As the chaos erupted, the German ships also thought they were under a British

air and submarine attack. Eventually, after half an hour of confusion and mayhem, they realised they had mistakenly killed 578 German sailors and sank two of their own ships.

CHAPTER 72

A Good General Does Not Advance Recklessly

And they rose up early in the morning, and gat them up into the top of the mountain, saying, Lo, we be here, and will go up unto the place which the Lord hath promised: for we have sinned.

And Moses said, Wherefore now do ye transgress the commandment of the Lord? but it shall not prosper.

GO NOT UP, FOR THE LORD IS NOT AMONG YOU; THAT YE BE NOT SMITTEN BEFORE YOUR ENEMIES.

For the Amalekites and the Canaanites are there before you, and ye shall fall by the sword:because ye are turned away from the Lord, therefore the Lord will not be with you.

BUT THEY PRESUMED TO GO UP UNTO THE HILL TOP: nevertheless the ark of the covenant of the Lord, and Moses, departed not out of the camp. Then the amalekites came down, and the Canaanites which dwelt in that hill, and smote them, and discomfited them, even unto Hormah.

Numbers 14:40-45

The children of Israel advanced into battle recklessly. They did not do it wisely, carefully and humbly. They did not seek the will of God and they did not go at the right time. This is a perfect example of recklessly advancing. Recklessly advancing will lead to your defeat. It is true that God wants your church to grow. It is true that God wants you to go out into the world and preach the gospel. But if you advance into these things without due caution, you will be defeated and forced to come back licking your wounds.

Reckless Advancing

Recklessly advancing is caused by three main things.

1. **Recklessly advancing is caused by hubris born of success**: Hubris means pride! Hubris born of success is the pride and confidence that comes because of your past successes. Your past successes have a way of feeding you with confidence. You somehow feel that what lies ahead will be defeated as easily as what you just conquered.

2. **Recklessly advancing is caused by the undisciplined pursuit of more**: Pursuing more fruit is God's will. Doing more for the kingdom of God is the right thing. As you pursue it, you must maintain the disciplines that brought you to where you are. There is no time in your life that you will not need the disciplines of humility, holiness, love, forgiveness, spirituality and faith. These hidden disciplines of honesty, truth and wholeness are necessary as you pursue more achievements for the kingdom. Unfortunately, people recklessly advance without regard for their own safety. You must take heed to yourself. You must take heed to your doctrine. You must take heed to your own prayer life. Walk closely with God. Do not simply advance because everyone else is moving on.

3. **Recklessly advancing is caused by a denial of risk**: The denial of risk speaks of the intentional closing of your eyes to dangers. To say that you are not at risk as you get

older and as you pursue more is to deny the reality. In fact, many problems that could not overcome you when you were young are sometimes able to overcome you when you are older. We all know that there are youthful lusts and youthful problems but there are also problems that come to older people. It is important to say to yourself, "I am at risk! I am in danger! I am still in danger!" As you march forward with the consciousness that you are still in a dangerous place, you will ensure many safety precautions are always in place. You will deliver yourself from many evils by acknowledging the risks.

The Reckless Advance of Hitler

Adolf Hitler recklessly advanced into Russia whilst he was fighting a war in Britain. This was a clear example of the undisciplined pursuit of more. He had been successful in overpowering Poland, Czechoslovakia, Austria, France, Holland and Belgium. The defeat of France within a few weeks was one of the greatest shocks at that time. He was now the master of Europe. Obviously, these successes had fed him the confidence that, he would do to Russia what he did to France.

At the time Adolf Hitler conquered France, France had one of the most powerful armies in the whole world. Adolf Hitler then recklessly advanced into Russia.

Denial of risk and the undisciplined pursuit of more were the causes of Adolf Hitler's defeat in Russia. Because he thought Russia would be as easy to defeat as France he did not prepare for a long campaign and his army was destroyed in the Russian winter. Hitler continued to deny the risks by continuing his invasion of Russia the next year. His entire army was surrounded and annihilated. Recklessly advancing and the undisciplined pursuit of more plus the denial of risk are clearly played out by Adolf Hitler.

No Reckless Advance of Hannibal

On the other hand, another famous general sensing danger, refused to advance recklessly to his destruction. Hannibal was the Carthaginian general who came from Africa to terrorise the Roman Empire. He rode his elephants across the Alps, entered into Italy and defeated the legendary Roman army on several occasions.

There are three notable victories of Hannibal over the Roman armies: the victory at the Trebia River, the victory at Lake Trasimene and the victory at Cannae. No one had advanced into Roman territory the way Hannibal did. After the defeat of Cannae where 80,000 Roman soldiers were killed, he was 250 miles from Rome. He was now within striking distance and everyone expected that he would advance on Rome and actually conquer Rome itself.

Somehow, Hannibal did not advance on to Rome. He stayed within striking distance of Rome but never attacked Rome. No one knows why he did not actually invade Rome when he had the opportunity. Perhaps, he knew this principle of not recklessly advancing. He could have fallen for the mistake of undisciplined pursuit of more. He had had victories in Trasimene, the Trebia River and Cannae. He could have added Rome to the tally.

But he was cautious and stayed back. He actually lived within the Roman Empire for eight years, moving around with his armies but never attacking Rome. Perhaps if he had attacked Rome he would have been destroyed. Perhaps if he had attacked Rome he would have been killed and his armies destroyed. There are times your successes should not inspire you to recklessly advance into more!

CHAPTER 73

A Good General Makes Special Efforts to Know about the Enemy

And Moses sent them to spy out the land of Canaan, and said unto them, Get you up this way southward, and go up into the mountain:

And see the land, what it is; and the people that dwelleth therein, whether they be strong or weak, few or many;

And what the land is that they dwell in, whether it be good or bad; and what cities they be that they dwell in, whether in tents, or in strong holds;

And what the land is, whether it be fat or lean, whether there be wood therein, or not. And be ye of good courage, and bring of the fruit of the land. Now the time was the time of the firstripe grapes.

Numbers 13:17-20

Make every effort to know your enemy: to know where he lives, to know what he looks like, to know what he does, to know what he has and to understand him. This is what Moses did when he sent out the spies into the Promised Land. He was making special effort to know about his enemy. Moses did not want to fight a war with someone he did not know a lot about.

The Stolen Plane

Make special efforts to now about your enemy. Those efforts you make to know all about your enemy will pay off in the long run. The Mossad, Israel's secret service, is famous for carrying out missions that gave Israel the upper hand.

One of the most daring operations by the Israeli secret service was the stealing of Russia's multi-million dollar plane, the MiG-21 fighter jet. This particular plane has been manufactured more than any other jet and an estimated ten thousand have flown in more wars than any other plane in the world. The rationale behind the stealing of this jet is encapsulated in the words of Israel's General Dan Tokowsky who said, "It is a basic principle of warfare that knowing the weapons the enemy has, is already beating him."

Israel had already tried to steal a plane through an Egyptian-born Armenian called Jean Thomas. Israel had offered an Egyptian pilot a million dollars to fly his MiG-21 to Israel. The pilot refused and Jean Thomas and his accomplices were arrested and hanged. On another occasion, Israel tried to convince two Iraqi pilots to fly another MiG-21 to Israel and this attempt also failed.

Finally, Israel got an opportunity when a stranger contacted the Israeli Embassy in Tehran. This stranger offered to convince his relative, squadron leader Munir Redfa to fly his MiG-21to Israel. For a sum of one million pounds sterling, as well as the resettlement of his family in Israel, protection for his family,

Israeli citizenship, a home and a job for life, the squadron leader agreed to the deal. Munir Redfa's large family was then moved out of Iraq.

On the day in question (August 16,1966), Munir Redfa asked his ground crew to fill his tank to full capacity, which was against the rules. (Normally, pilots were allowed to have only half-filled tanks to prevent them from defecting). After taking off, Munir Redfa suddenly turned his plane towards Israel, put on his after burners and rocketed towards Israel. He immediately received a call on his radio, "Turn round or we will shoot you down". Munir Redfa turned off the radio and continued his journey to a base in the Negev desert. Israel sent a flight of mirages to escort him on the last leg of his 500-mile journey to Israel.

The Israelis then tested the MiG-21 extensively and learned all its secrets. It is believed that this effort paid off in the 1967 six-day war when Israel shot down six Syrian MiGs with no losses of their own. During the six-day war, Israel's air force gained absolute air supremacy, which helped them to win the war. Make special efforts to know about your enemy! That is exactly what Israel and America did. They paid the price, took the risks and made the investment to find out as much as they could about their enemy.

Demons and Entities

A minister of the gospel must make some special efforts to know about evil spirits and their activities. You must make special efforts to understand the enemy spirits we are at war with. Who are they? Where do they come from? Where do they live? How do they affect us? What do they do to us? Do they have power over us or do we have power over them?

Make special efforts to read and to study all you can about these evil spirits. I once spoke to the principal of a Bible school and asked him which books they use in the study of demonology. He answered, "There are no demons in this school! There is nothing like demonology in our curriculum!" I almost felt stupid for asking him a question about demonology.

In a war with an invisible enemy, you must make special efforts to know and understand your enemy. Many years ago, I was listening to a teaching by Kenneth Hagin on demonology. He was explaining how evil spirits affect Christians today. He explained a vision in which he saw an imp-like figure sitting on the shoulders of a pastor's wife and ministering thoughts and ideas to her. He shared how this lady began to enjoy and accept those thoughts until the spirit moved into her head and down into her heart. This lady, now fully under the influence of the demon, left her husband and went out into the world. She committed adultery with several different men until she finally renounced Christ.

The Lord showed him the process which led to this woman being captured by the enemy. This story riveted in my spirit and I became much more aware of the activities of evil spirits in the dark world.

After this, I made even more efforts to learn about the enemy and the dark world. I read more books on demons by Kenneth Hagin such as, *The Triumphant Church*. The knowledge I gained about evil spirits has helped me to combat evil in my life for many years.

It will do you a world of good to read books on demons and how to deal with them. Do not think you know everything. You will discover that many things you struggle with are demonic in their nature. Make special efforts to know every detail about your enemy.

CHAPTER 74

A Good General Is Good at Both Fighting and Dodging Evil

FLEE ALSO YOUTHFUL LUSTS: but follow righteousness, faith, charity, peace, with them that call on the Lord out of a pure heart.

2 Timothy 2:22

For the love of money is the root of all evil: which while some coveted after, they have erred from the faith, and pierced themselves through with many sorrows. But thou, O man of God, FLEE THESE THINGS; and follow after righteousness, godliness, faith, love, patience, meekness.

1 Timothy 6:10-11

Agood general knows how to fight and will not shy away from a good fight but also knows how to dodge evil. The Scripture teaches us to flee youthful lusts, fornication and idolatry. Fleeing is a strategy to defeat an enemy whom you cannot fight effectively and directly. Youthful lust is an enemy you must learn to dodge. There is no point in confronting it head-on. It is too powerful to take on. It is too powerful to try a frontal attack.

There are two reasons we must flee youthful lusts. The first is that the flesh is a very strong force that you will grow to respect. It is good that you have a proper respect for the flesh and its capabilities. You may never know what you are capable of doing till you have done it. It is therefore best to keep the flesh contained and directed. Those who take their flesh for granted will live to regret it! The flesh is your door to sin and disgrace.

The second reason for fleeing youthful lusts is that tampering with the flesh causes it to develop certain tastes, and creates an abnormal form of "monster flesh" that is even more difficult to control. The "monster flesh" that is created through serial fornication, pornography, masturbation and homosexual contact is very difficult to control. A true pastor will have compassion for anyone who struggles with these temptations. Many people who have tampered with their flesh have developed weird desires and tendencies.

There will always be powers that you cannot defeat by a direct confrontation. This is where the art of dodging evil comes in! Notice how the mighty Napoleon was defeated by the art of dodging evil.

How to Dodge Napoleon

Just as Europe was under the grips of Hitler in 1941, Europe was under the grips of Napoleon in 1812. It then occurred to Napoleon that he should invade Russia and teach them a lesson. The same idea occurred to Hitler in 1941.

Napoleon gathered the largest army Europe had seen for hundreds of years and began his invasion of the Russian empire. Just like Hitler, Napoleon envisaged a quick victory. He only imagined Tsar Alexander I kneeling before him in surrender. But he was to be proved wrong. The Russian generals, realising that a head-on battle with Napoleon would not serve them well, decided to dodge the French man by retreating.

This retreat avoided a direct contact with the bulk of Napoleon's army. As the retreat progressed, the Russians burnt the farms and villages, leaving nothing for Napoleon's men to eat. Supplying Napoleon's troops with food became more and more difficult as Napoleon pursued the Russians deeper into Russia. After one or two battles, Napoleon focused his energy on capturing Moscow. He thought to himself, "If the French army enters Moscow, Russia will be forced to surrender."

Finally, when Napoleon was almost in Moscow, the Russians led by General Kutuzov made a stand and fought against Napoleon at a place called Borodino. Borodino was just a few miles from Moscow. At the battle of Borodino, many of the French soldiers lost their lives and Napoleon's army was weakened even more.

Napoleon won this battle, though at great cost and proceeded to Moscow, thinking that the Tsar would be there to surrender. But there was no Tsar and there were no officials to hand over anything. They had all decided to dodge Napoleon. The only people left in Moscow were prisoners who had been released from prison to terrorise the incoming troops.

The French army was terribly disappointed that the Russians were nowhere to be found. They began looting and pillaging the city. Fires were started in various districts to destroy any remaining resources. Even the Kremlin was burned down.

After occupying Moscow for five weeks, the situation became critical and Napoleon was left with no choice but to begin the long journey back home. Napoleon entered Moscow on the 15th of September and by the 18th of October he left Moscow in defeat having never even seen the enemy.

The expert strategy of dodging Napoleon had worked.

During the journey back to France, most of Napoleon's troops were killed and his army was destroyed. By dodging Napoleon, General Kutuzov had gained the upper hand. Napoleon was neutralised and destroyed by the strategy of dodging evil.

CHAPTER 75

A Good General Fights in Four Dimensions

... and seated us with Him in the heavenly places in Christ Jesus...

Ephesians 2:6 (NASB)

W e live and operate in different worlds at the same time. As you can see from the Scripture above, we are on earth but at the same time seated in heavenly places. We are operating in the earthly realm but we are also operating in the spiritual realm at the same time. This is how a spiritual war is. You operate in different dimensions, realms or worlds at the same time. I once asked some young men what difficulties they thought they would encounter as missionaries on the field. They all spoke of problems and difficulties in the public dimension. I realised that they did not know that there were three other dimensions in which they would be severely tested.

There are four different dimensions that you must fight to gain control of, if you are to be successful in the ministry: *the personal dimension, the family dimension, the leadership dimension* and *the public dimension of the ministry.* Let's look at these dimensions of ministry.

The First Dimension: the Personal Dimension

The war in the first dimension is the war for your personal wholeness. There are many battles that have to be fought to establish your personal wholeness and integrity. The war in the first dimension is therefore a war for your personal holiness.

The war in the first dimension is a war for your personal purity.

The war in the first dimension is a war to establish your humility as an individual.

The war in the first dimension is a war to establish your ability to love and forgive.

Your war in the first dimension is a war where you fight against depression and bad attitudes in yourself.

The war in the first dimension is a war against bad domestic habits and inappropriate behaviour.

At every stage of your life you will be fighting in the first dimension. In your younger years, the enemy will fight against your holiness. The enemy will fight to make you unable to live a holy life. There are four practices that Satan would love to impart to you as a young person. Once he is successful in planting these in you, you will struggle for the rest of your life to remain holy. Satan would like to infect you with pornography, masturbation, fornication and homosexuality.

a. Pornography, once planted in you is difficult to overcome both now and in the future.

b. Masturbation is also a negative practice that is difficult to overcome and has multiple negative effects.

c. Fornication with delightful and strange women sensitizes your taste buds to delicious sex. Such evil women will always be attractive to you once you have tasted what they are like as a youth. You may get married to Simple Sally and not have the exotic adventures and delicious escapades you had with Slippery Susie.

d. The fourth practice that Satan would like to plant in you is the taste for homosexuality. This is a terrible practice and once the taste for homosexual behaviour is established it is difficult to uproot.

Throughout your life, you have to fight to establish yourself in holiness and purity. Whether you are in your twenties, thirties or fifties you will have a fight in the first dimension. At different phases of your life, you may have to fight to establish yourself in humility and forgiveness, depending on what has happened in your life.

Another fight in the first dimension is the fight to be spiritual. The war in the first dimension has nothing to do with the externals. It is all about the unseen, the personal and the internal. If you win the war in the first dimension, you are more qualified to fight on in the second and third dimensions of war.

The Second Dimension: the Family Dimension

War in the second dimension has to do with your spouse, your marriage and your family. Once you get into a relationship, you have opened up a war on another front. Whilst Adolf Hitler was fighting with Britain, he opened another war in the east with Russia. It is not easy to fight a war on two fronts. It was this bad decision to fight a war on two fronts that destroyed Adolf Hitler. Indeed, after 1941 the German army fought on two fronts.

As soon as you get married, a war begins on a second front or in a second country.

Marriage promises many good things but also many battles.

The battle to be the head of the house is a battle in the second dimension. If you look around, you will see many men who have lost this fight and are not actually the heads of their homes. Because they are not the heads of their homes, they are unable to gain control in the ministry.

There are sexual battles waiting for you in the second dimension. The presence of your wife does not dry out all your sexual problems. In fact, it opens the door to other problems. Some Christian wives play hard to get, unlike strange women who are eager to use their sexuality.

Once you are married, there are battles to bring you down through strife. Marriage opens the door to conflicts, quarrels and strife. The battle to remain loving and forgiving begins as soon as you marry. The marriage relationship is not the same as a boyfriend-girlfriend relationship. You will fight in the second dimension to deal with conflict.

The Third Dimension: the Leadership Dimension

The third dimension is the war to bring your fellow commanders and team members into unity, oneness and loyalty. The battle in the third dimension begins when you start to have a team and to exercise leadership. Good leadership requires helpers and assistants. The battle to gain control over your helpers and assistants is a big one. This is where loyalty and disloyalty is important.

The battle to be a good leader, in whom people trust, is the first battle in the third dimension. Many leaders fail in the third dimension. This leads to poor growth, poor administration and no establishment. My books, *Loyalty and Disloyalty, Those Who Are Dangerous Sons, Those Who Accuse You, Those Who Leave You, Those Who Forget, Those Who Are Ignorant* and *Those Who Pretend* are books dedicated to the fight in the third dimension.

The Fourth Dimension: the Public Dimension

The fourth dimension is the battle for the public ministry. When fighting in the fourth dimension, you are seen in the open, preaching teaching and ministering. In this dimension, you will have to fight with familiarity in the people.

The battle for the fourth dimension is the battle to be anointed. It is the battle to be prepared to preach. It is the battle to know what to say, how to say it and when to say it. The battle in the fourth dimension may be the easiest of the four wars that you will fight.

Today, I look back and remember certain times and events in my life. People are impressed with victories they see in the fourth dimension, but I often remember some of the battles I was having in the first, second or third dimensions. Those first and second dimensional battles were so severe that they overshadowed any victories I experienced in the fourth dimension. Perhaps God allows us to fight in the first and second dimensions to protect us from pride. It is easy to become proud after victory in the fourth and public dimension of ministry. You need some first dimensional battles to cool you down.

Paul and the Four Dimensions of War

In the first dimension, Apostle Paul battled with his personal weaknesses, offenses and burning.

Who is weak, and I am not weak? who is offended, and I burn not? If I must needs glory, I will glory of the things which concern mine infirmities.

2 Corinthians 11:29-30

In the second dimension, Apostle Paul spoke of the battles that ministers have in marriage. He predicted that ministers would have anguish and difficulty because of their marriages and families.

But if you marry, you have not sinned; and if a virgin marries, she has not sinned. Yet such will have trouble in this life, and I am trying to spare you.

1 Corinthians 7:28

In the third dimension, Apostle Paul spoke of how he battled with false brethren who came in to destroy the church. You will always have to battle to maintain order in the close-knit team that work with you.

But it was because of the false brethren secretly brought in, who had sneaked in to spy out our liberty which we have in Christ Jesus, in order to bring us into bondage. But we did not yield in subjection to them for even an hour, so that the truth of the gospel would remain with you.

Galatians 2:4-5 (NASB)

In the fourth dimension, Apostle Paul spoke of his battle to take care of the churches. This battle would include preaching, teaching, travelling and training of the people.

Beside those things that are without, that which cometh upon me daily, the care of all the churches.

2 Corinthians 11:28

A Secular General

A secular general differs from a spiritual general in the sense that the secular general often does not need personal holiness and righteousness to fight in the public dimension. This is why many politicians live very immoral lives but are heads of state and leaders of nations. Indeed, some of them are very successful public leaders in spite of their depraved personal lives.

In some countries presidential candidates are forced to step aside when it is discovered that they do not have perfect lives. However, in many countries, public office holders are far from moral. In such places, the personal dimension has no bearing on their public career. We, as ministers of the gospel, cannot ignore the personal dimension. When you become a minister of the gospel, you cannot live anyhow and you cannot do what you want. You must follow God's way!

CHAPTER 76

A Good General Knows
When to End the War

A time to kill, and a time to heal; a time to break down,
and a time to build up.

Ecclesiastes 3:3

T here is a time to stop fighting. There is a time to fight and there is a time to stop fighting. Even war has seasons. You can see from the Scripture below that there were actually seasons when wars were fought, and times when everybody held back from conflict.

> **Then it happened in the spring, AT THE TIME WHEN KINGS GO OUT TO BATTLE, that Joab led out the army and ravaged the land of the sons of Ammon, and came and besieged Rabbah. But David stayed at Jerusalem. And Joab struck Rabbah and overthrew it.**
>
> **1 Chronicles 20:1 (NASB)**

There comes a time you must rest from war. Everybody needs to pause. Everybody needs to take a break. There comes a time when you must know how to exit from wars that you are engaged in. There are times you must decide to stop quarrelling. There are times you must decide to stop fighting. There are people who feel that they are so principled that they will never change their stance on an issue. What is the use of a mind if it cannot be changed? Perhaps you are fighting to be a doctor and all doors are closed. Why continue fighting endlessly against a stonewall?

Whenever you meet a stonewall or a hard-hearted and unyielding person, remember that the heart of the king is in the hand of the Lord. You will learn by experience that a hardened, unyielding person is usually used by God for His purposes. Pharaoh was hard and unyielding. The hardness of Pharaoh's heart was to bring about the will of God. God wanted to destroy Egypt and punish them for mistreating Israel. God wanted to have fun displaying signs and wonders in the earth. He needed somebody like Pharaoh whose heart was hardened.

> **And the Lord said unto Moses, Go in unto Pharaoh: for I HAVE HARDENED HIS HEART, and the heart of his servants, that I might shew these my signs before him:**
>
> **Exodus 10:1**

Why is it that some people never stop fighting? The answer is very simple. Pride! It takes humility to bow out of long-standing quarrels. It takes humility to back down. It takes humility to say sorry. It takes humility to accept that there may be another way, other than the way you have been fighting for.

Why is it that some people fight on endlessly to destroy themselves? The answer is also simple. Demons! When a man fights so that everyone around him is destroyed, you must understand that evil spirits are at work. Adolf Hitler embodies the madness of fighting without ending! Adolf Hitler embodies the insanity of fighting until there is nothing left.

The Nero Decree

At the end of the Second World War, Adolf Hitler realised that all was lost. Germany was defeated and he was about to be captured.

On the 19th of March 1945, Hitler issued the famous "Nero Decree". In this Nero Decree, he called for the complete destruction of Germany's infrastructure. He wanted the approaching British, American and Russian forces to find nothing but scorched earth when they arrived in Germany.

Adolf Hitler also had the intention to destroy the German population as a punishment for its defeat. There was to be no future for anyone after the defeat of his national socialism.

But the responsibility for carrying out this crazy instruction fell on Albert Speer, Hitler's Minister for Armaments. Speer was appalled by the order and lost faith in the dictator. Albert Speer deliberately failed to carry out the order. Upon receiving the instructions from Hitler, he requested to be given exclusive power to implement the plan. Instead he used his power to convince the generals to ignore the order.

Hitler remained unaware that his instructions had been disobeyed until the very end, when Speer admitted to Hitler that he had deliberately disobeyed the instructions. Speer knew that it was time to stop fighting. But the mad man wanted to go on and kill everyone.

A Time to Heal

There is a time to fight and there is a time to stop fighting. There is a time to fight and there is a time to heal. There is a time to plant and a time to pluck up that which has been planted. Perhaps it is time for you to fight. Perhaps it is time for you to stop fighting. Humble yourself! A good general knows when to end the war! A good general knows how to end the war! [77]A good general exits when it is time to go!

PREPARE WAR,
Wake up the
mighty men,
Let all the men of
war draw near…
Let the weak say,
I am strong

Joel 3:9-10

References

Chapter 5

"We Shall Fight On The Beaches". *En.wikipedia.org*. N.p., 2017. Web. 18 Mar. 2017.

Chapter 8

"Principles Of War". *En.wikipedia.org*. N.p., 2017. Web. 18 Mar. 2017.

Chapter 9

Historyguide.org. N.p., 2017. Web. 19 Mar. 2017.

Pitt.edu. N.p., 2017. Web. 19 Mar. 2017.

"Rwandan Genocide". *prezi.com*. N.p., 2017. Web. 19 Mar. 2017.

"World War 1". *Blog Project*. N.p., 2017. Web. 19 Mar. 2017.

"Six-Day War". *En.wikipedia.org*. N.p., 2017. Web. 19 Mar. 2017.

Schoppert, Stephanie. "10 Ongoing Territorial Conflicts With No End In Sight". *HistoryCollection.com*. N.p., 2017. Web. 19 Mar. 2017.

Chapter 13

"The Atlantic Wall - History Learning Site". *History Learning Site*. N.p., 2017. Web. 20 Mar. 2017.

Chapter 14

"Sparknotes: World War II (1939–1945): Japan And Pearl Harbor (Page 2)". *Sparknotes.com*. N.p., 2017. Web. 20 Mar. 2017.

Chapter 16

"The National Archives | Exhibitions & Learning Online | First World War | Aftermath". *Nationalarchives.gov.uk*. N.p., 2017. Web. 20 Mar. 2017.

Chapter 20

"Opposition In Nazi Germany - History Learning Site". *History Learning Site*. N.p., 2017. Web. 20 Mar. 2017.

Chapter 23

Speeches, Hitler. "Hitler Speeches". *Worldwarii.org*. N.p., 2017. Web. 20 Mar. 2017.

Chapter 25

Perez, L. G. (2013). Japan at war: an encyclopedia. Santa Barbara, CA: ABC-CLIO.

Chapter 28

General, The. "Rantings Of A Civil War Historian » John Ferling'S Almost A Miracle: The American Victory In The War Of Independence". *Civilwarcavalry.com*. N.p., 2017. Web. 20 Mar. 2017.

Chapter 33

"Fall Of Constantinople". *En.wikipedia.org*. N.p., 2017. Web. 20 Mar. 2017.

Chapter 37

"What If The Allies Had Not Broken The German Naval Code? | Historynet". *HistoryNet*. N.p., 2017. Web. 20 Mar. 2017.

"Why Did Germany Lose WW2? - Forum Page 62". Military-quotes. com. N.p., 2017. Web. 20 Mar. 2017.

Chapter 41

"About Bomber Command." *https://www.rafbf.org/bomber-command-memorial/about-bomber-command* N.p. 2017 2017. Web 20 Mar.2017

Chapter 44

"Alexander the Great". *En.wikipedia.org.* N.p., 2017. Web. 20 Mar. 2017.

Chapter 47

"Last will and testament of Adolf Hitler". *En.wikipedia.org.* N.p., 2017. Web. 20 Mar. 2017.

Chapter 51

"Adolf Hitler ". En.wikipedia.org. N.p., 2017. Web. 20 Mar. 2017.

1938 Newspaper Archives. (n.d.), *https://newspaperarchive.com/ historical-events/1900s/1938* N.p., 2017. Web. 20 Mar. 2017.

Chapter 53

Constantine I. (n.d.). *http://www.ancient.eu/Constantine_I/* N.p., 2017. Web. 20 Mar. 2017.

Siege of Constantinople 1453. (n.d.).http://en.metapedia.org/wiki/ Siege_of_Constantinople_1453 N.p., 2017. Web. 20 Mar. 2017.

Chapter 54

CPL Herbert Blum: Hitler as the Modern Haman. (n.d.). *https://nmajmh. org/* N.p., 2017. Web. 20 Mar. 2017.

Chapter 56

"Genghis Khan ". *En.wikipedia.org.* N.p., 2017. Web. 20 Mar. 2017.

Chapter 58

"Gallic Wars ". *En.wikipedia.org.* N.p., 2017. Web. 20 Mar. 2017.

"Military Campaigns of Julius Caesar". *En.wikipedia.org.* N.p., 2017. Web. 20 Mar. 2017.

Chapter 59

"Invasion of Poland". *En.wikipedia.org.* N.p., 2017. Web. 20 Mar. 2017.

The History Place - Defeat of Hitler: Catastrophe at Stalingrad. (n.d.). *http://www.historyplace.com/worldwar2/defeat/catastrophe-stalingrad.*htm N.p., 2017. Web. 20 Mar. 2017.

Chapter 64

Propaganda in Nazi Germany. (n.d.). *http://www.historylearningsite.co.uk/nazi-germany/propaganda-in-nazi-germany/* N.p., 2017. Web. 20 Mar. 2017.

CPL Herbert Blum: Hitler as the Modern Haman. (n.d.). *https://nmajmh.org/* N.p., 2017. Web. 20 Mar. 2017.

Chen, C. P. (n.d.). Joseph Goebbels. *http://ww2db.com/person_bio.php?person_id=201* N.p., 2017. Web. 20 Mar. 2017.

Joseph Goebbels. (n.d.). *http://www.newworldencyclopedia.org/entry/Joseph_Goebbels N.*p., 2017. Web. 20 Mar. 2017.

Chapter 65

"Indian campaign of Alexander the Great". *En.wikipedia.org.* N.p., 2017. Web. 20 Mar. 2017.

Chapter 67

"Trojan War". *En.wikipedia.org.* N.p., 2017. Web. 20 Mar. 2017.

Chapter 68

"Angolan Civil War". *En.wikipedia.org.* N.p., 2017. Web. 20 Mar. 2017.

Chapter 69

Alexander the Great. (n.d.). *https://www.britannica.com/biography/* Alexander-the-Great . N.p., 2017. Web. 20 Mar. 2017.